Harvard Business School

Research Colloquium

Principals and Agents:
The Structure of Business

Contributors

Kenneth J. Arrow
Robert C. Clark
Frank H. Easterbrook
Robert G. Eccles
Richard A. Epstein
John W. Pratt
Harrison C. White
Mark A. Wolfson
Richard J. Zeckhauser

Principals and Agents:
The Structure of Business

Edited by John W. Pratt
and Richard J. Zeckhauser

Harvard Business School Press

Boston, Massachusetts

Library of Congress Cataloging in Publication Data

Main entry under title:

Principals and agents.

(Research colloquium / Harvard Business School)
Proceedings from one of a series of conferences held
at the Harvard Business School in 1984.
Includes index.
Contents: The agency relationship. Overview / John
W. Pratt and Richard J. Zeckhauser. The economics of
agency / Kenneth J. Arrow—Institutional responses.
Agency costs versus fiduciary duties / Robert C. Clark.—
[etc.]
    1. Management—Congresses. I. Pratt, John W.
(John Winsor), 1931–   . II. Zeckhauser, Richard.
III. Series: Research colloquium (Harvard University.
Graduate School of Business Administration)
HD29.P735   1985   658.4'013   84-29039

Harvard Business School Press, Boston 02163
Printed in the United States of America.

89 88 87 86 85   5 4 3 2 1

ISBN 0-87584-164-3

Contents

Foreword

Founded in 1908, the Harvard University Graduate School of Business Administration celebrated its seventy-fifth anniversary in the academic year 1983–84. We chose to take this opportunity to involve our faculty in thinking seriously about the challenges and opportunities ahead in important fields of management research and teaching.

Field-based empirical research, within and across organizations, has always been fundamental to Harvard Business School's ability to meet its objectives of educating business managers and helping to improve the practice of management. In some respects, we are creating a distinctive model of research. We have often broken through the bounds of traditional disciplines and methodologies to borrow whatever tools and concepts were needed for a particular inquiry. In addition, we have been less concerned with testing existing theory than with generating new insights. And while we often find ourselves drawn to problems that are broad in scope, we strive for results that are operationally significant to managers.

Because Harvard Business School faculty members are committed to pursuing research on the way business actually *does* function, as well as theoretical explorations of how it perhaps *should* function, they can give students and practitioners a vital perspective on the real world of professional practice. Their continuing close contact with operating businesses keeps Harvard Business School faculty at the frontiers of management practice. Research conducted by the faculty often yields insights that are of considerable practical benefit to managers in both day-to-day operations and longer-range planning.

In sponsoring the colloquium series of 1983–84, we hoped to set the course for research development over the next decade, and in particular to encourage greater emphasis on multiperson, multiyear studies of major issues. The complexity of many issues confronting business today almost requires that academicians find more effective forms of collaboration in doing our research. The problems we study are often beyond the capacity of any individual researcher.

In addition to encouraging a reshaping of researchers' work habits, the conferences promised to help strengthen the ties between Harvard Business School and the outside academic and business leadership communities. The series comprised sixteen conferences held at the Harvard Business School campus, each lasting two to five days. Papers were presented by eighty members of the HBS faculty and an approximately equal number of practitioners and academics from other institutions. Altogether, some 450 academics and practitioners were involved as discussants and participants.

Some of these colloquia focused on current research topics, such as U.S. competitiveness in the world economy, productivity and technology, global competition, and world food policy. Others concentrated on establishing agendas for the coming decade's research and course development in a particular field. Clearly, these were not tasks to be attempted in isolation. Rather we wanted to work jointly with others in business, government, and the academic world who could contribute and would themselves gain from the undertaking. The papers presented in this volume have all benefited from the thoughtful discussion they received at the colloquium.

Beyond exploring research findings in particular areas, we hoped that these colloquia would sustain and enliven the continuing dialogue between students and practitioners of management. From that melding of perspectives, we have found, insights emerge that can revitalize the education of future managers and refine current professional practice. In that spirit of cooperative endeavor, I am proud to introduce this collection of essays.

John H. McArthur
Dean of the Faculty
Harvard Business School

Part One
The Agency Relationship

Chapter 1
Principals and Agents: An Overview

John W. Pratt and Richard J. Zeckhauser

In writing this overview, we are acting as your agents. On behalf of our principal (you, the reader), we will try to offer an informative introduction to this volume. The first part of our overview describes the agency relationship itself, and the second provides a reader's guide to the articles in this collection.

As is often the case in agency relationships, we the agents are closer to the subject than you the principal. But it is your interest that should be served. Can you be confident that we will inform you in the best possible manner? Not necessarily. First, we must serve many masters simultaneously. The best overview for a mathematical economist is not the best for a business executive. Second, there is some natural divergence of interest between the agents (the volume editors) and the principal. Yet there is also reason for you to think that we would not purposely mislead you.

You may be reading this to determine whether you should buy the book. Might we as volume editors, eager to make a sale, assure you, an executive, that an examination of our book can boost your profits and improve your labor relations? Probably not. There are at least two inhibitions to such a subterfuge: the market and personal reputation.

Books of this sort are sold through outside reviews and word of mouth. A disingenuous opening might well prove counterproductive. More important, your editors would sacrifice a substantial portion of their academic reputations were they found to misrepresent in this way. Such a loss of reputation would in no way benefit the misled reader. But it represents a threat sufficient to keep the present agents true to their principals' interests. Hence we make no claim for our book except that it will contribute to your understanding of a wide variety of economic and social relationships.

The Agency Relationship

The success of a modern enterprise, however small its scale, is likely to rely on the actions of many individuals. Even "solo" street performers have their shills. The one-man grocery store has to be assured of good produce by its suppliers. And the giant auto manufacturer, as America learned over the past decade, cannot expect that if its unionized employees merely perform as specified in their contracts, high-quality output will be the result.

A predominant concern for an economy, discussed since the time of Adam Smith, is to assure that production is conducted in the most efficient manner, taking advantage of the benefits of specialization, appropriately conserving scarce factors, and so on. But even if we could figure out, or were willing to let the market figure out, the most efficient way to produce the goods, there would be the problem of ensuring that each individual performs his or her agreed-on task. If information flowed costlessly and perfectly, superiors would know what their subordinates knew and what they were doing, the stockholder could be confident that managers were operating the corporation as if it were their own, and retailers would know that suppliers would provide goods of appropriate quality. But in real life full information rarely is freely available to all parties, and so the problem becomes how to structure an agreement that will induce agents to serve the principal's interest even when their actions and information are not observed by the principal.

Whenever one individual depends on the action of another, an *agency relationship* arises. The individual taking the action is called the *agent.* The affected party is the *principal.* In common parlance, the doctor is the agent, the patient the principal. The consultant is the agent, the client the principal. The corporate executive is the principal, his subordinates the agents. The corporate executive in turn is an agent for the shareholders; the general partner plays that role vis-à-vis the limited partners.

In many contexts, the agency relationship may be reciprocal. The client, if satisfied, is expected to make favorable references for the consultant; he is also expected to act in good faith in providing information and in receiving and implementing recommendations. And the superior must fight to get his subordinates promotions.

The challenge in the agency relationship arises whenever—which is almost always—the principal cannot perfectly and costlessly monitor the agent's action and information. The problems of inducement and enforcement then come to the fore. For most of our discussion, we take the agent and principal as the only relevant parties. Thus, for example, we seek the new commission arrangement that makes both the corporation and its sales representative better off, without worrying whether its sales growth injures a rival firm.

The agency relationship is pervasive in business. Recognizing this recurrent pattern, which underlies a variety of surface forms, helps explain a great deal about how business is organized. That is, businesses' relationships are structured so as to enable principals to exert an appropriate influence on the actions of agents.

Two arguments weave through this volume. First, given information asymmetries—agents typically know more about their tasks than their principals do, though principals may know more about what they want accomplished—we cannot expect any business enterprise or business institution to function as well as it would if all information were costlessly shared or if the incentives of principal and agent(s) could be costlessly aligned. This shortfall is sometimes called the *agency loss* or *agency costs*. The challenge in structuring an agency relationship is to minimize it. In economic parlance, since the first-best outcome could be achieved only in the unrealistic world of costless information flow, our goal must be to do the best we can, to achieve what is sometimes called a second-best solution.

Second, business participants have been fairly successful in structuring mechanisms and arrangements to deal with agency problems. Still, a world struggling for a second-best solution is full of imperfections and shortfalls one might hope to reduce. Salespeople almost starve when they encounter a run of bad luck, so strongly is their compensation based on commissions. Corporate management deals itself golden parachutes. Employees loaf and call in sick when they want to go fishing.

Such occurrences do not necessarily imply that the world is not performing as well as it can. Three questions must be asked: (1) Is there another structure that would do better? Clearly it is undesirable for salespeople to be subjected to risk when the company could better bear it, but a commission system may be the only way to motivate them when they are beyond the view of the employer.

(2) Is the imperfect structure occurring in a new and unforeseen situation, so that there has not yet been an opportunity to develop appropriate responses? Golden parachutes are relatively recent as a

salient development and may wither away as better mechanisms are developed to serve the same function.[1]

(3) Are we looking at the aberrant case? The employee who loafs or fabricates an illness or even a disability claim may be one of a very small number who exploit a system that on the whole works fairly well with individuals with representative preferences or values. We must structure systems for their overall performance, not for unusual and unfavorable circumstances. (Even the would-be exploiters, be they individuals or companies, will be deterred if they would ultimately suffer substantially when found out.)

Our theme then is that businesses, workers, consumers, and indeed all participants in society at large regularly struggle to deal with the intractable problems that arise in agency relationships, that organizational forms evolve to deal with them, and that on average these forms perform reasonably well. Although we must expect waste, slothfulness, and even dishonesty to be with us always, the question is whether we can keep them to manageable proportions.

Our overview of the agency relationship begins with its economic building blocks, information and incentives. We then turn to agency structures themselves to illustrate how abstract formulations can help us understand real-world incentive mechanisms and perhaps improve upon their performance. The chapters in this volume focus on microeconomic phenomena such as corporate governance, labor contracts, and transfer prices. A proper understanding of the agency relationship, we would argue, provides insight into broader questions as well. Our discussion of the agency relationship concludes with a section on the organization of society, commenting on the appropriate roles of the private and public sectors as agents of the citizenry in providing for their welfare.

Information

In most social and business relationships, the parties have different information available to them. Relationships vary in the degree of informational asymmetry they involve. At one extreme we have the fabled perfect-market transaction, with standardized products and all information fully shared. At the other end of the continuum are situations in which the agent has full discretion and is not observed at all by the principal. The pure version of the latter pole is rarely observed in the real world, for the principal could not rely on the agent unless their interests coincided.[2] Family businesses are frequently run with considerable discretion and little monitoring, for with them there is probably a confluence of interests, as well as such nonmarket sanctions as family disapproval.

In their encounters with auto repair shops or plumbers, many laypeople feel they are dealing with unmonitored, hence unrestrained, agents. But we shall argue that in many circumstances where information does not flow freely, quite a few moderating devices are actually available, and that most of us are familiar with them.

Monitoring. The market is an effective monitor in many circumstances. We all know that in a strange city we should dine in a restaurant that is reasonably full. The fact that a gas station has survived suggests that it is doing something right. But if the owner can overcharge you while dealing fairly with his usual customers, you may be in trouble. The protection to the casual or one-time shopper is that most vendors do not make this distinction, but follow standard operating procedures. Thus the large department store has an advantage with out-of-town customers, and antiques stores without posted prices tend to scare away neophytes. (An approach to consumer protection that relies on the market would penalize not for high prices or low quality, but for discriminating among customers in prices or treatment.)

A central task of this volume is to explain why different relationships entail different levels of monitoring and types of incentives, and why we observe the monitoring and incentive structures that we do. Several principles emerge from our analyses. Some are self-evident, but have implications that are frequently overlooked:

1. We tend to get less monitoring, or monitoring of poorer quality, when monitoring is expensive and/or substitutes for monitoring are cheap.
2. The agency loss is the most severe when the interests or values of the principal and agent diverge substantially, and information monitoring is costly.

Some principles are less obvious, or counterintuitive, but no less important:

3. Ideally the agent's information and action would both be monitored. However, in a range of real-world situations, much more limited monitoring—say of an indicator of output—is relatively or fully successful.

4. A large stock of value that could be lost through bad behavior, such as reputation or assets subject to suit, is a strong incentive for good behavior.

5. Long-term relationships, among other benefits, develop the stocks of value needed for "enforcement," and make limited monitoring more effective.

6. The benefits of any reductions in agency loss will be shared between principal and agent in most market situations, including competition and monopoly. Therefore:

7. The principal and agent have a common interest in defining a monitoring-and-incentive structure that produces outcomes as close as possible to ones that would be produced if information monitoring were costless.

Most of these principles, and others that we shall come to as we proceed, would be accepted by the writers who have contributed to this book. But their application to specific situations can be controversial, as our later discussion of the individual chapters should reveal.

Untangling Market Information. A favorite pastime of economists and other students of markets is to assess market phenomena and speculate why they exist. A fundamental premise underlying most such discussions is that the participants within the markets are rational, intelligent beings. But conundrums then arise. Why, if capital markets are efficient, are firms or individuals engaged in corporate takeovers willing to pay substantial premiums over previous market price for companies they are acquiring? Or why do massive advertising campaigns—which seem to have little informational content— succeed in "creating" demand?

Inherent in these discussions is a more general paradox. How is it that the participants in these markets, few of whom are trained in information economics, can understand phenomena that are at the forefront of sophisticated discussion and debate among economic theorists?

One possible answer is that market participants do not have a conscious understanding of what they are doing, but have arrived at their solutions through a trial-and-error process, with the forces of natural economic selection letting only the most sophisticated strategies survive. This model, however, would not seem to apply to many of the situations studied. Only a limited number of trials are available for most forms of enterprise. The big oil mergers, the introduction of personal computers, and the merchandising of new products are relatively unique events. The type of groping toward superior outcomes that is associated with evolutionary processes could not explain these examples of sophisticated behavior.

At least a few alternative possible explanations are in order. First, the strategies themselves may not be so sophisticated after all. Perhaps perfectly efficient outcomes are not achieved. The market may be a lenient enforcer if market power tempers the forces of competition. Second, in a world with imperfect information, there may be many possible equilibrium outcomes. Once the first big oil merger goes through at an inflated price, the second one may become more likely. Everyone's expectations of what will happen, as Keynes stressed so long ago, play a major part in determining what actually does happen.

If expectations are a critical element, then the path breaker, the entrepreneur, will be the individual who has twin skills: (1) recognizing the expectations that currently exist in the market—knowing where the parade is going—and (2) getting at the front of the parade and influencing its direction just a bit. The big players in modern capital markets have to gamble as much on human psychology as on whether the oil well is dry or whether the fifth-generation computer will make it.

Imperfect Untangling. People make inferences about factual reality based indirectly on the actions of others they observe. Thus, for example, if a Massachusetts resident is asked what price he would accept in exchange for the mineral rights under his home, he might say $1,000; yet if a representative of Exxon comes to his door and offers him $50,000, he is expected to refuse. "Why is a sophisticated company offering me $50,000?" he wonders, and quickly concludes, "They must know something I don't. My mineral rights must be worth much more than that." To counter such suspicions, the would-be purchaser soon learns to conceal his true valuation.

Those who study these matters usually assume that every participant untangles information perfectly. But do they?[3] Given the interactive complexities, the world often does a highly imperfect job of untangling information. The problem is just too complicated, and few of us are sufficiently insightful poker players to discern the truth, or an appropriate probability distribution on the truth, from each other's observed strategies. Yet, we would argue, much untangling does take place, particularly in repeated or long-term relationships. Mark Wolfson's chapter in this volume provides an elegant example of how certain oil well drilling operators manage over time to create and gain from reputations for "unselfishly" following the interests of their limited partners.

Incentives

Each person performs his or her task in Adam Smith's pin factory. The sum of the achievements of a large collection of specialists is greater than the total of what each could achieve on his own. But the specialization of labor that has created the possibilities for productive modern industrial societies has also created the need for organizations larger than the crafts shop or family. The new challenge becomes how to motivate the participants within the organizations that make up society so that they will be as productive as they would be if they were the owners.

Microeconomic theory addresses this issue, of course. It assures us that given certain conditions for efficient market function (which appear to be reasonably approximated in the real world), the product of society will be maximized if individual actors are paid according to value of their marginal product and then maximize only for themselves.

Productivity and Rewards: The Separation. The simple prescription of microeconomic theory is difficult to apply in practice. It is hard to measure an individual's marginal product—what he or she adds to the total picture—in an organization of any size. If Company A's sales go up, is it because of the perseverance of the salesperson, the workers' greater attention to quality, or blind luck? And do we really think that deans can get a good measure of improved teaching performance by counting extra tuitions?

Indeed, the problem of measuring marginal product has become so intractable that the vast majority of Americans are paid on salaries. Though salaries in many positions are adjusted from year to year, and though good performance can be rewarded with promotions, there is a widespread feeling that this is a rather crude process with many inherent difficulties even under the most favorable circumstances.

Paying by product is further handicapped by institutions that restrict rewards. Unionized workers and civil service employees work in grades with restricted salary scales, limitations on speed of promotion, and so on. Bonuses are not permissible in many organizations. That is, we have created various restrictions that level reimbursement schedules. Some of these restrictions have been imposed by unions. Notice the fierce opposition of teachers' unions, for example, to merit pay.

A traditional justification for such restrictions, including opposition to piece work, is that workers will otherwise kill themselves through excessive efforts to earn more money. But if that were the problem, excessive wages would be needed to lure entrants to the rat race, and employers and workers would have a common interest in imposing sensible limitations and reasonable rewards. An alternative explanation is that level wages are favorable to the union organization itself. Otherwise, its members' solidarity would be broken by competition among them. Moreover, the union would then be presented with a difficult task: for whom would it bargain? This has already proved a serious problem for many unions that represent individuals with different crafts, skills, and longevities.

Those who administer salary scales, such as personnel officers in large corporations, may also have an incentive for leveling. When they can limit salary ranges, they have control. They can also limit competition within the organization for talented workers. If each manager could promote or reward as he or she wished, the role of a central personnel system would be substantially diminished.

In modern business enterprises, we cannot in general expect that individuals' rewards within a period will vary directly with their productivity. The natural obstacles to pay based on productivity, together with forces seeking to diminish the relationship between the two, are such that one cannot expect to get paid commensurately more if one produces more.

Naively we might think that a person on salary can simply commit to how much work he or she will put in. But if work input is difficult to measure, the employee may have an incentive to shirk. Some *indicator* of inputs, such as hours on the job, is likely to be used in evaluating the employee instead of a measurement of *actual* inputs, which would include the diligence and quality of those hours. And given that quality is difficult to measure objectively, and that workers differ in backgrounds and natural abilities, there will be a tendency to magnify one's past accomplishments and overestimate one's capabilities. Contemporary wage compensation systems, in which compensation is not closely tied to productivity, pose a sizable agency problem for the motivation of workers. (See Richard Epstein's chapter in this volume, which argues that because compensation and productivity may diverge, all labor contracts should be terminable at will by either side.)

Incentives Restored. The corporation and the modern economy have found ways to respond to this separation of rewards and productivity. Part of the solution is monitoring by superiors. The reward differentials they can impose within any period may be insufficient. But significant cross-period rewards can be employed. Promotions, for example, offer an individual higher future wages for the indefinite future. And dismissal imposes a major cost on the worker.

If motivation is particularly important and monitoring is costly, wages may be set above the amounts workers could earn elsewhere; the small chance of termination will then be a powerful incentive. Presumably wages above those available elsewhere will also be employed where there is a substantial opportunity for dishonesty, yet little ability to impose penalties. (This might be the case with employees of cash businesses for which revenues are hard to monitor.)

Unlike labor, capital need not be motivated. But informational asymmetries still can create interesting agency problems for capital, be it dollars or machines. The quality of a machine can be overstated; consider the used car or the new computer. And the owner of the capital, such as the outside shareholder in a small closely held corporation, may have difficulty determining what his capital has produced. The chief executive is often able to make accounting elections, such as FIFO over LIFO, that boost earnings, hence his bonus. Such a choice is inefficient for the principal-agent pair, however, since the government will receive more in taxes. (Robert Clark's chapter shows how the legal concept of fiduciary duty has been employed to restrain corporate-executive agents from slighting shareholders' interests.)

Difficulties in monitoring the productivity of capital, or even its level (e.g., quality of a machine), have led to the development of a number of institutions. Machines that can be abused or overused, but whose condition is difficult to monitor, are sold rather than leased. And a production process is likely to be vertically integrated if there are severe quality uncertainties at various stages.

Modern accounting attempts to keep track of capital and the profits it produces. However, accounting techniques cannot accurately assess many contributors to a firm's long-term profitability, such as reputation for quality, condition of equipment, or research accomplishments. An agency loss may be the consequence, with managements pursuing measured outputs, such as reported profits, at the expense of those that are difficult to tally. Some critics have identified this distortion as a major factor contributing to lagging American productivity.

The types of informational asymmetries that lead to agency loss make it difficult to reward labor or capital with the value of its product. Having the factors of production in a single business entity such as a corporation is advantageous. Long-term residence there allows for more creative reward structures, such as internal promotion opportunities. It also makes it clear that the factors are expected to work to a common purpose.

Combining diverse resources within a corporation or single organization may also help diminish losses due to breakdowns in bargaining. Consider a not unlikely situation in which each of a half-dozen units is vital to the long-term success of a corporation. If any one of these units pulled out, corporate profits would be diminished by at least one-half. The units must have a long-term involvement with the corporation so as to know its business and maintain confidentiality. A competitive structure, in which the company purchased the services of these units from the outside, could never work, because it would be impossible to find two or three marketing or basic research units with sufficient background to be realistic competitors in doing the job. But an organization that relied on just one outside supplier would be at its mercy. Those outside suppliers, one in each of six areas, could each make demands for up to half of the organization's profits. The problem is not that such demands will be satisfied—no organization can pay out three times its profits—but that substantial costs, including interruptions in production, will be incurred in the bargaining process. Bringing the agents under one roof, ostensibly with unified goals, may diminish such bargaining losses.

Conservative and Nonconservative Transactions. An ingenious element of the exchange mechanism for organizing economic relations is that what the buyer pays for an object, the seller receives. Assuming no resources are used up in the transfer, a continual process of exchanging goods and services can assure that the resources will end up in the hands of those who value them the most.

Exchange is not always costless. Forms must be filled out; credit must be checked; goods must be transported at a cost to A and then reshipped to B. Information is a primary source of transactions costs. For example, contrary to perfect-market assumptions, individuals do not always know about the quality of goods on the market. Hence we have sales representatives to tell us about goods and employment agencies to inform us about people, and we have advertising in general.[4]

In an ideal world, all transactions would be conservative, in the sense that exchanging resources would not in any way diminish the total pile. That is, transactions would conserve resources. Yet we find many instances of nonconservative systems. A bank cannot demonstrate solidity through financial statements alone, for example, but must reside in an impressive structure—a far from costless way of communicating its reliability. The customers have to pay for marble pillars as well as financial services. Whenever resources are expended to signal or convey information, the transaction is nonconservative.

Some resource exchanges are designed to provide incentives for behavior. If the payment is made solely in cash, conservation is maintained (leaving aside bookkeeping costs). Frequently, however, we observe the nonconservative use of incentives. Parents do not fine their naughty children; they send them to their rooms. The child's displeasure becomes a deadweight loss, benefiting no one.

Our criminal justice system relies on fines primarily for relatively minor crimes. For more serious violations, we seek to imprison individuals. This costs society a goodly amount. Few argue that rehabilitation is accomplished within prison walls. A naive economic view might suggest that we should merely find the appropriate fine and impose it on each criminal. But we all know that this could not work in practice, and agency theory helps explain why.

To provide efficient incentives, a fine or award for damages must exceed the gain by a factor reflecting the probability of discovery. A purse snatcher who gets $200 on average, with one chance in five hundred of being caught, would appropriately be fined $100,000, an uncollectible amount given prohibitions on slavery.[5] Nonconservative penalties are frequently employed if it is unlikely that a misrepresentation or other form of misbehavior would be discovered and if institutional factors rule out the use of draconian conservative penalties. To provide adequate inducements in such situations, we must employ penalties that hurt the transgressor significantly. Hence, imprisonment, not fine, is the risk for the typical thief. And businesspeople know that a reputation of standing in the community is a good way to assure their associates of honest dealing, for a valued asset is at hostage in any business transaction.

Similarly, we would assert, many traditional business transactions employ penalties that are far from conservative. The dealer on the New York diamond exchange who fails to keep his word is forever banned from trading. The family member who does not live up to a commitment loses face, not money. The supplier who fails to deliver a critical product on time may have to pay under a penalty clause (a conservative transaction). More likely, though, he will lose a customer, and become the subject of a whispering campaign. Those who gain from the whispering campaign (or the loss of face, or the ban) probably reap far less than what was lost.

These penalties are in the nature of performance bonds intended to assure good behavior by means of a threat that is rarely carried out. Their nonconservative nature entails little deadweight loss because the probability that the penalty is paid is small. This contrasts with the typical incentive schedule used for employment, where some incentive is always paid and if that incentive is not conservative there is an efficiency loss.

In many circles, past plays of the game add to one's personal reputation. In virtually every industry there is a gossip circle that tells who is honorable, tough, sleazy, and so on. These reputations play a major role in determining what future deals will be struck, and on what terms. In reacting to the financial forays of Rupert Murdoch, Carl Icahn, and T. Boone Pickens, for example, the market will be guided by what they are known to have done in the past.

In recent years, it has become commonplace to launch major new products with extensive advertising campaigns. These campaigns are nonconservative. Since the customers receive nothing but information, would these companies make bigger profits if they spent their advertising budget instead on improving product quality or lowering prices? Possibly. But in most cases we suspect the companies know what they are doing. To see why, a richer understanding of information transfer is imperative. A Veblenesque explanation would look to the status and prestige conferred on the product by advertising. (Owning a shirt with a little polo player becomes something significant.) More important factors related to agency theory may be the inferences that can be drawn from the very fact of advertising: (1) the company has confidence in its product quality (it would not spend so much promoting a new product unless it was expected to sell well), and (2) there are substantial resources behind the product.

Consider the success of IBM in introducing its personal computer. Although virtually every expert suggests that some competitor products offer a superior price-quality package, IBM is by far the best seller. It is IBM's reputation—for quality and resources—that explains its success with this product. It is difficult to judge a personal computer, in particular to know about its likely repair record, reliability, and the like. With IBM, customers know that either the machine is reliable or IBM will stand behind it to make it reliable. Its ample resources are an assurance that the company will be in business a number of years from now. There will be no problem with service contracts or replacement parts.

Obviously, IBM has other advantages as well. More software will be written for its PCs and more facilities will be able to repair them. But these advantages are all due in part to the primary ingredients, quality assurance and adequate resources. In like manner, the mere expenditure of resources in an advertising campaign, even if only a deadweight loss, conveys the information that the company has confidence in its product and expects to be around for a while.

We need these nonconservative mechanisms because fully efficient contracting is not feasible. In an ideal world, a computer manufacturer would merely make attestations about product quality, with an assurance of compensation should they not be met. But such claims—particularly about generalized product quality—are difficult to make and convey precisely, suits about product claims are costly and difficult to bring, and in the unlikely worst case, bankruptcy is an ultimate protection for the manufacturer.

In short, agency theory, we would suggest, provides a much richer understanding of the use of rewards than is provided by the traditional competitive model of microeconomics, in which each factor of production is paid the value of the product it produces and, leaving aside the minimal cost of making transfers, rewards are conservative.

In the real world, the product of a factor is difficult to measure, there are significant pressures to divorce immediate reward from productivity, and monitoring considerations make it desirable to employ nonconservative transactions. In response, most business is conducted within the context of long-term relationships. Subtle mechanisms involving reputations, promises of future promotions, and the surplus gained from less than fully competitive long-term contracts help an economy in which information is not costlessly shared to struggle to second-best solutions.

Alignment of Objectives. The intriguing element of the agency relationship arises when principal and agent have divergent objectives. But intellectual interest is merely a lagniappe; productivity is the goal. Hence, principals and agents will seek situations in which purposes line up naturally. If we can get work that we like, we needn't worry about our boss's standing over us. Moreover, if we do not shirk, and there is no need for monitoring, we can share in the resulting cost savings. Harvard University's real estate operation has discovered that student athletes make prized summer maintenance workers. For their own purposes, they want to do a lot of hard physical labor. Religious cults and family businesses frequently get a level of dedication from their members that would not be possible without a strong alignment of perceived interests.

The alignment of interests helps not only to assure an appropriate level of effort, but to promote the right choices. Politicians always try to appoint people who share their goals, who will make the choices regarding welfare or the environment that they would make. A college president who is seeking to attract more scholars and fewer athletes to the student body is likely to appoint an admissions director who shares that goal. And the corporate executive who thinks the future lies with product A, not B, can be expected to place like-minded managers in positions of responsibility. Those who share one's objectives tend to carry them out; monitoring and conflict are reduced, and such people may even make themselves available at a cheaper price.

Alignment of objectives is beneficial to the performance of the agency relationship. Both agent and principal have an incentive to seek a good match. If either judges the match satisfactory, he can be expected, as a recruitment mechanism, to exaggerate a natural confluence of interests. On the social front, a successful date knows enough to express delight in his or her partner's favorite recreations. Similarly, when Wall Street law firms recruit at prestigious liberal law schools they stress the possibilities they offer for pro bono work. And all parties make clear their commitments to fair dealing, integrity, and long-term relationships. Even when these masquerades of natural alignments of interest can be untangled, they must be expected. Any firm knows that the talented new college graduate who claims to be looking for a permanent job may well be going back to graduate school. But that applicant is a better bet for the position than one who announces graduate school intentions, and thus is more likely to get it; hence many candidates conceal their true plans.

Agency Structures

With perfect competition or perfect contracting, there would be no need for continuing business relationships or indeed business organizations. We could construct the required entities as we went along.

But most of the commerce in the real world is conducted in long-standing relationships, and most production takes place in long-lived business institutions. These arrangements not only reduce contracting and monitoring costs, they build trust, facilitate the flow of information, make it possible to make trade-offs at the last minute, and offer some risk-spreading advantages.

Yet long-term relationships are not unmixed blessings. Why is it that many manufacturing establishments rarely seek competitive bids for many of their basic supplies? One factor is the absence of appropriate incentives. The manager who spends considerable time and energy shopping around gets little credit if costs are reduced, but will certainly be blamed if something goes wrong with the new supplier.[6] The agent (manager) may sacrifice the welfare of the principal (corporation) to assure the performance of his own agent (supplier), which will in turn protect him from the types of unfortunate outcomes that could be monitored. The surplus profits that the long-term supplier can expect to reap over a period of time make it worth his while to maintain quality and to provide limited extra services when needed.

Though they are perhaps happiest when dealing with extreme cases, such as the competitive market paradigm, economists can contribute something of value to a discussion of the real-world relationships that are the focus of this volume. The analytic foundations of microeconomics address a great variety of real-world situations, including monopoly, government regulation, imperfect product information, and so on. But when venturing beyond the boundaries of the simplest case, economists have often maintained some of its more comforting assumptions. In particular, it has been common to assume that contracts could be drawn readily and enforced costlessly. In fact, however, contracting difficulties are a central feature of many agency relationships.

In his evaluation of agency theory, which follows, Kenneth Arrow points out that the principal-agent relationship in the real world frequently diverges sharply from what is derived in economic models. In particular, the models frequently prescribe complex fee schedules, whereas observed schedules are almost always simple. Even where the models produce relatively simple suggestions—for example, that a physician's payment should depend at least in part on medical outcome—the real world produces different answers.[7]

The divergence is explained in part by the difficulty in specifying and enforcing contracts in the real world. Practical arrangements simply can't reproduce the complexities that agency theory, in its exact form, requires. Moreover, in many instances the gains from complication are small. But there is another explanation that has a quite different thrust. The real world has many more instruments available to reward its players than are found in most analytic models. Arrow stresses social rewards, such as reputation in the community or the returns that come from adhering to a set of ethics. Friendship, family, and connections also play a substantial role in creating additional types of incentives. The real world, we would argue, may be much more sophisticated than economic models in using its rich palette of instruments.

The Design of Agency Structures. In considering the agency problem, it is perhaps natural to focus on the question of how the principal can reap the greatest advantage through incentives that influence the agent's behavior, yet reward the agent enough so that he will not quit. Two central assumptions are implicit in this formulation: first, that the principal is in a position to design the monitoring and incentive mechanism; second, that all the benefits from improvements in performance go to the principal.

We wish to argue that agency situations often satisfy neither of these assumptions and that the most important issues do not depend on them. In fact, the agent and principal are merely two (or more) individuals (or organizations) in some sort of explicit or implicit contractual relationship. The mechanism of oversight and reward may be designed by either the agent (most lawyers, for example, define the terms of their financial relationships with clients) or the principal (the store manager probably sets the employment conditions for retail clerks). There may be a joint negotiation, as we see with labor agreements under collective bargaining. Or some external party may set the terms, as the government does in structuring many of the rules by which corporations are governed in the United States.

Prospective Changes. Agency costs—the fact that employees leave and steal customers, or that no broker will be as careful with one's money as oneself, or that automobile repairpeople do slipshod work— are as much the problems of employees, brokers, and repairpeople (the agents) as of their respective principals. How the inefficiency costs will be borne depends on alternative supplies and demands.

In agency relationships, better monitoring and incentive structures produce outcomes closer to what might be achieved in a world of costless contracting and perfect information flow. Reducing the costs created by information asymmetries enhances efficiency. Who benefits when these costs are reduced depends on such matters as the availability of other agents and principals, not primarily, if at all, on who sets the terms for the agency relationship. (The principle is the same as in nonagency situations: for example, competition will force a manufacturer to share with his retailers the benefits from any reductions in freight costs.)

Consider the hypothetical taxi company that for years has leased its taxis in return for 50 percent of revenues. On average it has received $50 per shift. A consultant's report reveals that its drivers would hustle more if they rented for a fixed fee and kept all of the revenues. Moreover, the gains in revenue would be sufficient to compensate the drivers for the additional risk they would be bearing and the gas they would be using, and still leave a $5 per shift surplus. This surplus will be split between the drivers and the company. The division, as in the freight-cost case, will depend on the shapes of the company's demand and supply curves for drivers.[8]

We propose that the following principle governs prospective changes:

> Any changes in the rules of the game in an agency relationship will either benefit or hurt all players if no contracts have yet been drawn, no capital or labor is yet committed to particular industries, all factors can move costlessly to their highest-valued use, and players are rational and self-interested.

If we accept this principle, we see that the search for superior instruments for allocating resources in a world where information does not flow freely is predominantly a search for efficiency rather than a struggle over distribution.[9] We should expect to find no debates as to whether employees should be paid time and one-half for overtime. If the gain in production efficiency can compensate the employee for the marginal loss of leisure, it should. The manager need not worry whether centrally provided services should be charged against his shadow budget. The worker and manager should agree on the circumstances in which the worker can be dismissed. (See Epstein's chapter in this volume.)

Retroactive Changes. In fact, of course, disputes over such issues are commonplace. Part of the problem arises because the contractual arrangements are not negotiated entirely at one time. Consider labor-management negotiations. The union and management strike a three-year deal in 1985. In 1986, a case of possible wrongful dismissal arises.

It can be expected that the union will be solidly on one side, management on the other. It is too late now to go back and suggest that if the union will be more flexible on this issue, higher wages will be awarded. If issues come up piecemeal, mutually beneficial trades may be precluded.

This problem arises with a vengeance in the context of government regulation. Most workers and unions, and even some managements, believe that what is awarded through government regulation, say on conditions for occupational safety, comes free to one party at the expense of the other. Thus, a labor-oriented administration will serve as an agent for labor in pushing the role of the Occupational Safety and Health Administration (OSHA). A probusiness government will attempt to rein in that agency. Such policies help their intended beneficiaries only to the extent and for the reason that they are in essence changing conditions after contracts have already been drawn.

If contracts had not already been drawn, if labor and machines were not in place, the government would not be able to pick and choose which constituencies it wished to represent. All constituencies would have a common interest in reaching the most efficient possible solution.

In the real world, however, we are seldom dealing with a clean slate. When OSHA insists on higher standards in the workplace, we already have well-trained workers and machines in place. If we strengthen the product liability laws, the thousands of manufacturers who already have their products out in the marketplace are all hurt. When a corporation unexpectedly reduces fringe benefits, it hurts employees with limited mobility, perhaps due to ties to the community. Changes in contracts or policies have retroactive features. This suggests another principle, with a quite different implication.

> To the extent that capital is in place, contracts drawn, and commitments made, any rule change will have retroactive implications. That is, it will have effects that, if anticipated, would have affected previous decisions. This feature of rule changes has redistributive consequences. The more important the retrospective implications of a change relative to its efficiency gains, the closer it comes to being purely redistributive in its consequences.

Redistributive effects usually help the individuals on one side of the principal-agent relationship at the expense of those on the other side. To bring about a rule change that would increase efficiency, it may be necessary or desirable to neutralize the redistributive effects due to its retroactive implications. Two common methods of doing so are offsetting monetary redistributions and grandfather clauses. (The latter may sacrifice efficiency gains to preserve contractual integrity for past agreements. Such integrity in itself represents a stock of value.)

Heterogeneous Agents or Principals. If there is heterogeneity among the participants on one side of the agency relationship, it will create a natural source of dispute over rules changes. The energetic taxi drivers will like the switch to a rental system; lazy drivers will prefer the former revenue-split arrangement. Hypochondriacs will resist a change to a lower insurance premium in conjunction with a per-visit charge at the medical clinic.

When principals cannot distinguish among heterogeneous agents or vice versa, we see different kinds of effects of information asymmetry. Instead of affecting the principal-agent arrangement, asymmetry here affects the relationship between two different classes of individuals on the same side of the fence. This type of asymmetry, which arises frequently, has distributional implications even when changes are prospective. The agent who performs less well for the principal—say a manager who makes excessive use of centrally provided services because they are "free" to him—would like to see the asymmetry in information persist.

Knowing that principals cannot readily distinguish between effective and ineffective performers, weak agents seek to blend with strong agents. Similarly, weak principals like to be confused with strong ones. For example, companies with less marketable products would try to withhold that information from potential sales representatives.

Legal or institutional barriers to drawing distinctions play the same mixing role. Prohibitions against piece rates, grading, civil service examinations, and merit rating of insurance all have the effect of blending heterogeneous populations of agents. It is important to recognize that the primary losers in this process are not the principals—the employers, the teachers, the taxpayers, or the insurance companies. (Their well-being is maintained by a change in price for the services they receive.) Rather, those losing most are the workers, students, job applicants, and insurees who could have benefited by differentiating themselves from the mass. The process may also entail a loss of efficiency, whose distribution across the members of society will depend on the competitive situation. But in this form of market transaction, masquerading mainly hurts not the one who is deceived, but the one who is imitated.

How Are We Doing? Two major lessons emerge from an analysis of agency structures. First, if one is starting afresh in an agency relationship, the principle governing prospective changes applies: both principal and agent can gain by looking for more efficient monitoring and incentive structures. This argument recently convinced the entrepreneur in a start-up venture that because his investors would be in higher tax brackets than he, he should give up his tax benefits from the expected initial period of losses. He could expect to more than recover this sacrifice through an agreement giving him a greater share of stock when the partnership was converted to a corporation.

Second, it is frequently possible to improve on standard agency structures. Some of these structures are the product of political decisions affecting contracts already in place. Some are good for past circumstances, but not the present. Many just have not been thought out clearly. The Lehman formula for compensating investment bankers who arrange mergers is a clear example of an inferior arrangement. The formula offers a 5-4-3-2-1 schedule; that is, the banker gets 5 percent of the first million of total price, 4 percent of the second million, and so on, with 1 percent of anything over $5 million. This arrangement creates little incentive for the banker to work hard at the margin or risk the deal in the attempt to get a better price. If a company is expected to sell for roughly $4 million, all parties might be better off if the fee were $100,000 plus 4 percent of the amount over $3 million. Not only would incentives for effort be stronger at the margin, but the presumably expert investment banker would be much more willing to advise the firm to turn down an insufficient offer. With the Lehman formula, the investment banker who brings the client $5 million as opposed to $4 million gets only 7 percent more in fees.

In like manner, incentives are better aligned if the principal pays the expenses of an outside paid agent, whether a lawyer, a real estate broker, or a consultant. Those expenses mainly benefit the principal; if their full cost is borne by the agent, who receives only a tiny percentage of the benefit, skimping must be expected. Though this principle is incorporated into most legal relationships, and many consulting relationships, it is rare with real estate brokers.

Agents are often paid on an hourly basis; excessive effort is the natural result if, as is often the case, the agent is receiving more than his reservation wage (the lowest sum for which he would be willing to work). Such contracts can be improved. The agent should be granted a lump-sum amount and a lower hourly rate. Say a consultant with a reservation wage of $30 per hour has accepted a project expected to take 100 hours at a fee of $50 per hour. The improved contract would give the consultant $2,000, his existing surplus, and then pay at the rate of $30 per hour, his true cost of input. Home decorators correctly employ the principle of avoiding distortion when they charge a fixed amount and pass on their decorator's discount price on materials.

In sum, the world struggles to do a good job, and does quite well in many areas. But with a little thought, and a willingness to go against convention, one can frequently come up with creative ways to do better.[10]

The Organization of Society

In 1985 more than a quarter of the United States' gross national product flows through the government. Perhaps the most central political debate in our society, as well as in other developed and underdeveloped nations, is which sector shall produce what. Will government or the private sector perform better in the interests of the citizenry?

Part of the answer is provided by a consideration of market performance. The theory of competitive equilibrium is the most beautiful edifice of economics. Although incompletely understood and appreciated by the general public, its suggestion that competitive markets promote the general good has become the philosophical underpinning for free market societies. Moreover, faith in the benevolence of the invisible hand—and evidence that governments make decisions for political, not efficiency, purposes—is the primary intellectual restraint on the growth of the public sector in mixed-enterprise societies.

Microeconomics can be a dispassionate servant. The theory of market failure and the ramifications of the new welfare economics have helped provide an intellectual justification for a variety of government interventions in the marketplace, including antitrust legislation, the regulation of toxic waste disposal, disclosure requirements for securities, occupational safety legislation, pension vesting rules, and the provision of public goods, such as national defense.

Some of these interventions, such as disclosure requirements, are intended to facilitate the functioning of the private market. Others, however, involve the government directly in allocating resources. It can regulate patterns of production (pollution control), finance an output (purchase of medical services through Medicare), or produce the good itself (public education). Sometimes, in a rather substantial extension of the agency concept, the government identifies a merit want such as medical care and on a paternalistic basis influences individuals to purchase goods they would not choose for themselves.

Though enlightened by the simple models of economics, which provide logical arguments for and against government participation, we still confront the agency side of the question: How well do business and government perform their respective tasks when viewed as agents for the citizens? What are the structures for monitoring and providing incentives in each sector, and how effective are they?

The advocates of government decry the practices of businesses, particularly big businesses. They see management as self-serving, view the workplace as dehumanizing, and complain that products are well packaged but shoddy. It is quite obvious, they argue, that we should not let the profit motive drive such vital industries as health care and education. Those are industries where information asymmetries abound, customers have a difficult time judging output, and agency problems come to the fore. A for-profit organization must be expected to take advantage of unknowledgeable customers.

The rival camp sings the praises of business and believes that stockholders' interests are well represented and that customers in general need not beware, for the market protects. This group suggests that special interests, including government workers, manipulate the government to their own benefit, and that bureaucrats are frequently lazy, incompetent, downright dishonest, or so numerous that they simply trip over one another. The absence of a bottom line to measure performance, and of a base of paying customers that will demand satisfaction, means that when government purchases or produces goods and services, the cost will be too high and quality too low.

The arguments on both sides point up deficiencies in the citizen-principals' ability to impose appropriate incentives for the agent, be it the public or private sector, and in the relevant sector's motivation and competence to structure itself to produce efficiently. It would be comforting to conclude that this fundamental debate on how society should be organized revolves around issues of appropriate incentives and comparative performance. Then it might be subject to empirical resolution.

But another, more fundamental, factor may be at work. Society is by no means homogeneous. The opposing sides in this political debate for the most part not only espouse different principles, but also favor different principals. Many private-sector detractors, for example, decry corporate irresponsibility. They believe that managements should not just be responsive to shareholder interests, but should take account of the welfare of workers, customers, and society at large. The counter-argument is that the market imposes appropriate penalties if management neglects worker welfare (namely higher wages) or consumers' demand for quality products (reduced sales), and that leaving it to corporate good intentions to promote society's interests will penalize those corporations that respond. No one would propose that corporate income taxes be voluntary. To promote any societal goal, fairness and efficiency demand that uniform incentives should be imposed, whether through taxes or regulations.

The government is also accused of catering to the wrong principals. When it is a supplier, for example, as it is with education, it is alleged that its monopoly position relieves it of the burden of satisfying the intended principals: the students, their parents, and the taxpayers. Instead it caters to those who are in the arena full-time and for the longest duration, the teachers and school administrators. Similarly, regulatory agencies cater to their industries, the Defense Department to its contractors.

The debate must also recognize that the public and private arenas tend to weight principals' interests rather differently. Government responds to ballots and political influence. Their distribution is quite different from that of endowments of dollars and marketable skills, the basis of private sector weights. Both advocates and opponents of greater centralized participation in our economy appear to believe that the more the government controls rewards, the more even will be the ultimate division of spoils. But if government involvement inevitably reduces efficiency, the size of the pie and its division may prove to be inseparable considerations.

These issues raise strong passions. It is not our purpose to settle them or express our own views. We do point out that much of the debate on private versus public control over resource allocation revolves around the performance of the two sectors as agents. But the principals for the two sectors differ; and that is a more fundamental source of disagreement.

This Volume

This volume is a product of a conference convened to celebrate the seventy-fifth anniversary of the Harvard Business School. Not surprisingly, there is no course at the Business School with the word *agency* in its title. But we believe that most members of the faculty, whether they teach international business or management accounting, would acknowledge that they spend a good part of their time talking about agency relationships, in our sense of the term. How did Japan manage to convert a national reputation for shoddy goods into a worldwide reputation for quality? Is an accounting firm required to police its clients in interpreting accurate but misleading information? These are questions of agency.

Our conference crossed disciplines and professions. To assure ourselves of relevance, and to keep us from soaring too often to the stratosphere of abstraction, we invited practicing business decision makers as active participants and discussants. Thus, for example, Malcolm Brachman, an independent oil man (and physics Ph.D.), discussed the investigation of oil and gas tax shelters by Mark Wolfson, an accounting professor. Roger Stern, a New York City attorney and American Stock Exchange chief executive officer, addressed law professor Robert Clark's discourse on the fiduciary duties of corporate managers and directors. Robert Scott, Harvard's vice president for administration, tackled sociologist Harrison White's exegesis of the use of agency as a mechanism for exerting control within organizations. Michael Brewer, an executive of Cummins Engine Company, reviewed the work of business school professor Robert Eccles on transfer prices. And theatrical and movie agent Sam Cohn drew on his own experiences to assess the agency relationship. Cohn's career demonstrates that with objectives appropriately aligned—i.e., with the agent passionately committed to his client's (principal's) welfare—agency losses can be avoided.

Law professor Richard Epstein's analysis of collective bargaining was discussed by Herman Leonard, an economist whose down-to-earth orientation comes from teaching accounting and finance. Economics professor Kenneth Arrow's discussion of the economics of agency was addressed by law professor Frank Easterbrook, who turned his comments into his chapter on insider trading. Andrew Nevin and Mary O'Keeffe recorded our proceedings. Nancy Jackson, our editor, moderated any tendencies to the pedantic or obscure.

The Agency Relationship

The first section of the volume, including this "Overview" and Kenneth Arrow's chapter, "The Economics of Agency," focuses on the agency relationship in general.

Arrow, the world's foremost contributor to the economics of information (and a Nobel Laureate), explains the foundations of the agency relationship. Even readers with little taste for abstraction will benefit from Arrow's evaluation of the agency literature. He stresses that "the agency relationship is a pervasive fact of economic life . . . at least one significant component of almost all transactions." But he questions whether economists' conceptual models have yet done a good job in describing the principal-agent relation in actuality. He suggests that we must move beyond the usual boundaries of economic analysis—for example, looking at social values that might be internalized during an education process, not just monetary incentives—if we are to achieve adequate explanatory and prescriptive formulations. Arrow thus provides a challenge that is taken up in the remainder of this volume. The subsequent chapters all confront real-world phenomena and employ them as a means to develop general lessons about agency relationships.

Institutional Responses

The second section of this volume examines various institutional responses to agency problems. Robert Clark turns his legal mind to the operation of the modern corporation. Shareholders entrust their money to corporate managements, but have little practical control. Given the asymmetry of power in this relationship, corporations probably could not survive unless the environment placed constraints on this use of power. The rise of the modern corporation, therefore, would not have been possible without some external check or control, in this instance provided by the legal system, which creates stringent concepts of fiduciary duty for directors and managers.

Clark's analysis takes us well beyond the traditional economic models, in which agency relationships are defined through explicit or implicit contract. He points out that it would not be possible to make enforceable commitments to all relevant elements of the contract. The solution has been to create the fiduciary's responsibilities to disclose information pertinent to the shareholders' (principals') interests. Corporate managers have an open-ended fiduciary duty to act on behalf of the principal. Their rights to capitalize on their positional advantage are restrained. In particular, they have a moral duty to follow the spirit of the law governing their position.

Clark focuses on the modern corporation and the relatively success-ful mechanisms that have evolved to enable it to survive. It is worth speculating, however, on the numerous business institutions and transactions that cannot establish themselves because there is no in-herent equivalent to the external framework provided by law and its concept of fiduciary duties. Many entrepreneurs, for example, must slowly accumulate their own capital because they can provide no convincing reassurance to investors that: (1) they have sufficient faith in their idea, (2) they are presenting their initial knowledge honestly and fully, and (3) they will not exploit their position of superior knowl-edge and power once they get control of their investors' money.

Unsolved agency problems of this kind are worth further considera-tion, for they raise a thematic question of the volume. To what extent can we be confident that existing institutions—possibly laissez-faire—deal with asymmetries of information and interest optimally or nearly optimally? If experimentation is readily undertaken, a search for superior outcomes should assure high-quality performance. But if an institutional structure is imposed by custom, common law, or legisla-tion, there can be substantially less confidence that a desirable out-come has been reached. First, even with the help of human imagina-tion and blue-ribbon panels, societies do not easily search a terrain to discover preferred mechanisms. In the natural world, the evolution of the species has been a slow process, even though it has proceeded through millions of near-simultaneous trials. The task is still more difficult for agency structures. We can experiment with only one fed-eral legal system at a time. Moreover, the human environment is changing rather more quickly than the natural environment. Surely there has been a change in the postwar era—with the advent of com-puters, modern communication systems, and highly developed capi-tal markets—in the best way for corporations to run themselves.

Second, because resources have already been committed and con-tracts drawn, the introduction of superior institutional forms, particu-larly if they are imposed by the society as a whole, may have sub-stantial redistributive consequences. (See our earlier discussion of retroactive changes.) Experiments will be fiercely fought by those who stand to lose. The power of the status quo will exert itself. Clark cautions us against the "facile optimism" that assumes that the arrangements we observe are in fact optimal, even though he focuses on an institution that has been largely successful, the development of the concept of fiduciary duties as an underpinning of the modern corporation.

Frank Easterbrook examines insider trading, an emotional issue in the field of corporate governance and fiduciary duties. Whether insider trading should be allowed, and if so under what restrictions, is clearly a question of identifying a preferred structure within an agency relationship. In itself such trading will not necessarily increase or decrease efficiency.

Easterbrook dismisses appeals to the "fairness" or "morality" of an agreed-upon structure. Insider trading is not inherently "unfair" to the shareholders, he argues, for the market will discount this practice in the pricing of securities. However, because we are operating in a world where many contracts have already been drawn, and where different executives would have quite different attitudes toward capitalizing on inside information, any changes in the rules will have substantial redistributive effects. Thus a reversal of rules that is not reasonably in accord with prior expectations (i.e., a retroactive change) may well be unfair.

Easterbrook's analysis provides an interesting twist on the "whatever is, is right" argument. He observes that in those places where insider trading has not been prohibited by law, it has persisted. If it were not an efficient form of compensation, he asks, would not private contracts between managers and shareholders be written to eliminate this practice? The answer to his question is assuredly yes, if it would be relatively straightforward for shareholders to monitor insider trading and to exact contractually agreed-upon penalties. But if monitoring is imprecise, and if draconian penalties (which could compensate for a low detection probability) are ruled out by social norms, then insider trading might flourish even if inefficient, a possibility that Easterbrook recognizes. If so, managements would favor a self-denying ordinance, but would be unable to put it into place.

Perhaps only society, which has such enforcement advantages as economies of scale in monitoring and nonconservative criminal penalties, is able to commit to prohibit insider trading. Logical regulatory alternatives include a ban (no insider trading), certification (insider trading unless a firm or individual commits not to), and no regulation (unrestricted insider trading). However society makes its choice, it will not be through free competition among the alternatives; thus there can be no assurance that the existing system is near-optimal.

The Clark and Easterbrook papers explore situations in which principals may be unable to structure contracts directly. One may only be able to contract within the structures that the economy and society as a whole have produced. In a more limited context, this is the dilemma of the fully open and straightforward used-car dealer. However he structures his contracts and advertising, it will be difficult for him to convince potential customers that his intentions and actions are very different from what they believe to be the norm of his profession. One way around this problem, presumably, is collective action, either undertaken by the participants or enforced through the society. The first tack has been taken by the member firms of the New York Stock Exchange, who police their own members. The second is the way of virtually every professional group that can impose some form of licensing requirement.

It is worth observing that policing or self-policing can only work (assuming that the major available penalty is banishment) if there is some prize to be lost. The competitive market system does not generate prizes, however. The ability to enforce good behavior on the part of agents thus may require that there be some element of monopoly profit.

Mark Wolfson examines the oil and gas industry, an arena peppered with agency problems due to severe informational asymmetries. Moreover, the U.S. tax code has encouraged investment in oil and gas drilling by limited partnerships—a classic agency relationship. The limited partners (the principals) put up most of the capital, while the general partner (the agent) makes most of the decisions. The limited partners are typically far from the scene of action, and most of them have no experience or expertise in the business.

Conflicts of interest abound. The general partner frequently sells services to his limited partners. He may also have related investments nearby and may benefit personally from the information gained from drilling. Most important, the traditional functional allocation form of partnership imposes all of the immediately deductible costs on the limited partners (to capitalize on tax advantages), whereas completion costs are shared between the limited and general partner, or may even be fully the responsibility of the general partner. In essence, the general partner has too much incentive to drill and, for some revenue splits, too little incentive to complete.

The agency problems in drilling are well known to both operators and limited partners. Prospectuses detail them at length, and point out as well that monitoring by the limited partners is not really feasible. To reassure prospective investors, general partners explain verbally that they are more interested in their long-term reputation and relationships than in short-term profits.

Wolfson tests a number of empirical assertions about the outcomes we should expect in this arena. For example, the problem of distorted incentives is less severe in exploratory than developmental drilling. Hence, more limited partnerships should operate there, and they do.

Wolfson's most intriguing hypotheses relate to the role of reputation and its use as a mechanism to overcome agency losses. If an operator/general partner can build a reputation for success, Wolfson demonstrates, he can secure investment funds on more favorable terms. To build his reputation, he takes actions to benefit the limited partners at the expense of his own immediate profits. Wolfson's data reveal that operators with records of success for limited partners do receive more favorable terms from investors.

A good reputation, as we remarked earlier, is an asset that can be squandered through bad behavior. The agent who has one will be loathe to sacrifice it, for it offers considerable reassurance to others that the agent will behave well. IBM demonstrated such behavior when it upgraded its unsatisfactory PC/Jr. computer keyboard free of charge. Pillars of the community find that their reputations assist in their business dealings. Wolfson shows that even, or perhaps particularly, in the treacherous world of oil and gas drilling, reputations can help overcome contracting difficulties and the resulting inefficiencies.

Richard Epstein's paper examines employment and labor contracting, the field in which agency relationships have been most widely studied. Labor resources have numerous special features that make agency problems a concern. Unlike capital holdings, labor resources cannot be readily diversified. Usually an individual must take just one job. And unlike machines, workers are far from standardized and must be motivated to work. They are likely to accumulate capability over their careers through training and experience. Such improved capability may or may not be portable to other firms.

Employers have various means to control their employees, including direct supervision and monitoring; piecework, bonus, and promotion schemes; and, most severe, hiring and firing. Assuming once again a situation in which no contracts have yet been drawn, these could equally well be viewed as mechanisms by which workers can assure employers that they will work appropriately. In a free labor market, presumably employer and employee would agree on the most efficient oversight and reward mechanism.

Epstein asks, what types of labor contracts would we expect to find in an unregulated market? In particular, what would be the basis for dismissals or firings? He suggests that what such a market would produce is likely to be optimal: the contractual forms that will minimize the adverse impacts of the agency costs that arise because of informational asymmetries.

Both worker and employer confront considerable risk when they enter into an employment contract, each knowing relatively little about the other. Epstein argues that it is in the two parties' mutual interest to maintain as much flexibility as possible. Thus he believes that either party should be able to cancel the employment contract at any time. The fact that at-will contracts have predominated through history, Epstein suggests, indicates that they are efficient.

Contracts at will, he says, represent "the best means of responding to the problems of controlling agency costs and imperfect information about employment. Their great strength is that they allow each side continuously to monitor the other for violations of the original understanding."

Epstein's essay raises once again the question of whether what is, assuming that it is freely arrived at through contract, is best. This issue motivates both Clark's discussion of the need for fiduciary duties enforced by law and Easterbrook's questioning of making insider trading a matter of legislation rather than contractual agreement. The editors believe that an in-between position is appropriate. We cannot be confident that what we observe is best if: (1) parties affected by the contract do not fully participate in drawing it (as happens with externality or free-rider problems), (2) the contract has not been freely arrived at, but imposed by government or some interest group, (3) environmental conditions have been changing rapidly over time, (4) opportunities available to try out new contractual forms have been limited, or (5) the parties would like to include certain provisions in a contract that they cannot enforce by themselves, but they might be able to do so with the assistance of custom, law, or other external mechanism.

This last possibility relates to Epstein's assessment of arbitrary firings. He argues that they would not be in the interests of employers, because they would give the firm a reputation that would make it difficult to attract good employees in the future. But what if potential employees find it difficult to monitor employers' firing records? Employers then cannot build a credible reputation for not firing unjustly and thus may be willing to accept a self-denying ordinance—for example, to accept legal penalties if they cannot demonstrate "cause" in a dismissal.

In an era when the principal new feature of the latest United Auto Workers-General Motors agreement is substantially increased job security, and the fabled lifetime contracts of Japanese workers are widely cited for their positive effects on productivity, Epstein's argument is arresting.

Agency in Organizations

The last two chapters of this volume look at agency relationships as they are embedded in continuing organizations. As we have said, continuing organizations can be viewed as a response to informational asymmetries. If all information were costlessly shared, and if perfect contracting were feasible, no organizations would be needed to produce goods and services. All production would be subcontracted down to the level of single factors of production. Instead of a corporation, we would have thousands of individual contracting agents (though agents might combine for other reasons, such as shifting bargaining relationships).

In practice, of course, the economic world is filled with organizations whose primary purpose is to produce goods and services. Business entities such as corporations and partnerships are the examples that come most quickly to mind. But, as Harrison White reminds us in the concluding chapter, other organizations, such as organized religions, are also involved in production. Moreover, many of the central functions performed by quite disparate organizations are much the same. Though it is not stated in these terms, one might take a part of White's message to be that organizations are needed to fulfill various control functions that cannot be achieved in arms-length transactions because information is not costlessly shared.

Forming an organization only internalizes agency relationships. It does not eliminate problems of coordination, incentives, and so on. Presumably, though, it should substantially lessen them, for now we are all working on the same team and can be rewarded accordingly—

unlike say the supplier and purchaser, who ordinarily represent different interests.

Robert Eccles examines the interior of the corporation and provides us with an empirical study of the use of transfer prices in coordinating the activities of profit centers within it. Transfer prices have long been an economist's dream solution to a variety of agency problems, theoretically achieving within the firm the types of decentralized efficient decision making that the market provides in external transactions. When moving resources back and forth within an organization, use the principle of the market. Charge the user what the resources are worth in terms of opportunity cost. Then we can be confident that the divisions will be employing capital wisely, not overusing company-made intermediate products or centrally provided legal services, and so on. Efficiency will be assured. But Eccles, who has been studying the question over a period of years, says that transfer prices are actually employed to pursue a far richer agenda of goals than mere economic efficiency.

Agency relationships pervade the management structures of modern corporations. The CEO is the principal, in effect. Because he cannot supervise every aspect of the business, he must delegate to division managers, who are his agents and the agents for the firm as a whole. Organizing the firm by profit centers, as is common, assumes that the overall interests of the firm are best served by decentralizing profit responsibility to the division manager agents.

But in many divisionalized firms there is some synergy, hence interconnection among the units. Sales between divisions are a logical outgrowth. But at what prices? An economist would argue that if divisions merely charge the opportunity cost of the resources they trade, which might be the external market price, incentives for overall corporate profit maximization will be in place. Eccles labels such a situation, with divisions free to buy internally or externally, market agency.

But Eccles's research reveals that transfer pricing can be much more complex. First, appropriate prices are rarely well defined. Second, and more important, transfer prices are often employed to fulfill many functions beyond merely aligning incentives. Vertically integrated firms often rely on hierarchical agency relationships. The agent is required to buy or sell internally, usually with full-cost prices employed as transfer prices. It is appropriate to evaluate such agents on their actions, not primarily their results.

Eccles highlights a mixed case of second-order agency. Internal sourcing is required, but external prices or full-cost prices plus a profit margin are employed to generate profit-center results. To define appropriate prices involves a social process that is sure to generate conflict. It may even be fostered by central management as a means to generate information and encourage its flow to the top. The divisions can be expected to monitor each other's actions and performances.

Eccles's investigation shows that transfer prices play a much more complex role than merely promoting efficiency. They are an instrument for facilitating the overall function of the organization. They stimulate information flow, provide an instrument for discussion of corporate objectives, and allow for transfers of wealth between divisions. He observes that the elusive concept of fairness joins efficiency as a major concern when transfer prices between profit centers are constructed. In sum, though transfer prices allow for decentralization, they also allow top management to exert influence between its divisions in controlling their behaviors.

Harrison White's concluding chapter steps well beyond the confines of economics and the narrow concerns of efficiency. He starts with the question of what enables an organization to function, observing the critical need to establish control over diverse parts of the organization and the actors within it. This is true whether the organization has a traditional economic purpose, as a corporation or partnership does, or is a political campaign organization, an organized religion, or an army. An implication of White's argument is that those who focus on the purely economic are missing the kernel of the problem. The question is what enables the organization to operate, not what enables it to produce efficiently. Many organizations fall short of an outstanding performance on economic efficiency, but they could not even survive had they not incorporated some elements of control, White's primary focus.

White identifies the maintenance of control by the principal as the central purpose of the agency relationship. For him agency is a "solution, a neat kind of social plumbing. The problem is the ancient one of how to attain and maintain control in order to carry out definite but varying purposes." He shows that control issues and the agency solution have been employed in settings ranging from the Roman Empire and early Christian Church to modern business enterprises.

White's organizational perspective enables him to look at elements of the agency structure from the inside out. For example, he views compensation packages as a way to send a signal to the agent to indicate what is expected of him; they define his role. White stresses the dynamic nature of agency relations. Thus compensation packages structure the elusive and changing nature of the agency situation. He also identifies some natural patterns of evolution. For example, as the agent accumulates specialized skills and knowledge, there is a movement toward role reversal. The principal begins to come under control of the agent, and strategic and operational control become separated.

White's analysis looks at fabrics of relationships, not single threads. He observes that agency is rarely a single relation. Rather it is a complex set of roles and mutual expectations embedded in markets and hierarchies. Proceeding beyond the paper in this volume, White is now engaged in a major research project using agency to understand the structures of our society.

* * *

From the time of the first gods to be served, the first families to be nurtured and supported, there have been agency relationships. In business such relationships are as old as the earliest productive process involving more than one worker. What do contemporary formulations tell us beyond the experiences of billions of man-years? First, the real world has been inventive in developing subtle mechanisms, such as career expectations and product reputations, to overcome the difficulties posed by informational asymmetries. In this realm our models must learn from the world. Second, the evolutionary processes for institutional structures are quite different from those for species. Desirable contracts are impossible to draw. Human environments change swiftly. Hence there is no assurance that the institutions we observe are best. Third, conceptual thinking has improved structures for important agency relationships and can continue to do so in the future.

The real world has provided substantial nourishment for the theory of agency. Now it is time to reciprocate. We hope our decision-maker readers, now acting as agents, will apply the concepts of agency theory and the lessons of this volume to the improvement of business practice and hence ultimately to the benefit of society.

Chapter 2
The Economics of Agency

Kenneth J. Arrow

The agency relationship is a pervasive fact of economic life. Even in the limited sense in which the concept has traditionally been understood in ordinary and in legal discourse, the principal-agent relation is a phenomenon of significant scope and economic magnitude. But economic theory has recently recognized that analogous interactions are virtually universal in the economy, representing a significant component of almost all transactions.

The common element is the presence of two individuals. One (the agent) must choose an action from a number of alternative possibilities. The action affects the welfare of both the agent and another person, the principal. The principal, at least in the simplest cases, has the additional function of prescribing payoff rules; that is, before the agent chooses the action, the principal determines a rule that specifies the fee to be paid to the agent as a function of the principal's observations of the results of the action. The problem acquires interest only when there is uncertainty at some point and, in particular, when the information available to the two participants is unequal. The economics literature has focused primarily (but not exclusively) on the case in which (1) the agent's action is not directly observable by the principal, and (2) the outcome is affected but not completely determined by the agent's action. (Were it not for the second condition, the principal could infer the agent's action by observing the outcome.) In technical language, the outcome is a random variable whose distribution depends on the action taken.

More generally, a single principal may have many agents. Each takes an action, and the output of the system is a random function of all the actions. The principal cannot observe the actions themselves but may make some observations, for example, of the output. Again the principal sets in advance a schedule stating the fees to be paid to the individual agents as a function of the observations made by the principal.

A similar but not identical principal-agent relation occurs when the agent makes an observation not shared with the principal and bases his or her action on that observation. In this case, the principal may be able to observe the action itself, but does not know whether it is the most appropriate one.

The principal-agent theory is in the standard economic tradition. Both principal and agent are assumed to be making their decisions optimally in view of their constraints; intended transactions are realized. As is usual in economic theory, the theory functions both normatively and descriptively. It offers insights used in the construction of contracts to guide and influence principal-agent relations in the real world; at the same time it represents an attempt to explain observed phenomena in the empirical economic world, particularly exchange relations that are not explained by more standard economic theory.

The Two Types: Hidden Action and Hidden Information

Before specifying the model more completely, it is useful to distinguish a few examples of each of the two kinds of principal-agent problems and give a few examples of each. As will be seen, many situations that are not classified under that heading in ordinary discourse can be considered as such. I will call the two types of principal-agent problems *hidden action* and *hidden information*, respectively. In the literature, they are frequently referred to as *moral hazard* and *adverse selection*. These terms have been borrowed from the practice and theory of insurance and are really applicable only to special cases.

The most typical hidden action is the effort of the agent. Effort is a disutility to the agent, but it has a value to the principal in the sense that it increases the likelihood of a favorable outcome (technically, the distribution of the outcome to a higher effort stochastically dominates that to a lower effort; that is, the probability of achieving an outcome that exceeds any given level is higher with higher effort). The physician-patient relation is a notorious case. Here the physician is the agent who chooses actions affecting the welfare of the principal (the patient). The very basis of the relation is the superior knowledge of the physician. Hence, the patient cannot check to see if the actions of physicians are as diligent as they could be.

A second, less obvious example is that of torts. One individual takes an action that results in damage to another—for example, an automobile collision. The care taken by the first driver cannot easily be observed, but the outcome is very visible indeed. Although it may seem an odd use of language, one has to consider the damager as the agent and the one damaged as the principal. Again, in pollution control, society may be regarded as the principal, and the polluter, whose actions cannot be fully monitored, as the agent.

An example of very special economic importance is the relation between stockholders and management. The stockholders are principals, who certainly cannot observe in detail whether the management, their agent, is making appropriate decisions. In a different context, sharecropping represents a formally similar relation. Instead of paying straight wages, the landlord (the principal here) prefers a relation that supplies incentives for better production, since the tenant's diligence cannot be directly observed; on the other side, the tenant, too poor to bear excessive risks, wants to avoid a fixed rent, which would maximize incentives but would expose him or her to all the risks of weather and price.

Fire insurance dulls incentives for caution and even creates incentives for arson; this is the origin of the term moral hazard. Health insurance creates similar problems, for it creates an incentive to use excessive medical care. If medical fees are paid by the insurer, the patient may elect more costly treatments than he or she would be willing to pay for individually. The employment relation in general is one in which effort and ability acquired through training and self-improvement are hard to observe. In one view, firms exist as a means of measuring effort.

In the hidden information problems, the agent has made some observation that the principal has not made. The agent uses (and should use) this observation in making decisions; however, the principal cannot check whether the agent has used his or her information in the way that best serves the principal's interest. A case much studied from various points of view in the economic literature is that of a decentralized socialist economy. Because the knowledge of productivity cannot be centralized, the individual productive units have information about the possibilities of production not available to the central planning unit. The productive units may well have incentives not to reveal their full potentiality, because it will be easier to operate with less taxing requirements. The problem for the central planning unit (the principal) is how to tap the agent's information. A similar problem occurs in decentralization within a firm. This topic in the literature has acquired the name of *incentive compatibility*.

The problem of adverse selection was originally noted in insurance of several kinds. The population being insured is heterogeneous with respect to risk; in the case of life insurance, for example, some have a higher probability than others of dying young. In at least some cases, the insured have better knowledge of this probability than the insurance company, which is unable to differentiate. If the same premium is charged to everyone, then the high-risk individuals will purchase more insurance and the low-risk ones less. This will lead to an inefficient allocation of risk bearing (Rothschild and Stiglitz 1976). Public utilities, such as telephones, also face heterogeneous populations; as in insurance, the utility provider cannot know to which class a given purchaser belongs. Nevertheless, as has been pointed out in recent literature, some differentiation can be made by offering alternative rate schedules and letting the customers choose which to follow. In these cases, the insurance company or the public utility is the principal; the customer, with more knowledge not available to the principal, is the agent (Spence 1977; Roberts 1979; Maskin and Riley 1984a).

Example: Public Utility Rate Setting. To illustrate the theoretical issues for the hidden information model, consider a monopolistic public utility facing two types of customers, designated H and L for high and low demanders respectively. Assume there are no income effects. Let $U_t(x)$ be the money equivalent of amount x of the public utility for type t ($t = H, L$), so that $U_t(0) = 0$, and characterize high and low demand by the condition that $U'_H(x) > U'_L(x)$ for all x. It is assumed that the characteristics of the product preclude resale.

The public utility knows the proportion of high demanders but not the identity of these individuals. It offers a total payment schedule, $T(x)$, a function of the amount purchased. Assuming a constant marginal cost of production, c, the monopolist's markup, M, for x units is $M(x) = T(x) - cx$. For convenience, let $V_t(x) = U_t(x) - cx$, the consumer's surplus over social cost. Since $V'_H(x) > V'_L(x)$, for all x, there is a difference in willingness to pay, which the monopolist can exploit.

Since individuals are free to refrain from purchase, there will never be a negative consumer's surplus, no matter what pricing scheme the utility adopts. The monopolist can try to extract all consumer's surplus by all-or-none offers. Let $\bar{x}_t$ maximize $V_t(x)$. If the monopolist can identify the type to which each consumer belongs, it will offer buyers of type t $\bar{x}_t$ units and charge a markup of $\bar{M}_t = V_t(\bar{x}_t)$.

If identification is not possible, however, this scheme breaks down. If the monopolist offers the consumer a choice between $(\bar{x}_L, \bar{M}_L)$ and $(\bar{x}_H, \bar{M}_H)$, the high demanders will always choose the former. Since $V'_H(x) > V'_L(x)$, it follows that $V_H(\bar{x}_L) > V_L(\bar{x}_L) = \bar{M}_L$, so that type H individuals get a positive consumer's surplus by choosing the offer appropriate to type L individuals; if they accept $(\bar{x}_H, \bar{M}_H)$, their consumer's surplus is zero. To induce type H individuals to buy $\bar{x}_H$, the markup must be reduced so that they are no worse off than they would be by choosing $(\bar{x}_L, \bar{M}_L)$. That is, the markup demanded must satisfy the condition,

$$V_H(\bar{x}_H) - M_H^0 = V_H(\bar{x}_L) - \bar{M}_L. \tag{1}$$

This can be accomplished without knowing individual consumer types by choosing $M(x) = \bar{M}_L$ for $x \leq \bar{x}_L$, $= M_H^0$ for $x > \bar{x}_L$.

This allocation is Pareto efficient, since all consumers are paying marginal cost. The monopolist is extracting all surplus from the low demanders but not from the high demanders. To realize maximum profits, however, the monopolist must set prices in a manner that creates inefficiency. The amount to be bought by the low demanders will be reduced by a small amount. This will reduce the surplus to be extracted from them. On the other hand, the constraint imposed on extraction of surplus from the high demanders to prevent them from switching to the offer intended for the low demanders will become easier to satisfy. It turns out that the loss in profits due to the reduction in amount purchased by the low demanders is much smaller than the gain from higher markup obtainable from the higher demanders. In symbols, let the amount to be purchased by type L consumers be reduced from $\bar{x}_L$ to $\bar{x}_L - dx$. This is enforced by locating the discontinuous increase in markup at that point. The markup must be reduced correspondingly; choose $M_L^* = V_L(\bar{x}_L - dx)$. Since V_L is maximized at $\bar{x}_L$, it must be that the difference, $M_L^* - \bar{M}_L$, is of the second order in dx.

To induce the type H consumers to choose $\bar{x}_H$ rather than $(\bar{x}_L - dx, M_H^*)$, the markup to them must be set so that

$$V_H(\bar{x}_H) - M_H^* = V_H(\bar{x}_L - dx) - M_L^*.$$

By comparison with (1), it is seen that

$$M_H^* - M_H^0 = (M_L^* - \bar{M}_L) + [V_H(\bar{x}_L) - V_H(\bar{x}_L - dx)].$$

The first term on the right is, as stated, of the second order in dx. But since $V_L'(\bar{x}_L) > 0$, the second term is positive and of the first order. Hence, for dx sufficiently small, the loss in markup from the type L consumers is of the second order, the gain in markup from the type H consumers is of the first order, and there is a net gain. This is true no matter what the proportions of the two types of consumers are, though of course the optimal policy of the monopolist depends on those proportions. The optimal monopoly policy can be enforced without identification of the types of consumers by letting $M(x) = M_L^*$ for $x \leq \bar{x}_L - dx$, $M(x) = M_H^*$ for $x > \bar{x}_L - dx$.

Constraints, such as (1), that ensure that the different types are induced to accept the allocations allotted to them are referred to as *self-selection* constraints. The example illustrates a very general principle in hidden information models; the optimal incentive schedule typically requires distortions (deviations from first-best Pareto-optimal) at all but one point.

Another instance of hidden information in economic decision making is the auction with private information (Vickrey 1961; Maskin and Riley 1984b; Milgrom and Weber 1982). Bidders for oil leases, for example, may be permitted to engage in exploratory drilling and other geophysical studies. Each then has an observation unknown to the others and to the seller, which in the United States today is usually the government. The problem is to design auction rules to achieve some objective. Much of the current literature is devoted to maximizing the seller's revenues, rather than social welfare in some broader sense.

A final illustration of hidden information is the problem of optimal income taxation (Mirrlees 1971). Any income tax distorts the choice between labor and leisure. This deficiency could in principle be overcome completely if the social price of leisure (i.e., the productivity or wage rate of the individual) were observable. In general, however, this information is available to the taxpayer but not to the government. Like the geophysical estimates of oil field size in the earlier example, individual wage rates are known only to the agents; from the principal's perspective they are hidden information.

Multiple Principals

The hidden information principal-agent problem becomes more complicated when multiple principals compete for agents (Spence 1973; Rothschild and Stiglitz 1976; Riley 1975). Suppose a large number of potential principals will enter the market to exploit any profitable alternative. This might be the case, for example, in an insurance market with a large number of competing insurance companies, each of which, because of risk pooling, is approximately risk neutral. As argued earlier, any given offer (so much coverage at such a premium) will be more attractive to those with higher loss probabilities; insurance companies will then have an incentive to sort risk classes by offering lower premiums per dollar of coverage to those willing to accept higher deductibles. However, unlike the monopoly utility, each insurance company must take into account the effect of other available alternatives on the type of individuals attracted to its own offerings. To use Spence's terminology, it is not enough that low risk classes can "signal" their differences by accepting larger deductibles; such signals must also be competitively viable.

The issue of what kind of signaling survives competitive pressures turns out to be a delicate one. In general, there does not exist a Walrasian (or Nash) equilibrium with the property that no principal has an incentive to introduce new profitable alternatives. However, recent work by Wilson (1977) and Riley (1979) has argued that equilibrium can be sustained if principals rationally anticipate certain responses to their behavior.

The Hidden Action Model

Let me now turn to a simple formulation of the hidden action model. The agent (for the moment, assume there is only one) chooses an action a. The result of this choice is an outcome, x, which is a random variable whose distribution depends on a. The principal has chosen beforehand a *fee function*, $s(x)$, to be paid to the agent. For the simplest case, assume that the outcome x is income—that is, a transferable and measurable quantity. Then the net receipts of the principal will be $x - s(x)$. Because the principal and agent are both, in general, risk averters, each values whatever income he or she receives by a utility function with diminishing marginal utility. Let U be the utility function of the principal, V that of the agent. Further, let $W(a)$ be the disutility the agent attaches to action a. It will be assumed separable from the utility of income; that is, the marginal utility of income is independent of the action taken (the amount of effort). Note that the action is taken before the realization of the uncertainty and is therefore not uncertain to the agent, though it is unknown to the principal.

Since, even for a given action, the outcome, x, is uncertain, both principal and agent are motivated to maximize the expected value of utility. Given the principal's choice of fee function, $s(x)$, the agent wishes to maximize the expected value of $V[s(x)] - W(a)$. In effect, therefore, the principal can predict the action taken for any given fee schedule. The choice of fee schedules is, however, restricted by competition for agents, who have alternative uses for their time. Hence the principal must choose a fee schedule that offers the agent a utility at least equal to what he or she could achieve in other activities. (The literature has usually referred to this condition as that of individual rationality, a term first used by J. von Neumann and O. Morgenstern, but this name is easily misinterpreted. The term *participation constraint* has come into use recently and seems more appropriate.)

The principal-agent relation defined, as here, by a fee function is a significant departure from the arm's-length fixed-price relation among economic agents usually postulated in economic theory. The principal does not buy the agent's services at a fixed price set by the competitive market nor does the principal simply buy output from the agent. The relation cannot even be described as a contingent contract, in which payments and services rendered are agreed-on functions of an exogenous random variable; rather the principal observes the outcome but cannot analyze it into its two components, the agent's action and the exogenous uncertainty. Even though the underlying principles are impeccably neoclassical, in that both parties are acting in their own self-interest and are subject to the influence of the market, the variable to be determined is not a price but a complicated functional relationship.

The principal-agent problem combines two inextricable elements, risk sharing and differential information. Even if there were no problem of differential information, there would be some sharing of the outcome if both parties are risk averse. Indeed, if the agent were risk neutral, the principal-agent problem would have a trivial solution: the agent would bear all the risks, and then the differential information would not matter. That is, the principal would retain a fixed amount and pay all the remainder to the agent, who therefore would have no dilution of incentives (Shavell 1979). In the terminology used above, the fee function would equal the outcome less a fixed amount, $s(x) = x - c$, where the constant c is determined by the participation constraint. Thus a landlord renting land to a tenant farmer would simply charge a fixed rent independent of output, which in general depends on both the tenant's effort, unobservable to the landlord, and the vagaries of the weather. However, this solution is not optimal if the agent is risk averse. Since all individuals are averse to sufficiently large risks, the simple solution of preserving incentives by assigning all risks to the agent fails as soon as the risks are large compared with the agent's wealth. The president of a large corporation can hardly be held responsible for its income fluctuations.

In the general case of a risk-averse agent, the fee will be a function of the outcome, in order to supply incentives, but the risk will be shared. If the ability of the agent to affect outcomes approaches either zero or infinity, then the efficiency level that could be achieved under full information to the principal can be approached with an optimally chosen fee function. More generally, there is a trade-off between incentives and efficiency of the system (considering both principal and agent) (Shavell 1979).

For an application, consider the case of insurance with moral hazard. Some insurance will be written, but it will not be complete. In the terminology of the insurance industry, there will be *coinsurance;* that is, the insured will bear some of the losses against which the insurance is written. Coinsurance is customary in health insurance policies, where the insured has considerable control over the amount of health expenditures. Similarly, in a system of legal liability for torts (assuming no insurance), the required payment should increase with the amount of damages inflicted, to provide incentive for avoiding the inflicting of damages, but by an amount less than the increase in damages, so that the unavoidable risks are shared.

Monitoring

More recent literature has stressed the possibility of monitoring. By this is meant that the principal has certain information in addition to the outcome. If this observation, y, conveys any information about the unobserved action, a, beyond that revealed by the outcome, x (technically, if x is not a sufficient statistic for the pair, x, y with respect to a), then one can always improve by making the fee depend upon y as well as x. In the case of torts, it is held in many cases that a damager is not liable if due care has been exercised. Therefore the plaintiff is required to show negligence on the part of the defendant, so that additional knowledge beyond the outcome is available. It turns out that if the liable party (the agent in this interpretation) is risk neutral, then a strict liability standard, which requires only knowledge of the outcome, is optimal (in the sense of economic efficiency). But otherwise an appropriate negligence standard is an improvement (Shavell 1979; Holmström 1979). Harris and Raviv (1978, 1979) have argued that the custom of paying lawyers (in most circumstances) on the basis of time spent, as well as by a contingent fee, is an example of monitoring. If this idea were applied to health insurance, it would suggest that an improvement could be achieved by making insurance payments to the provider of care depend on some measure of the amount of medical services provided, such as frequency of visits.

It has been shown that if the monitoring information is essentially an imperfect measure of the action taken (i.e., $y = a + u$, where u is a random variable with mean zero), then an optimal fee policy is to pay a very low figure, independent of outcome, if the measured action is sufficiently low, and to pay according to a more complicated schedule otherwise.

Multiple Agents and Repeated Relations

New possibilities for incentives arise when there are many agents for a single principal or repeated relations between agent and principal. The many-agent case offers new opportunities for inference of hidden actions (or of hidden information) if the uncertainty of the relation between the action (or the agent's observation) is the same for all the agents. In that situation, the uncertainty can be estimated by comparing the performances of the different agents; thus individual actions can be approximately identified. One can meaningfully compare the performance of each agent with the average, for example, or use the ordinal ranking of the agents' outcomes as a basis for fees (Holmström 1982).

A different and as yet only slightly explored problem can arise in the case of many agents with a single principal. Suppose the principal cannot observe the outcome of each individual agent's action but only the output of the group of agents as a whole. This is obviously an important case in production carried out jointly, with many complementary workers. Even when the relation between actions and collective outcomes is certain, there are difficulties. Holmström (1982) has considered the problem of a team, whose output depends on the unobservable actions of all members. Each team member has a disutility for his or her action. Assume for simplicity that utility is linear in the output. Then one can speak of a social optimum, that vector of actions that maximizes total output minus the sum of disutilities for actions. The question is whether the team can devise some incentive scheme that will induce the members to perform the socially optimal actions. This will necessarily be a game, since the reward to each is a function of the output and therefore of the actions of all.

When there is no uncertainty, an incentive scheme can be devised with the desired outcome in mind. Let a_i be the action to be chosen by individual i, $x(a_1, \ldots, a_n)$ the production function that gives the output of the team as a function of the actions of all members, and $W_i(a_i)$ the disutility of individual i as a function of his or her action. Then the socially optimal set of actions is that which maximizes $x(a_1, \ldots, a_n) - \Sigma W_i(a_i)$. Call the actions so defined, $a_1^*, \ldots, a_n^*$, and let $x^* = x(a_1^*, \ldots, a_n^*)$ be the output at this optimum. Choose any set of lump-sum rewards, $b_1, \ldots, b_n$, which add up to x^*, subject to the condition that $b_i > W_i(a_i^*)$ for each i. Then set up the following game: Each individual i chooses a_i. If the result of all these actions is to produce an output that is less than optimal, no one receives anything. If the total output, $x(a_1, \ldots, a_n)$, is greater than or equal to x^*, then individual i receives b_i.

A Nash equilibrium of this game is for each individual to choose the appropriate action, a_i^*; that is, for each individual i, choosing a_i^* is optimal given the payoffs, providing each other individual, j, chooses a_j^*. But the proposed game is hardly satisfactory. It involves in effect collective punishment. More analytically, there are many Nash equilibria, of which $(a_1^*, \ldots, a_n^*)$ is only one. If some individuals shirk a little, it pays the others to work somewhat harder to achieve the same output. Hence the scheme does not enforce the optimal outcome, though it permits it.

Repeated relations between a principal and an agent provide new opportunities for incentives. Experience rating in insurance illustrates the situation; the premium rate charged today depends on past outcomes. In effect, the information on which the fee function is based is greatly enriched. Radner (1981) has demonstrated the possibilities for achieving almost fully optimal outcomes in hidden action situations. Suppose the principal wishes the agent to implement a certain level of action, a^*. In any one trial, the action is hidden, in that the outcome differs from the action by a random variable; that is, $x_t = a_t + u_t$, where the random variables, u_t, are identically and independently distributed, with mean zero. If the agent is in fact performing the desired action a^*, then the distribution of the x_t's is known. Hence, if enough are observed, the principal should be able to detect statistically whether the agent is performing actions below the desired level. Specifically, the principal can keep track of the cumulative sum of the outcomes. If it ever falls below a known function of time, then the principal can assume that the performance of the agent is below that desired. More exactly, the principal imposes a very severe penalty if there is some time, *T*, such that,

$$\sum_{t=1}^{T} x_t < Ta^* - k \; log \; log \; T.$$

For properly chosen *k*, the probability of imposing a penalty when the agent is in fact carrying out the desired action can be made very low, while the probability of eventually imposing the penalty if the agent is shirking is one.

An Evaluation of Agency Theory

I have sketched some of the leading ideas in the rapidly burgeoning literature on the economic theory of the principal-agent relation. We may step back a bit from the pure theory and ask in a general way to what extent our understanding of economic processes has been enhanced. On the positive side, there is little question that a good many economic relations inexplicable in previously standard analysis can now be understood. Contractual relations are frequently a good deal more complicated than the simple models of exchange of commodities and services at fixed prices would suggest. Sharecropping, incentive compensation to executives and other employees, the role of dismissal as an incentive, coinsurance, and other aspects of insurance all find a place in this literature not found in standard economic analysis.

But it is perhaps more useful to consider the extent to which the principal-agent relation in actuality differs from that in the models developed to date. Most importantly, the theory tends to lead to very complex fee functions. It turns out to be difficult to establish even what would appear to be common-sense properties of monotonicity and the like. We do not find such complex relations in reality. Principal-agent theory gives a good reason for the existence of sharecrop contracts, but it is a very poor guide to their actual terms. Indeed, as John Stuart Mill pointed out long ago, the terms tend to be regulated by custom. They are remarkably uniform from farm to farm and from region to region. Principal-agent theory, in contrast, would suggest that the way the produce is divided between landlord and tenant would depend on the probability distribution of weather and other exogenous uncertainties and on the relation between effort and output, both of which certainly vary from one region to another; the latter has varied over time as well. Similarly, the coinsurance provisions in health insurance policies are much simpler than could possibly be accounted for by principal-agent theory.

In some cases where principal-agent theory seems clearly applicable, real-world practice is very different from the model. In many respects, the physician-patient relation exemplifies the principal-agent relation almost perfectly. The principal (the patient) is certainly unable to monitor the efforts of the agent (the physician). The relation between effort and outcome is random, but presumably there is some connection. Yet in practice the physician's fee schedule is in no way related to outcome. Liability for malpractice can be seen as a modification of the fee schedule in the direction indicated by principal-agent theory, but it is not applicable to what might be termed run-of-the-mill shirking, and it requires very special kinds of evidence. In general, indeed, compensation of professionals shows only a few traces of the complex fee schedules implied by theory.

Even in situations where compensation systems seem closer in form to the theoretical, there are significant differences. Consider the incentive compensation schemes for corporate executives. They invariably have a large discretionary component. What is the purpose of this? Why should the incentive payment not be based entirely on observable magnitudes, profits, rates of return, and the like?

These difficulties can be explained within the terms of the principal-agent logic but in a way that points beyond the usual bounds of economic analysis. One basic problem is the cost of specifying complex relations. There is a large, though not easily defined, cost to a contract that specifies payments that depend on many variables. Costs are inherent in the very statement of the contract, in understanding it and its implications, and in verifying which terms apply in a given situation. Hence, there is a pressure for simple contracts, the more so since any of our models is actually much too simple to capture all aspects of a relation that would be thought relevant by participants.

There are a variety of means of monitoring, and it is difficult to define exactly what they are. The world is full of performance evaluations based on some kind of direct observations. These evaluations may not always be objective, reproducible observations of the kind used in our theories (perhaps the only kind about which it is possible to construct a theory). Executives are judged by their superiors and students by professors on criteria that could not have been stated in advance. Outcomes and even supplementary objective measures simply do not exhaust the information available on which to base rewards.

A third limitation of the present models is the restricted reward or penalty system used. It is virtually always stated in terms of monetary payments, although the present literature has begun to go beyond this limit by considering the possibility of dismissal. Still further extensions are needed to capture some aspects of reality, for there is a whole world of rewards and penalties that take social rather than monetary forms. Professional responsibility is clearly enforced in good measure by systems of ethics, internalized during the education process and enforced in some measure by formal punishments and more broadly by reputations. Ultimately, of course, these social systems have economic consequences, but they are not the immediate ones of current principal-agent models.

All three of these limiting elements—cost of communication, variety and vagueness of monitoring, and socially mediated rewards—go beyond the usual boundaries of economic analysis. It may ultimately be one of the greatest accomplishments of the principal-agent literature to provide some structure for the much-sought goal of integrating these elements with the impressive structure of economic analysis.

I wish to express my gratitude to John W. Pratt, John G. Riley, and Richard Zeckhauser, whose comments have materially improved the exposition of this paper.

References

Gjesdal, F. 1982. "Information and Incentives: The Agency Information Problem." *Review of Economic Studies* 49:373–90.

Grossman, S., and O. D. Hart. 1983. "An Analysis of the Principal-Agent Problem." *Econometrica* 51:7–46.

Harris, M., and A. Raviv. 1978. "Some Results of Incentive Contracts with Applications to Education and Employment, Health Insurance and Law Enforcement." *American Economic Review* 68:20–30.

———. 1979. "Optimal Incentive Contracts with Imperfect Information." *Journal of Economic Theory* 20:231–59.

Holmström, B. 1979. "Moral Hazard and Observability." *Bell Journal of Economics* 10:74–91.

———. 1982. "Moral Hazard in Teams." *Bell Journal of Economics* 13:324–40.

Marcus, A. J. 1982. "Risk Sharing and the Theory of the Firm." *Bell Journal of Economics* 13:369–78.

Maskin, E. S., and J. G. Riley. 1984a. "Monopoly with Incomplete Information." *Rand Journal Of Economics* 15:171–196.

———. 1984b. "Optimal Auctions with Risk Averse Buyers." *Econometrica,* 52:1473–1518.

Milgrom, P. R., and R. J. Weber. 1982. "A Theory of Auctions and Competitive Bidding." *Econometrica* 50:1089–1122.

Mirrlees, J. 1971. "An Exploration in the Theory of Optimum Income Taxation." *Review of Economic Studies* 38:175–208.

Radner, R. 1981. "Monitoring Cooperative Agreements in a Repeated Principal-Agent Relationship." *Econometrica* 49:1127–48.

Riley, J. G. 1975. "Competitive Signalling." *Journal of Economic Theory* 10:174–86.

———. 1979. "Informational Equilibrium." *Econometrica* 47:331–60.

Roberts, K. 1979. "Welfare Considerations of Nonlinear Pricing." *Economic Journal* 89:66–83.

Rothschild, M., and J. E. Stiglitz. 1976. "Equilibrium in Competitive Insurance Markets." *Quarterly Journal of Economics* 80:629–49.

Shavell, S. 1979. "Risk Sharing and Incentives in the Principal and Agent Relationship." *Bell Journal of Economics* 10:55–73.

Spence, A. M. 1973. *Market Signalling: Information Transfer in Hiring and Related Processes.* Cambridge: Harvard University Press.

———. 1977. "Nonlinear Prices and Economic Welfare." *Journal of Public Economics* 8:1–18.

Vickrey, W. 1961. "Counterspeculation, Auctions, and Competitive Sealed Tenders." *Journal of Finance* 16:8–37.

Wilson, C. A. 1977. "A Model of Insurance Markets with Incomplete Information." *Journal of Economic Theory* 16:167–207.

Part Two
Institutional Responses

Chapter 3
Agency Costs versus Fiduciary Duties

Robert C. Clark

A closer focus on actual rather than presumed legal doctrines and concepts might do much to refine our current theory of the firm. This paper begins by exploring some problems with economists' customary presentation of agency costs theory, and then examines the law's concept of the fiduciary duty of loyalty as an attempted solution to the so-called problem of agency costs.

Pitfalls of the Agency Costs Approach

Lawyers and economists often study the same phenomena but approach them in different ways. In some contexts their awareness of these differences can be mutually enlightening. The received agency costs literature describes managers as "agents" of stockholders and the corporation as a "center of contracts."[1] But the important relationships and real problems that engage the "agency costs" commentators are conceived by legal authorities in a subtly different way, because the legal system has evolved its own unique strategy for dealing with them. The precise characteristics of the legal strategy, I believe, are often unknown or misunderstood, and could usefully be subjected to a close economic analysis.

Much of the economic literature talks about "firms" rather than "corporations," and does not distinguish sharply between closely held business organizations (whatever their legal form) and publicly held corporations. For a number of reasons, failure to make this distinction clearly can be a source of almost fatal confusion.[2] Throughout this paper, I will be referring only to publicly held (or "public") business corporations, which of course account for the great bulk of business revenues in the United States. Some apparently different approaches by legal commentators to the theory of business organizations, such as William Klein's emphasis on bargaining under constraints, may be compatible with mine, once this restriction is appreciated.[3]

Managers Are Not Agents of Stockholders

To an experienced corporate lawyer who has studied primary legal materials, the assertion that corporate managers are agents of investors, whether debtholders or stockholders, will seem odd or loose.[4] The lawyer would make the following points: (1) corporate officers like the president and treasurer are agents of the corporation itself; (2) the board of directors is the ultimate decision-making body of the corporation (and in a sense is the group most appropriately identified with "the corporation"); (3) directors are not agents of the corporation but are sui generis; (4) neither officers nor directors are agents of the stockholders; but (5) both officers and directors are "fiduciaries" with respect to the corporation and its stockholders.

These legal characterizations are not just semantic differences from the usual terminology of the agency costs literature. To see the distinction, let us first contrast the legal conception of the agent with that of the corporate director and then examine the more general legal concept of the fiduciary.

Though lawyers use the concept of agency in a variety of senses, the core legal concept implies a relationship in which the principal retains the power to control and direct the activities of the agent.[5] Typically, the principal sets the ultimate objective and general strategy for the agent to pursue, occasionally specifies details of the agent's behavior, and stands ready to countermand specific acts of the agent.

A review of elementary corporate law shows that this power of the principal to direct the activities of the agent does not apply to the stockholders as against the directors or officers of their corporation.[6] By statute in every state, the board of directors of a corporation has the power and duty to manage or supervise its business. The stockholders do not. To appreciate the point fully, consider the following activities: setting the ultimate goal of the corporation—for example, whether its legal purpose will be to maximize profits; choosing the corporation's lines of business—for example, whether it will engage in retailing general merchandise or refining oil; hiring and firing the full-time executives who will actually run the company; and exercising supervisory power with respect to the day-to-day operations of the business.

Stockholders of a large publicly held corporation *do not* do these things; as a matter of efficient operation of a large firm with numerous residual claimants they *should not* do them; and under the typical corporate statute and case law they *cannot* do them.

The first of the four activities is the work of the incorporators, when they choose the state corporation statute—"business," "nonprofit," "mutual," or other—under which they will incorporate. The other three activities reside ultimately in the decision-making power of the board of directors. Directors can and often do delegate or abandon these decision-making chores to corporate officers and lower-level employees, of course, and custom or case law often makes the delegation for them. But the ultimate power is still with the directors. For example, they can countermand specific past or proposed actions of the chief executive officer, and the court will uphold their decision. Under appropriate conditions, as when proper notice is given or readily available, their decision will even bind third parties dealing with the corporation through the executive. None of this is true of stockholders with respect to the directors or officers of their corporation. Moreover, the board can withdraw delegations of authority that it has made in the past. It may even get in trouble by delegating too much power for too long to corporate officers, employees, or contracting parties.[7] Stockholders cannot withdraw authority they delegated to the board of directors, for they never delegated any authority to the directors.

As a matter of statutory law, stockholders' powers in a public corporation are extremely limited. They can vote for or against candidates for directorships. They can even nominate possible directors, if they are willing to pay the costs of a proxy campaign out of their own pockets. Under unusual circumstances, they can vote to remove directors. They can vote for or against so-called organic corporate changes—mergers, charter amendments, and the dissolution of the corporation—but only if the board has formally voted to approve the change and to put it before the stockholders for approval. Thus, even a 100 percent vote of the stockholders cannot initiate or force through such a change or put it before a stockholders' meeting for a legally valid vote, if the board of directors resists.

Admittedly, stockholders have other rights besides those already mentioned. The most valuable is the right to bring a derivative lawsuit—a lawsuit on behalf of the corporation—against dishonest or disloyal directors and officers. A more modest right is the power, under appropriate circumstances, to inspect certain corporate books and records. But these rights do not give stockholders the power directly to control or specify the acts taken by directors on behalf of the corporation.

Some of the more modern business corporation statutes do permit management by stockholders if the certificate of incorporation or some other specified document provides for it. But this permission is generally restricted to closely held corporations—as it is in the important state of Delaware—and even in states where the permission is formally available to all corporations, it is clear that the legislature was simply trying to alleviate the burden of the rigid corporate form for closely held businesses.[8]

To influence corporate managers, then, stockholders can vote for directors and approve or veto director-initiated organic changes, but cannot do much else. The important part of this description is the negative clause.

The contrast between this set of arrangements and true agency relationships is seen very starkly and concretely when one dips into the vast ocean of legal opinions involving questions of "agency law," such as whether one person had "actual" or "apparent" authority to act on behalf of another in connection with a particular disputed transaction.[9] Generally, the alleged agent and principal have met each other face to face, or have talked on the telephone, or have otherwise communicated with each other in a specific, individualized way. Courts trying to determine the scope of their relationship often scrutinize the actual course of dealings between the particular parties and try to determine what their actual understanding of their particular relationship was. In corporate law or securities regulation cases involving alleged misbehavior of corporate managers with respect to a publicly held corporation and its stockholders, there is almost never a comparable inquiry.

Thus, the legal relationship between the stockholder and the manager is very different from the legal relationship between the ordinary principal and agent. So what? the reader might ask. Do these differences have any bearing on the kinds of problems that have been at the heart of the agency costs literature? To some degree, yes. Ignoring the legal restrictions on stockholders' decision-making power makes it easier to talk as if stockholders and managers "bargain" over and "contract" about the terms of their relationship, or "implicitly" or "virtually" do so—and this is the next, more serious pitfall of the agency costs literature (discussed below).

My basic proposition is that an important but neglected job for agency costs theorists is to try to understand, in economic terms, the main features of the actual legal relationship between stockholders and managers. They should theorize about the conditions under which such features are likely to come about, test their theories against empirical data, and assess whether these features are likely to be efficient or not. A modest stab at this problem is made later in this paper. Everyone will agree that there is still an ample virgin territory to be explored.

A Corporation Is Not a Nexus of Actual Contracts

While Coase saw the essence of the firm in coordination of activities by "fiat" rather than in "market" transactions, subsequent writers in the same general tradition have often gone out of their way to disagree.[10] Alchian and Demsetz insisted that the firm "has no power of fiat, no authority, no disciplinary action any different in the slightest degree from ordinary market contracting between any two people." They went on to say that the distinctive feature of the employer-employee relationship, as contrasted with that between a sole proprietor and his customer, lies "in a *team* use of inputs and a centralized position of some party in the contractual arrangements of *all* other inputs. It [the firm?] is the *centralized contractual agent in a team productive process*—not some superior authoritarian directive or disciplinary power. . . ."[11]

These remarks might be interpreted simply as an exaggerated way of pointing out that employees of modern firms are not slaves: they have the legal option of refusing to get into or stay in a relationship with someone who might give them orders (a boss). But the more important point seems to be a much broader one—that *all* relationships that make up a firm are "contractual." In their influential and often illuminating article on the theory of the firm, Jensen and Meckling drive home this point and are worth quoting at length:

> The private corporation or firm is simply one form of *legal fiction which serves as a nexus for contracting relationships and which is also characterized by the existence of divisible residual claims on the assets and cash flows of the organization which can generally be sold without permission of the other contracting individuals.* While this definition of the firm has little substantive content, emphasizing the essential contractual nature of firms and other organizations focuses attention on a crucial set of questions. . . . Viewed this way, it makes little or no sense to try to distinguish those things

that are "inside" the firm from those things that are "outside" of it. There is
in a very real sense only a multitude of complex relationships (i.e., contracts)
between the legal fiction (the firm) and the owners of . . . inputs and the
consumers of output.[12]

Jensen and Meckling's view that the corporation is "only" a multitude of contracts becomes important to them when they attempt to
establish certain conclusions. It helps them argue that the "original
owner-manager" of a firm that later goes public bears all of the agency
costs thereby generated, and that agency costs are at an optimal or
efficient level. Both of these propositions, and others that they assert
in their article, may have important consequences for policy making.

But is it realistic or useful to view the modern public corporation as
consisting only, or even principally, of a set of contracts? I think not.
This extreme contractualist viewpoint is almost perverse. It is likely to
blind us to most of the features of the modern public corporation that
are distinctive, puzzling, and worth exploring. To see this, we must
first consider the notion of contract, and then note the extent to which
the corporation, considered as a multitude of legal relationships, con-
sists of noncontractual legal relationships.

The term *contract* is more frequently used, even by lawyers, in varying senses than is the term *agency*, so it would be neither right nor
prudent for me to claim that one particular specification of the term is
the definitive legal notion of contract. For example, lawyers and judges
often talk of contractual terms that are "implied" by law or custom,
and courts often declare and enforce rights and duties between contracting parties that relate to matters neither party actually contem-
plated or bargained about. It is easy to speak of such rights and duties
as being "part" of the parties' "contract." Nevertheless, the core notion
of contract, and the most relevant for theorizing about the optimality
of commercial relationships, is that the rights and duties between the
two parties are specified and fixed by their own voluntary and actual
agreement. Let me refer to a set of legal relationships determined
solely in this way as constituting an "actual contract."

Most of the particular rules that make up the legal relationships
among corporate officers, directors, and stockholders—that is, the
relationships that constitute corporate law and give operational meaning to the legal concept of the corporation—are not the product of
actual contracts made by the persons subject to them. Furthermore,
they are often not the product of "implicit" contracts between these
people, if by that term we mean that the individuals actually under-

stood the governing rules but simply did not advert to them when entering their roles as officers, directors, or stockholders.

But some will insist that contracts may be implicit in a more remote but meaningful sense: Such as a contract exists if the parties, assuming they are rational and reasonable, would have agreed to the rules in question, if they had thought and bargained about them beforehand. Moreover, the whole set of legal relationships that make up corporate law may well be seen as a large-scale "standardized contract" or "form contract"—a miniature version of the libertarian philosophers' social contract—to which various people "consent" when they voluntarily step into the standardized roles of the officer, director, or stockholder. But I would insist that the use of the term contract in connection with "implicit contracts" and "standardized contracts" is metaphorical, and (as I will argue below) that the metaphor is seriously misleading.

Most corporate case law deals with alleged breaches of fiduciary duties by managers, though a given opinion might focus as readily on a question of procedure or process as on a question of definition or application of the duty. Fiduciary duties are sometimes waivable by stockholders and sometimes not waivable. But in either event the duties are highly unlikely to have been the result of any actual compact or understanding between manager and investor.

Since actual voluntary consent to the governing rules of a relationship is the essence of my notion of actual contracts, let me restate my view in terms of three grades of consent that might be given to corporate law by participants in the modern public corporation. The first level is consent to the *role* of officer, director, or stockholder. Many millions of people in the United States have voluntarily entered these roles, often with some vague awareness of, and lack of objection to, the fact that they thereby become subject to an unspecified, large, and perhaps arcane assortment of legal rights and duties. This acceptance of the legal rules, however, does not explain their origins. Most of these millions of people play no direct part in articulating, justifying, criticizing, changing, getting established as law, or enforcing the myriad particular rules that govern and define the roles they play.

The second level is consent to particular deviations from the otherwise governing rules in particular situations. Sometimes, for example, an officer will want to buy a "corporate opportunity" for himself—that is, to exploit for himself an opportunity that he would normally be expected to recommend to the corporation. In an earlier era, around 1900, directors who wished to engage in dealings with their corporations might have to, and often would, seek the explicit approval of the "disinterested" directors. But while such things do happen with some frequency, they do not explain the creation of the ground rules to which they are exceptions. Moreover, lawyers, courts, and commentators often argue over the extent to which such expressions of consent are informed, uncoerced, and untainted by conflicts of interest, and thus whether they should be declared legally valid.

The third level of consent is bargaining about and creation of the particular terms of a particular relationship among participants in a public corporation. A chief executive officer, for example, may bargain with a board of directors about compensation and terms of employment. Other important examples are hard to come by.

With these qualifications and understandings, I suggest again that the legal relationships among participants in the modern public corporation are not primarily the product of actual contracts.

Why It Matters Whether Contracts Are Actual Rather than Implicit or Standardized

At this point some readers may be ready to concede that a large firm is not a nexus of actual contracts in a strict sense, but would argue that the distinction does not matter much. The important point is that firms can be usefully understood *as if* they were sets of contracts. One can still maintain that firms are virtually contractual in all essential aspects.

But this response, which resembles a lawyer's defense strategy of confession and avoidance, is not adequate. Viewing corporations as essentially contractual may have at least four troublesome consequences.

Deflection from Close Study of Actual Rules and Processes. Economic analysis could help a great deal in the study of the law's special concept of the fiduciary, but a militantly contractualistic approach may make it difficult to realize this contribution. With some exceptions, agency costs theorists to date have done little to explain the concept of the fiduciary, to develop positive theories as to why fiduciary law has developed its particular doctrines and characteristics, and to assess whether particular fiduciary doctrines are efficient or sound.[13]

Moreover, only a modest effort has been directed to deciphering how corporate law is actually made, and to identifying the role of economic efficiency in that process. Most corporate law derives from two sources: business corporation statutes adopted by legislatures, and fiduciary and other doctrines developed by courts. No one has shown, and I believe it is clearly not the case, that legislative changes to corporate statutes typically represent efforts merely to codify as general presumptions certain rights and duties that have already become prevalent in actual contracts. Nor are court decisions elaborating the contours of particular fiduciary duties merely filling in the gaps and ambiguities of actual contracts between the litigants in question. Most corporate *law* is created and imposed by legislatures and judges, not by investors and managers. The lawmakers are, of course, influenced by lobbying groups and litigants. But this does not necessarily mean that the rules thus laid down are similar to those that would be produced by actual contracts between the relevant lobbying groups or litigants—much less by actual contracts between groups consisting only of investors and managers.[14] The possible existence and extent of such a similarity is a subject for theoretical and empirical inquiry. The results of such an inquiry should not be assumed in advance.

It may be objected that some corporate law rules seem to fit the model of "standard presumptions" adopted because they fit the normal case, and that it is intuitively plausible that the relevant participants would actually agree to them, if the issue were put to them for explicit consideration and bargaining. This group of rules is likely to include the more elementary structural features of the corporate form of organization, such as limited liability of stockholders and free transferability of shares, which are often embodied in statutes. I agree that there are such rules, and they constitute an important class. In my view, they result from (fairly slow, crude) processes of legal evolution that favor rules that reduce transaction costs. But I would note that with many other rules, it is not at all obvious that they can be analyzed this way; the analysis has to be made in detail before it becomes convincing.

Another objection might be that while most rules of corporate law are imposed on the parties subject to it, they are usually free to "bargain around" them. A stockholder, for example, can bargain around limited liability by expressly guaranteeing specific corporate debts. *Failure* to bargain around a rule then amounts to accepting it, and one might even argue that the nonbargainers "contract" to obey the rule.

(Similarly, one can argue that failure to reincorporate in another state implies real consent to those rules that could be changed by reincorporation.)

But some important corporate law rules cannot be bargained around (unless, perhaps, one is willing to depart from the manager or stockholder roles or to modify their parameters drastically). Basic fiduciary duties fall in this category, along with insider trading rules and the norm that directors rather than stockholders manage public corporations. Of course, one can often get around such rules by violating them and avoiding detection and sanctioning, or by disguising the nature and effects of a transaction. But this possibility is irrelevant to the issue at hand, which is whether the rules are created by contract.

Moreover, bargaining around is costly. If the cost of bargaining is expected to exceed the benefits, the standard legal rule is simply tolerated—but this does not mean that it is the best available rule to govern the behavior in question. An alternative rule might make some people better off and no one worse off. Yet the substitution need not occur. For example, bargaining around a waivable fiduciary duty, such as the doctrine of corporate opportunity as developed in some jurisdictions, might require the preparation and distribution of a special proxy statement and the collection of a stockholder vote. The associated expense may deter many such bargains with investors. A different version of the legal doctrine might eliminate the transaction costs and deterrent effects of the need to seek shareholder consent. Thus, at any given time, it is an open question whether the standard legal rule is better than some imagined or proposed one. The interested commentator will have to make an independent assessment of the costs and benefits of the opposing rules, rather than simply assuming that the existing rule must be fit because it has survived (so far) without provoking much bargaining around.

A similar caution applies to any tendency to assume that the lawmaking process, or some part of it, mimics actual contracting in its Pareto-optimal results and therefore need not be laboriously studied and evaluated.

Consider this puzzle: In his book on economic analysis of law, Richard Posner argues that the judicial process is such that the common law has usually developed so as to promote economic efficiency, while the opposite is often true of the legislative process and statutory law.[15] Yet in the same book he describes basic corporate law, by which he means the *statutes* governing corporate structures, as a kind of standardized contract that may be adopted by parties wishing to operate a business (to save the costs of actual contracting about details) and that embodies efficient general presumptions about the relationships among the participants in businesses.[16] His particular assessments of rules may well be valid. I certainly share his admiration for the utility of the basic principles of the corporate form of organization (namely, limited liability, free transferability of investor interests, strong legal personality, and centralization of management). But what mechanism leads to this happy—and, by Posner's developmental theory, unusual—result? How do we go about deciding whether the efficiency claim is valid or not, especially as to the myriad of particular rules of corporate law?

To the first of these questions, Ralph Winter has proposed an answer: competition among chartering states for the favor of both investors and managers.[17] It is hard to be sure, however, that this process will lead to efficient outcomes. It may, if both investors and managers can react effectively to variations in state law. It may not, if, as seems plausible, investors and managers face very different transaction costs of effective collective action in this regard.[18]

Facile Optimism about the Optimality of Existing Institutions and Rules. A strong general orientation toward contractual analysis will lead one to assimilate many particular legal relationships to actual contracts. Since actual contracts are usually presumed to be Pareto-superior moves, the contractualist may conclude that many such assimilated relationships are Pareto-efficient or "optimal." But the conclusion may seem more doubtful to one who (like myself) insists that equivalences to actual contracts be demonstrated.

Jensen and Meckling argue, for example, that when a 100 percent owner and manager of a firm sells equity interests to the public, he will always bear the entire wealth effects of the agency costs, "so long as the equity market anticipates these effects."[19] (They define agency costs as the sum of monitoring expenditures by the principals [i.e., the stockholders]; bonding expenditures of the agent [the owner-manager]; and the residual loss from unprevented deviation of the agent from his promise.) Since the owner-manager is going to bear the full brunt of the agency costs, regardless of who directly makes the expenditures, he has the proper incentive to minimize agency costs. The strongly suggested conclusion is that existing levels of agency costs are optimal. This implication is supported by Jensen and Meckling's critique of the hypothetical thinker who concludes that the agency relationship is nonoptimal, wasteful, or inefficient simply because agency costs are not zero. Clearly such a conclusion would be too hasty—but no one has seriously propounded it. The question is why Jensen and Meckling felt moved to create and destroy such a straw man. My guess is that they wanted to create the impression, by negative implication, that real-world "agency" relationships between managers and stockholders are close to optimal.

Yet this ultimate conclusion is open to serious criticism. Once it is acknowledged that the going-public transaction may not constitute a perfect actual contract, one could ask some critical empirical questions. Does the equity market anticipate agency costs well? Might there not be information asymmetries between owner-managers and potential investors in this regard?

More important than this line of attack, I think, is the suspicion that the size and distribution of agency costs are determined in many clearly noncontractual contexts. Beyond bargaining about the terms of the original going-public transaction, or shopping around for the best positions already defined by such bargains, the participants in corporations can themselves influence the distribution and level of agency costs in other ways. They may bring about the adoption of rules to which their would-be bargaining parties would never agree. These rules may decrease the costs imposed on those who get them enacted even though they increase the total level of agency costs.

For example, litigating managers obtained recent case law giving limited deference to the decisions of litigation committees formed to recommend dismissal of stockholders' derivative lawsuits against managers.[20] These results may make derivative suits more costly and risky, yet certainly were not anticipated by investors, managers, or lawyers fifteen years ago. The same is true of federal court opinions interpreting state law to give managers very wide discretion to spend corporate funds and take major corporate actions to defeat takeover attempts.[21] These victories will presumably increase or maintain the high level of takeover costs—which are a part of agency costs.

A related example is the successful lobbying efforts by management groups in the early and mid 1970s to get state legislatures to enact antitakeover statutes.[22] To be sure, some stockholders fought back by trying to invalidate these statutes in court, arguing that they were preempted by the federal Williams Act or represented unconstitutional burdens on interstate commerce. Eventually—after the state statutes had allowed managers a substantial period of unpoliceable slack and discretion—these suits met with significant successes.²³ Still, there is no good reason to think that the resulting tissue of rules on this subject is very similar to the set that managers and stockholders would have jointly agreed to in some hypothetical original position with abundant information and no transaction costs.

One could argue that even these lobbying and litigation efforts cannot halt the inevitable march to optimality. After all, when managers have raised and shifted monitoring costs, the costs are then borne by stockholders, who therefore have an incentive to reduce them. Indeed, the implicit main point of Jensen and Meckling must be that the parties to the relationship (not just the original owner-managers) bear all the agency costs (in whatever proportions among themselves), so there are no externalities to worry about.

Nevertheless, managers and investors can try to avoid agency costs by shifting rather than reducing them, and there is no good a priori reason to conclude that neither group can rationally expect to do better by following the shifting strategy. Clearly a system of rules and institutions that encourages cost shifting is less desirable than one that encourages cost reduction. Indeed, when the background conditions are sufficiently bad—for example, when they allow and encourage frequent litigation and lobbying to shift costs—it seems not inconceivable that total agency costs could drift higher and higher.

Cover-up of Judgments about Preferences. Strong-form contractualism may be favored by the political conservative in a spirit of optimistic or defensive affirmation of the status quo. But in many cases the adoption of the contractualist view is merely a response to a basic problem that arises when microeconomic analysis is used to support particular policy recommendations—namely, the practical necessity of judging and evaluating other people's preferences when verification is impossible. In the course of making these judgments, however, the underlying problem may simply be covered up.

One reason for using the concept of Pareto superiority in economic analysis of law is that it allows one to work with relative rather than absolute evaluations of the impact of different legal arrangements on people's utility or welfare levels. The same reason leads conservative analysts to construe legal arrangements as being "essentially" the product of contracts. If an arrangement is contractual it must make the parties better off: Why else would they have agreed to it? The arrangement therefore represents a Pareto-superior move, and one can say this without claiming insight into people's specific welfare levels or value systems.

When arguing for a particular proposed rule of corporate law as against the current actual law or other alternatives, however, policy makers face an especially severe problem in trying to maintain this stance. They may argue that the proposed rule is really part of the larger "implicit" contract that already exists between managers and investors of public corporations. Formal lawmakers like legislators and judges simply have to be educated so that they can see that the proposed rule is implicit in the implicit contract. Alternatively, policy makers may argue that rational, self-interested managers and investors, bargaining with each other in a hypothetical original position, would have agreed to this particular proposed rule. In either case, argument will be thoroughly unconvincing if it is based on a simple assertion that the proposed rule "is part of the implicit manager-stockholder contract" or "would be agreed to in the original position."

As policy makers are compelled to elaborate on these assertions, they almost inevitably make arguments that imply they have insight into the characteristics of people's utility functions. Indeed, they will often make intersubjective comparisons of utility or otherwise resort to cardinal evaluations of the impact of rules on people's utility. While this is hardly to be condemned just because neoclassical economists would rather avoid doing it—ordinary people and politicians do it all the time—it is desirable to be aware of what one is doing.

Indeterminacy of Results. The basic pitfall with implicit-contracts reasoning is that it is frequently indeterminate and therefore manipulable. This is true whether the purpose of the reasoning is to advance positive or normative theory. It is especially true of complex, multi-faceted relationships, such as those among directors, officers, stockholders, and the large bureaucratic organizations with which they are associated.

In arguments about which rules rational managers and investors would have agreed to, much depends on what one assumes about the characteristics of the bargaining parties, their knowledge, the bargaining process, and the state of the financial and business world. The implicit-contracts form of reasoning is often indeterminate precisely because there is no consensus about which assumptions to use.

For example, Frank Easterbrook and Daniel Fischel assert that socially optimal fiduciary rules "approximate the bargain that investors and agents would strike if they were able to dicker at no cost." Such a bargain, they argue, would not include rules of equal treatment or gain sharing in corporate control transactions.[24] Their basic intuition is that inequality is sometimes necessary to maximize share values, which is what investors really care about. One important part of their argument is that investors would not care about the division of gains between two corporate entities in such a transaction because they can cheaply diversify away the risk of being on the losing side.[25] Consider the merger of a partially owned subsidiary into its parent: Because the parent's managers control the transaction and their personal compensation may be tied to the stock market performance of the parent as a whole, they may—and case law suggests they sometimes do—arrange the transaction so that minority shareholders of the subsidiary get no share, or a disproportionately small share, of the value created by the merger.[26] But if those stockholders are fully diversified, what is denied to them in one role will be given to them in another. Legal rules to ensure fair prices in such a merger, with the goal of protecting investors who "choose not to diversify," penalize other investors.

One of several problems with this argument is its assumption that investors in the original position will understand the benefits of full diversification and the fallacy of stock picking. In the real world, many individual investors are not well diversified. Often, I suspect, they honestly believe their professional investment advisers and therefore discount as "academic nonsense" any advice to give up on stock picking and to invest in an index fund. They are not so much risk neutral as ill-informed. A change in their views will be costly: the investors must be educated in portfolio theory, and the obstructive power of the self-interested investment advisory profession must somehow be broken. By what reasoning should these educational and political costs be stipulated away in the original position? Shouldn't these costs, and the resulting reality of imperfect investor diversification, have some bearing when lawmakers consider whether the possibility of diversification should eliminate concern for unequal or uncertain treatment of investors?

The resort to implicit but assertedly actual contracts can also be taken to questionable lengths. Consider the chief executive of a publicly held bottling company who buys a bottling plant that the corporation could have bought and developed. In arguing for a lax rather than a strict rule to govern a manager who thus "takes a corporate opportunity," Easterbrook and Fischel contend, "Managers properly take opportunities for themselves when they can exploit them more profitably than the firm. The increase in the value of the opportunity creates the possibility of a mutually beneficial transaction between manager and firm: the manager takes the venture, and the firm reduces the manager's other compensation."[27]

Recognizing that this characterization seems quite unrealistic, since executives who take a corporate opportunity typically do not reduce their salaries on the spot or accept part-time employment, Easterbrook and Fischel argue that there will be a "settling up" either before or after the taking. Perhaps the executive's original salary was lower than it otherwise would have been, because the corporation is the sort of firm that "allows its officials to exploit business opportunities on the side." Or perhaps the executive will receive smaller compensation in the future. And it "will not do" to suppose that executives can avoid this settling up (i.e., the implicit contract), because such executive discretion is constrained by product markets, labor markets, and the market for corporate control.

This argument depends crucially on unproven and nonobvious empirical assumptions. To evaluate it, one should try to answer at least three questions: (1) How often, when managers take corporate opportunities, can they exploit them *better* than their corporations could? (2) How often does the postulated *ex ante* or *ex post* settling up actually occur? (By the way, why *doesn't* the settling up occur explicitly and simultaneously with the taking? Is there a good reason why the market for executives should operate so as to prefer contracts that are difficult for the outside observer to verify and measure? What is so difficult about making an explicit contract?) (3) How tight are the three market controls they rely on? That is, how much slack or discretion— to seize perquisites, take corporate opportunities without giving benefits in return, and so on—is possible even with these controls? If, as many economically oriented commentators now seem to think, the tightest controls are those supplied by the threat of takeover, the cost of a takeover might serve as a proxy for the amount of unpoliceable managerial discretion in a corporation. This measure would suggest that the scope for slack is quite large, and helps explain why the law has evolved fiduciary rules, enforceable by derivative lawsuits, as yet another control mechanism. It is quite possible that these rules complement market controls because they have comparative advantages in some kinds of situations.

The indeterminateness of implicit-contracts reasoning does not mean that it cannot be useful, especially in normative discussions. It only means that doing it well is a treacherous business.

Toward a Positive Theory of Fiduciary Duties

Thousands of reported legal opinions articulate some version of the concept of fiduciary duties or some particular fiduciary doctrine. Legal commentators have spilt many gallons of ink writing sharp observations about particular lines of cases and fuzzy banalities about the general concept. Perhaps because the subject matter is so sprawling and elusive, there has been little legal analysis of the fiduciary concept that is simultaneously general, sustained, and astute.[28] This is unfortunate, since the rational agency costs theorist who is an economist is likely to be unwilling to delve into the large legal literature on particular fiduciary doctrines in the corporate area. Accordingly, I will attempt to articulate the major distinctive attributes of the fiduciary relationship in fairly general terms and then speculate briefly on why courts may have thought it rational and efficient to impose these attributes on corporate managers.

Common Attributes of the Fiduciary Relationship

At least four legal attributes of the fiduciary relationship would be of interest to an analyst of agency costs. Each can be usefully contrasted with legal relationships between so-called independent contracting parties.

Affirmative Duties to Disclose. An independent contractor may not lie to another contracting party, and in some cases expressly warrants the truth of certain information. Corporate borrowers, for example, often expressly warrant the truth of their financial statements to lending banks. Breach of the warranty then excuses the other party from having to perform under the contract or gives him certain remedial rights. But apart from expressed agreement or special circumstances, the independent contractor is often free not to disclose business information that the other party would find relevant in evaluating a proposed deal. For example, a corporation about to sign a requirements contract with a supplier of raw material probably has no duty to disclose facts and plans that suggest its future requirements may greatly increase or decrease—unless, of course, the contract expressly calls for it to make some assertions about its future requirements.

Corporate managers are in a sharply contrasting legal position. They often have an affirmative duty to disclose to other corporate decision makers information that bears on whether the corporation is about to make a good or bad business decision. This duty does not arise from the express terms of an employment contract, the resolutions of the board of directors, the corporate articles and bylaws, or the relevant business corporation statute. It does not depend on whether any or all of the other directors or officers think managers have such a duty. It does not depend on what managers themselves think about the issue. Rather, it depends on their fiduciary status.

For example, the much-cited case of *Globe Woolen v. Utica Gas & Electric Co.* involved a nonstockholding director of a utility company who was simultaneously the president, a director, and the chief stockholder of a woolen company that entered into a requirements contract with the utility.[29] This director, Maynard, presided at the utility board meeting in which the contract was approved; he put the resolution but did not vote and said nothing about the substance of the contract. Under the terms of the contract, which put a ceiling on the amount the woolen company would have to pay during a given period, the utility company later began losing substantial sums of money—partly because the woolen company changed its production processes in a way that greatly increased its need for electricity.

Without deciding how precise or certain Maynard's foreknowledge of this change was, or how careful his understanding of other aspects of the contract, the court concluded that he must have realized that he held a one-sided contract that left the utility company at his mercy, yet did not warn the other directors or apprise them of all the relevant facts and possibilities. (The other directors knew of his conflict of interest and might well have foreseen the ultimate problem if they had read the terms of the contract carefully, but apparently they did not do so.) In Judge Cardozo's words:

> But "the great rule of law" . . . which holds a trustee to the duty of constant and unqualified fidelity is not a thing of forms and phrases. A dominating influence may be exerted in other ways than by a vote. . . . A beneficiary, about to plunge into a ruinous course by dealing, may be betrayed by silence as well as by the spoken word.

The trustee is free to stand aloof, while others act, if all is equitable and fair. He cannot rid himself of the duty to warn and denounce, if there is improvidence or oppression, either apparent on the surface, or lurking beneath the surface, but visible to his practiced eye.[30]

Open-ended Duties to Act. The independent contractor usually has relatively fixed obligations under his contract. If the contract does not call for a particular performance, he does not have to do it. To be sure, the law of contracts will insist that he proceed "reasonably" and "in good faith" in carrying out the contract, and these qualifications will make his task somewhat open-ended.

With corporate managers, the open-endedness of legally imposed duties is more substantial. Statutes and case law empower the directors to manage the corporation's "business and affairs," and impose a "duty of care" in the exercise of those powers. For example, many statutes require the directors and officers to exercise that degree of care, skill, and diligence which an ordinary, prudent man would exercise in the management of his own affairs. The manager's duty of loyalty is also quite open-ended.[31]

Closed-in Rights to Positional Advantages. Case law on managers' fiduciary duty of care can fairly be read to say that the manager has an affirmative, open-ended duty to maximize the beneficiaries' wealth, regardless of whether this is specified in any actual contract. But with respect to the fiduciary's rights, the law leans exactly the other way. These rights are bounded in a fairly definite way. Essentially, the fiduciary cannot take any compensation from the beneficiaries or any other advantage from his official position (even when doing so does not seem to deprive the beneficiaries of any value they would otherwise get) except to the extent provided in an above-board actual contract or in accordance with explicit statutory permissions. Thus, top executives' compensation is supposed to be *expressly* approved by the board of directors acting for the corporation. Usually the directors of a public corporation are well advised to get and process full information about the chief executive, and to have the compensation package passed by a majority of "disinterested" directors. The board of directors now typically sets the directors' fees for its own members, but this procedure is legitimized by specific statutes. (In earlier days, directors often served without pay.)

As older case law using express analogies to trust law would put it, the manager has a duty not to take "secret profits." By "secret" the law really meant something quite broad: not *expressly* provided to the manager in the governing statutes, charter and bylaws, and employment contract (if any). Indeed, the entire centuries-old tradition of fiduciary law displays an antipathy toward viewing the fiduciary's reaping of positional advantages as "implicit compensation." The fiduciary tradition is hostile, almost by definition, to *this* use of implicit-contracts reasoning. This hostility is the ultimate source of most of the particular legal doctrines that make up the fiduciary duty of "loyalty."

For example, it gave rise to rules governing self-dealing transactions. According to most case law authority in force today, when the corporation enters into a transaction with another party who is a director or officer, or in whom or in which a director or officer has a personal interest, the director or officer must prove, if called upon to do so in a derivative lawsuit, that the transaction was "fair" to the corporation. "Fairness" means in part that the transaction was at least as advantageous to the corporation as a comparable transaction in a reasonably competitive market or as a hypothetical arm's-length bargain. In this case, the positional advantage denied to the manager is the opportunity to try to outdo the market at the corporation's expense. By contrast, no legal principle prohibits an ordinary independent contractor from charging more or giving less than in the average comparable market transaction or in a judicially imagined hypothetical arm's-length bargain. If a hardware store sells me a lawnmower at a price that is two standard deviations higher than the average retail price for that lawnmower, I cannot rescind the contract or get damages simply because of that fact. But if a corporate president sold a batch of lawnmowers to his corporation at equally inflated prices, the corporation would have a remedy.

Similarly, a corporate director or officer may not buy and develop a "corporate opportunity" for himself, unless the corporation is unable to do so or its disinterested decision makers expressly agree to the director's doing so. In Delaware, where many large public corporations are incorporated, a business opportunity is a "corporate" one for a particular corporation if it is within the corporation's "line of business." (Practically speaking, an opportunity is more likely to be classified as a corporate one, as between the corporation and a particular manager, if the manager learned about it in a way that had some connection with his official duties—that is, if his knowledge represents a positional advantage.) For a broadly diversified conglomerate, "line of business" could include almost anything. Thus, a group of directors and officers of a savings and loan association might well be prohibited from buying or setting up a home insurance agency next to the association's office, if the association could find some regulatorily permissible way of setting up the agency itself.[32] By contrast, the outside accountants and lawyers who contract to provide services to the association would be under no such prohibition.

A third example of restriction on fiduciaries is the rules against insider trading. These rules aim to prevent managers and other corporate insiders from profiting in securities transactions on the basis of information acquired in connection with their official positions. This is a strong application of the rule against secret profits: Though the insider's gain may be a loss to public investors trading in the opposite direction, insider trading seems unlikely to cause clear direct harm to the corporation itself (that is, to its business operations or its total value in the securities markets). Thus, if a corporate president learns from his research staff that a big increase in demand for the company's widgets is in the offing but is not yet recognized by traders in the stock market, he is forbidden from going out and buying the corporation's stock. But no restrictions are placed on the consultant under contract to the corporation who learns about the demand from the research staff of the consulting firm.

As these examples suggest, position-related benefits are often denied to fiduciaries when similar benefits are available to ordinary contracting parties. Economic analysts ought to ponder why this pattern of rules has evolved.

Moral Rhetoric. Our society is reluctant to allow or encourage organs of the state to try to instill moral feelings about commercial relationships into its citizens. Lawmakers officially condemn outright fraud and theft, of course. Yet judges have sometimes seemed to believe that a contracting party should feel perfectly free, in a psychological and moral sense, to break a contract, so long as he or she is prepared to pay the damages that legal rules require. But in the case of fiduciary duties, courts have not been reluctant to go beyond external sticks and carrots; indeed, they commonly intrude into the psyches of fiduciaries (or of their lawyers, who are the ones who read the cases), try to create feelings of guilt for violation of duty and rectitude for fulfillment of duty, and even conjure up an aura faintly resembling that which churches try to put around the duties of ministers to their congregations or of parents to their children.

A good example of the rhetoric of fiduciary duties was given by Justice Douglas in *Pepper v. Litton*.[33] That case itself involved the duties of a manager of an insolvent corporation to its creditors—who in an insolvent firm assume a status functionally like that of stockholders—but the passage in question has been quoted in noteworthy later cases involving more ordinary breaches of duty by corporate managers to their corporations and stockholders.[34] After analyzing and characterizing the facts, Douglas wrote what might be called the Seven Commandments of the Fiduciary Relationship.

> He who is in such a fiduciary position cannot serve himself first and his cestuis second. He cannot manipulate the affairs of his corporation to their detriment and in disregard of the standards of common decency and honesty. He cannot by the intervention of a corporate entity violate the ancient precept against serving two masters. He cannot by the use of the corporate device avail himself of privileges normally permitted outsiders in a race of creditors. He cannot utilize his inside information and his strategic position for his own preferment. He cannot violate rules of fair play by doing indirectly through the corporation what he could not do directly. He cannot use his power for his personal advantage and to the detriment of the stockholders and creditors no matter how absolute in terms that power may be and no matter how meticulous he is to satisfy technical requirements. For that power is at all times subject to the equitable limitation that it may not be exercised for the aggrandizement, preference, or advantage of the fiduciary to the exclusion or detriment of the cestuis. Where there is a violation of those principles, equity will undo the wrong or intervene to prevent its consummation.[35]

Clearly this is sermonizing, not logically necessary to justify the result in the case. And Justice Douglas was by no means the only prominent judge to bring moral fervor to the discussion of fiduciary duty.[36] But as noted earlier, the law makes no such noises in the case of ordinary contracting parties. Some reasons for the differences in treatment of fiduciary and contractual relationships are explored below.

Summary. Fiduciary law is stricter on fiduciaries than contract law is on ordinary contracting parties in at least four fundamental respects. There are stricter rules about disclosure, more open-ended duties to act, tighter delineations of rights to compensation and to benefits that could flow from one's position, and more intrusive normative rhetoric. These elements of strictness do not arise from actual contracts but have been created by judges in the common law tradition.

Explaining the Attributes

Why have these four attributes of the fiduciary relationship evolved, and why have they been applied to corporate directors and officers? In a rough sense, they are all designed to help deter abuse of managerial discretion. (Or as the economist would say, they aim to reduce agency costs.) Management of the public corporation has several characteristics that make abuse of discretion a major problem. First, almost by definition, the manager's job is to act on behalf of others in carrying out corporate business activities. Second, managers must have great power and very wide discretion to carry out their jobs well. Third, because of their expertise and their full-time commitment to the corporation, managers usually have a great informational advantage over their beneficiaries, the many widely dispersed public stockholders who individually have only small stakes in the business. The information asymmetry is paralleled by an asymmetry in the transaction costs of taking effective collective action. Managers can act to promote their interests as a group more easily and more coherently than can thousands of dispersed public stockholders.

But from a cost-benefit point of view, how well do the attributes of the fiduciary relationship succeed in mitigating the problem of managerial discretion ("agency costs")? We can hardly be sure, but we can offer speculations as a guide to further research. One theme that I would emphasize pertains most clearly to the third attribute. Closed-in rights to compensation and positional advantages often have little or no cost in terms of business efficiency, yet they are apt to reduce *avoidable and unproductive uncertainty* in the capital markets.

For example, consider the manager who annually embezzles from the corporate treasury an amount equal to about a third of his explicit salary and benefits. Suppose his practice is finally discovered and challenged by a dissident stockholder. Why can he not argue that the embezzled amounts should be regarded as an implicit part of his total compensation and therefore legal? Why should only benefits voted upon by an independent board of directors be deemed to constitute valid compensation? One reason is that the embezzlement is unilateral, and so does not represent a market transaction; it may be inefficient—for example, because the manager takes more than his services are worth on a competitive market.[37] But let us suppose that embezzlement is widespread in his industry, that investors are aware of that fact, and that stock prices are discounted accordingly. Should these facts exonerate him? Have investors and the board of directors implicitly consented to the prevailing level of embezzlement?

One reason for a negative answer is that market prices in an efficient market will embody expectations, not only about managerial taking of "secret profits," but also about stockholder rights to a remedy when any particular manager is caught. Basing legal rights on expectations is circular; the right must be specified first.

Suppose that rights are to be specified by constructing a hypothetical contract between managers and investors. Why might the parties agree to a rule against embezzlement? One reason is that "secret profits" like embezzled funds increase uncertainty about levels of return on investment, without making possible significant value-creating transactions that could not otherwise occur. Unproductive uncertainty is a deadweight loss, clearly to be avoided. Moreover, the resulting secrecy about the precise amount of "remuneration" to particular executives makes it harder for the market to evaluate the productivity of executives (their performance in light of their remuneration) and to reward or punish them accordingly.

My intuition is that most higher-order fiduciary duties are variations on these basic themes. Analysis can be difficult because some regulated behaviors—for example, interested director transactions—may have redeeming features (value-creating potential) in some cases. But at bottom the economic analysis will be analogous to that of the case of embezzlement.

Why moral rhetoric is used to help bolster norms in some contexts but not others is a question that points to a vast area for research. I would suggest here only that moral opprobrium seems to attach to misdeeds for which the usual market and legal controls will not provide adequate deterrence.

Suppose deterrence of a rule violation is a multiplicative function of the probability and the magnitude of the market and legal sanctions, and consider two different kinds of rule violation: breach of contract and a fraudulent financial scheme. The probability of being sanctioned for breach of contract in one way or another is usually rather high—the other party will know of the breach, will have an incentive to do something about it, and will be able to do something (if only to warn other potential contracting parties). Only modest opprobrium attaches to ordinary breach of contract. By contrast, the probability of being sanctioned for fraudulent financial behavior is probably much smaller. (How much smaller, we do not know, since fully successful frauds are not discovered.) Moreover, the legal system seems unable or unwilling to impose a remedy that is sufficiently harsh—that is, sufficiently greater than the actual damages caused in particular frauds—to compensate for this low probability. Perhaps this is one reason why acts and expressions of disapproval, by both lawmakers and business people, are added to the arsenal of control mechanisms.

Whether these sketchy suggestions will help elucidate the legal concept of the fiduciary remains to be seen. My purpose here has been to argue that this is the concept that needs to be explained.

Chapter 4
Insider Trading as an Agency Problem

Frank H. Easterbrook

Economic discussions of the agency problem, which Arrow (1985) describes, are both enlightening and frustrating: enlightening because they show how difficult it is to induce agents to act in principals' interests, and frustrating because they do not establish whether the solutions they describe are effective. As Arrow observes, the agency models are unusually difficult to construct. The game-theoretic models never seem to have equilibria, and other models contain highly limiting, often quite implausible assumptions. The complications in the theory would not be troubling if there were good tests of the predictions of these models. There are not, however, and the agency literature is one of the few remaining parts of economic thought that depends almost entirely on the power of deductive logic. There has been some empirical work by people interested in finance, but this work so far looks only at the consequences of the structures within which agency relations are conducted. The evidence enlightens us, for example, on whether takeovers are beneficial for investors but not (yet) on what changes in agency or other arrangements produce these benefits.

I want to look more closely at one of the most interesting problems in agency: is trading by corporate insiders on material information (before its disclosure to the market) beneficial to investors? The subject has provoked substantial public debate, leading to administrative regulation and judicial decisions. This debate has been carried on with either indifference or hostility toward the sparse agency literature on the subject, and the literature itself has been inconclusive. I examine the competing arguments in order to bring out the unsettled questions. Because there have been changes in the law and the technology concerning insiders' trading, and many instances of the detection of such trading, it should be possible to design tests of the agency theories. I suggest a few such tests.

Economic Theory

Some History

Until 1961 trading by insiders in organized markets was almost always lawful, no matter what kind of information the insiders possessed. Section 16(c) of the Securities Exchange Act of 1934 prohibited short sales by some defined insiders, who also were required by section 16(b) to disclose after the fact and to turn over to their firms the profits from buy-sell transactions within six months. Some person-to-person trades of the stock of closely held corporations were improper because of the managers' implicit representations to their trading partners. These exceptions did not govern very many cases, however, and firms did not write contracts with managers that prohibited trading that the law allowed.

In 1961 the Securities and Exchange Commission (SEC) declared that trading by insiders was unlawful if the trades were based on "material" but undisclosed information. ("Materiality," a term of legal art, usually denotes substantial importance but has considerable ambiguity.) Courts came round to this point of view in the next few years, and in 1968 the court of appeals with jurisdiction of New York (and thus the principal exchanges) held that neither the insiders nor their "tippees" could trade on material, undisclosed information. The Supreme Court endorsed these rules in 1980, modifying them in ways that are not important to this essay.[1] It is still lawful and common, however, for insiders to own and trade large quantities of their firms' stock. They may trade as they please, provided that none of the undisclosed information they possess by reason of their positions of trust in the firms is "material."

The SEC's decision invoked two considerations. It said that trading was wrongful first because the inside information was intended for the benefit of the firm and not the private advantage of the traders and second because trading was "unfair" to the uninformed investors. The first of these is an economic rationale about the benefits of establishing property rights in information and assigning those rights to the firms rather than the agents. The second is vacuous. Fairness is an empty concept into which agencies, courts, and lawyers pour a miscellany of unexamined and inconsistent premises (Easterbrook 1981, 323–30).

Fairness arguments in the law too often serve as discussion-stoppers, permitting advocates to assert conclusions without reasons while branding those who think otherwise as moral dwarfs. Sometimes arguments based on fairness rest on a coherent theory of moral rights; usually, though, fairness arguments have no ascertainable philosophical foundation. The ease of invoking "fairness" as the beginning and ending of a legal argument was amply illustrated in discussions about insider trading. When Henry Manne (1966) offered the first careful economic treatment of insider trading, he was met not with scholarly answers but with ridicule: because insider trading is unfair and immoral, the economics do not matter, and anyone who says they do is immoral himself.[2] Courts and legal scholars ignored the economics; economists other than Manne ignored the subject altogether. Until the late 1970s, neither those working on the theory of the firm nor those writing about the economics of agency had much to say about the compensation devices actually observed in corporations, including insider trading.

Insider Trading and Agency Costs

Manne's initial argument about insider trading was that it rectified what we now call a problem of agency costs.[3] (See Jensen and Meckling 1976.) When managers of large corporations do not receive the marginal benefits of their labors, they will be less dedicated in the pursuit of new and better ventures. Shareholders, not managers, are the residual claimants, and both can gain from devices that ameliorate the ensuing divergence of interest. Now of course the potentially baleful consequences of the separation of ownership and control were not news (Berle and Means 1932; Schumpeter 1934). The existing literature, however, either treated the problem as insoluble or overcame it by fiat by assuming that managers were perfect agents of investors. Manne argued instead that although agency costs were a problem, the size of these costs had been greatly reduced by market mechanisms, including insider trading.

Manne saw insider trading as a form of contingent residual claim by managers. They could obtain substantial payoffs whenever they produced gains that were so much better than expected that the price of the stock would rise. Thus managers' incentives would be aligned with investors' interests; both would want the firm to select good projects and develop them efficiently. Managers would compensate investors by accepting lower base salaries, and, because increasing efficiency is a positive-sum game, what might appear to be "losses" to investors (who sold the shares to managers in advance of appreciation) would not be losses at all. Manne also offered arguments about why other contingent compensation systems, such as bonuses and stock options, are not as beneficial in addressing the agency problem. Stock options usually are issued at the beginning of a period, and the number of options awarded is not contingent on previous performance. As a result, he argued, they do not sufficiently motivate performance during the period. Bonuses generally depend on a manager's office (the chairman gets more than a vice president) and so are not well tied to performance.

Those who paid any attention to the economics argued in response to Manne that the payoffs from insider trading also are not tied very well to performance. Sometimes business success is the result of chance rather than effort and skill, and insider trading payoffs occur whenever the stock rises or falls, not when dedicated and skillful services are rendered. The insider gains from volatility, which can follow good or bad events. Moreover, the inside traders will be those who know the critical information about impending success, not necessarily the people whose efforts produced that success. The profits of insider trading may be nothing but windfalls.

These are not very good answers. No compensation device is perfect. We can evaluate the benefits of one only in relation to the benefits of others. Insider trading offers payoffs to those who learn the important information first. These insiders are apt to be those who create the information and profit for the firm. The fit will be imperfect, but it is at least as good as and probably better than the fit between the award of bonuses (or stock options) and the employee's creation of gains for the firm. Similarly, although insiders can avoid losses by selling before bad news comes out, the rewards go to the most astute analysis within the firm. Payoffs for quick learning and adaptation may be valuable though today's news is bad. Even when a firm does poorly it must pay its best managers the wage they could earn at other firms, for otherwise they will leave.

Indeed, the goodness of fit between information (or gain) production and opportunities for profit from trading has been the basis of a different challenge to Manne's thesis. Robert Haft (1982), drawing on the literature on organization theory, argues that subordinates will hoard information, to the detriment of the firm, if they can use it to their own advantage in trading. This line of argument assumes that those who gain from trading will be those who generate information.

Haft's argument is unsuccessful as a justification of legal prohibitions, because it cannot justify any restrictions on trading by those at the top of the hierarchy. More important, Haft's argument raises a problem that recurs in the agency literature. If insider trading is disadvantageous to the firm, why do employees not voluntarily agree to forego such trading? They could then increase their salaries. Law firms, printers, and many others with access to information pledge not to use it. A firm with an inferior organizational structure cannot endure in competition with better-organized firms. True, no organizational form displaces another immediately, but insider trading has survived for a very long time in very many countries. Why was it not forbidden in contracts? Why is the ban a matter of law? (That is, even if there is a presumption against insider trading, why can firms not opt out by contract and public declaration?) Why was the legal rule not adopted until 1961? An agency theory that finds insider trading to be inefficient but leaves these questions unanswered is not satisfactory. As I discuss below, reliance on evidence of survival also is unsatisfactory, but it is necessary to start there.

One can turn Haft's argument almost completely around to support insider trading. Perhaps firms are relatively poor at transmitting information internally unless those who obtain information can use it to their profit. Then the lure of insider trading causes top managers to seek out information held by subordinates, instead of sitting back and waiting for the bureaucratic pipeline to deliver a memorandum. Along similar lines, Dye (1984) argues that the availability of insider trading in a compensation package allows managers to give investors additional information about the menu of projects. The managers do this in Dye's model by selecting the features of the compensation package. Those who select a package that includes inside trading send a message different from that of those who do not.[4]

Perhaps, too, firms are relatively poor at delivering information (in credible form) to stock markets. If so, then insiders' trades may improve the market's assessment of a firm's prospects and so reduce its cost of capital (Kitch 1980, 718–19). The traders convey information to the market (slowly, to be sure), and the information they convey is credible because they are putting their own money on the line.

Insider Trading and Moral Hazard

Manne's book and subsequent articles did not offer a formal model of optimal compensation. Some of the recent work on insider trading has attempted to do that. Economists now take it as given that so long as managers work in teams, do not possess all residual claims, and are not supervised by residual claimants with complete information, there is bound to be divergence between investors' interests and managers' actions. The interesting question is whether a compensation scheme can reduce that divergence without incurring information costs exceeding the available benefits.

The occurrence of information costs joined with the independent operation of agents immediately creates a moral hazard. Easterbrook (1981, 332–33) and Leftwich and Verrecchia (1983) discuss this problem. Whenever the manager can claim part of the profits of a successful project, but the shareholders bear the entire cost of failure, the manager has an incentive to select high-variance projects even if they have a lower mean return than other options. This is just like the incentive equity investors have to increase the variance of projects because debt investors' payoffs do not increase in the event of especially favorable results, yet debtholders bear part of the loss from especially unfavorable results.

Recognizing moral hazard problems of this sort, Fama (1980) and Fama and Jensen (1983) argue that optimal managerial compensation packages will entail fixed rather than residual claims, supplemented by reevaluations ("*ex post* settling up") after performance has been completed. But such schemes depend on the timely possession of information by those fixing compensation, and when information is costly the best compensation scheme entails some payoff contingent on the outcome of the project as well as the managers' levels of effort and talent.[5] (See, for example, Holmstrom 1983; Diamond and Verrecchia 1982.) Thus the moral hazard problem may be unavoidable.

These moral hazard arguments are also regrettably indeterminate. Managers may shift to riskier projects, but it is not necessarily true that these riskier projects will have lower mean returns. One strain of agency literature (Holmstrom 1983; Shavell 1979) argues that managers accept too little risk, choosing low-variance projects even if they have lower mean returns. In part this happens because managers are more risk averse than investors. Investors can diversify, and they care about the risk of one firm's projects only if they cannot diversify that variance away. Managers, though, have a substantial part of their personal wealth tied up in the firms. They own their firms' stock (which helps align their interests with the shareholders'); more important, their human capital is undiversified. Denied the advantages of diversification, managers are apt to shun risks that other investors would want taken.

If insider trading gives managers an incentive to select higher-risk projects, this may be just what the doctor ordered. Unless the distribution of the mean returns of projects according to risk is very peculiar, the countervailing effects of pro- and anti-risk incentives will not drive the managers to look only at a portion of the firm's opportunity set that contains lower-mean projects. But we cannot be sure. Maybe managers are not effectively risk averse, so the risk-inducing quality of insider trading is detrimental, according to the Leftwich and Varrecchia arguments. Maybe other compensation devices would do better at inducing optimal risk-taking. Dye (1984) makes an interesting formal argument that compensation via insider trading is superior to compensation via these other outcome-contingent methods. Leftwich and Verrecchia say that Dye's assumptions are implausible and his results suspect. I am inclined to agree, but this is an empirical rather than a logical quarrel.

Perhaps the whole debate is pointless. If other compensation devices (such as bonuses and some kinds of stock options) have the same risk-inducing effects as insider trading, those effects linger, for good or ill, after insider trading becomes unlawful. Moreover, the adverse incentive effects may be trivially small. The principal welfare loss from insider trading may be the great sacrifice of ink, trees, and the time of academics, judges, and lawyers who dispute the subject. These costs are at least more readily quantifiable than many of the others discussed in the literature.[6]

Insider Trading and Adverse Selection

As Arrow (1985) reminds us, the information cost and monitoring difficulties that create moral hazard also may create adverse selection. So they do with insider trading.

Consider one of the available arguments to this end. Scott (1980) and Easterbrook (1981) argue that compensation through trading opportunities amounts to paying managers in lottery tickets. The price of stock reflects the expected outcomes of the firm's projects, so that only unusually good outcomes produce profitable trading opportunities for insiders. (Put to one side for the moment the fact that unusually bad outcomes create loss-avoidance opportunities.) The (effectively) risk-neutral investors are indifferent between paying the managers $100,000 in salary and paying them $50,000 in salary plus a one-in-ten chance of trading profits worth $500,000. They will choose whichever offer gives the manager the better incentive to select profitable projects. The manager, however, is undiversified (only one employer) and risk averse. He sees the offer with inside trading as worth less than the straight salary offer. Under inside trading, the firm pays more than the manager receives, and the difference is a deadweight loss.

Worse, there can be adverse selection even when inside trading is the superior device for motivating managers. If managers are not free to leave the firm, inside trading opportunities may be optimal incentive devices. But of course they are free to leave, and managers in the example just given may view the package with inside trading as worth no more than $90,000 with certainty. A firm that offers $95,000 will attract the manager, even though the manager's social product is $worth less with that firm (or worth less in the absence of the incentives provided by inside trading).

By a parallel process, a compensation package with inside trading will attract risk-preferring managers, which (for reasons discussed in the section on moral hazard) the firm may or may not want. Whether this process creates a lemons market is hard to say, because we do not know the optimal degree of risk preference by managers.

This adverse selection argument has been met by a signaling argument. Carlton and Fischel (1983, 870–72) contend that higher-quality managers "signal" their quality by accepting a compensation package that contains a risk of nonpayment. Because it is hard for firms to identify high-quality managers, they design compensation packages that let such managers identify themselves. If they are to work, the packages must be lucrative for top-quality managers but not remunerative to those less able. Carlton and Fischel argue that packages designed along these lines will have contingent payoffs, which only the high-quality managers will receive. Because prospective managers know more about their talents than the prospective employers, high-quality managers will be differentially attracted to such packages, because they believe they will receive the payoffs for excellent results.

This selection mechanism need not depend on trading profits; there are other ways (although perhaps not as effective) to give contingent payoffs. How well it works will depend on the degree of risk high-quality managers will tolerate and on the risk distribution of the available projects. If the firm is in a very risky business and many projects will pay off even under low-quality management (or will not pay off under high-quality management), the incentives do not work right. In a high-variance world, it is not irrational for low-quality managers to accept employment under a compensation schedule with payoffs contingent on outcomes. And for reasons developed by Holmstrom (1983), high-quality managers employed under such a schedule may find that their expected returns are greatest if they pursue low-variance projects with lower mean returns.

So we may yet get a lemons market, depending on risk preferences and the variance of the available projects. Once more, because no one knows what these preferences and variances are, the theoretical work is indeterminate. It is safe to say that compensation packages with inside trading would be more useful in some industries than others, since different markets have different risk distributions. Any uniform legal rule or economic treatment is questionable. Beyond that we know little.

How Can We Test the Models?

The principal problem that arises in evaluating the arguments set out above, and much of the rest of the agency literature, is that the models are almost hopelessly incomplete. Models focusing on how compensation packages influence managers usually treat the investment decisions as given, assume that there is only one compensation device (say, a state-contingent payoff at the end of the period), and limit to one or two the number of firms and periods of time. Often they also assume that the future is not discounted. None of the models of agency, and none of the treatments of insider trading other than Carlton and Fischel (1983), discusses more than a small fraction of the considerations I have brought out above.

I am not criticizing the use of exceptionally or even patently false assumptions in the models. Agency problems are so complex that the restrictions are necessary if we are to make any progress at all. But when a whole branch of economics uses implausible assumptions, the claim that the results are useful must rest on more than the purity of the deductive logic. There must be some effort to verify that the models' predictions describe the world (Friedman 1953; Stigler 1983). Efforts to verify the assessments provided by the agency models have been few and unsatisfactory.

What Do We Learn from the Survival of Insider Trading?

The dominant empirical theme in the inside trading literature has been survival. Manne (1966, 1970, 1974), Dooley (1980), and Carlton and Fischel (1983) all rely heavily on the fact that unregulated markets produced insider trading. Firms made little or no effort to suppress such trading. If it is an inefficient method of compensation, why did it not go away? Those who argue that insider trading is inefficient commonly ignore its survival (e.g., Haft 1982) or assume it away (e.g., Left-wich and Verrecchia 1983, 20).

The legal literature characteristically attributes the survival of inside trading to persistent advantage taking. Managers like insider trading, it is argued, because it enables them to fatten their purses at the expense of stockholders (e.g., Brudney 1979, which also discusses earlier writings). The managers hide most of the details of their compensation package from investors, and it is said that inside trading profits are easier to hide than other sources of income.

If incumbent managers can exploit their positions though, why do they not establish optimal compensation schemes, increase the worth of the firm, and then use their power to skim off part of the increased profits? They have no vested interest in inefficient behavior by the firm.

The view that incumbents are in a position to exploit investors also does not explain persistence of inside trading for more than one generation of managers. The incumbents have no reason to share any power to exploit investors with newly hired managers. They would maximize their own returns by ensuring that the younger managers cannot expropriate the firm's (and thus their) profits. The senior managers would insist that junior managers forswear any inefficient compensation package. Yet there is no evidence that senior managers have tried to prevent junior managers from engaging in insider trading.

No matter how much managers may be protected from scrutiny by investors, inefficient compensation methods cannot survive forever in competition. Managers of an upstart firm, seeking an advantage over rivals, could bind themselves not to engage in inside trading. If such a pledge benefited investors (as it might), the price of this firm's stock would rise. It would then be able to get capital at a lower price and sell its goods for less in the product market. The upstart and others that copied it would gain profits and market share; the older firms would be forced to follow suit. The evolutionary behavior of competitive markets makes it unlikely that the ability of managers to escape monitoring by investors could yield inefficiency in perpetuity (Alchian 1950; Becker 1961).

There is, finally, the observation of Jensen and Meckling (1976) that if managers want to be in a position to exploit investors, they must pay for that position. When a firm goes public (or issues stock), the investors have appropriate incentives to scrutinize what they are getting. The capital market is competitive, and investors with the ability to buy Treasury bills certainly will not take an inferior risk-return combination from a firm. If managers write inefficient compensation contracts or otherwise do not minimize the agency costs of the firm, they must pay for their choices by getting lower prices for the stock. The investors are neither fooled nor exploited.

Nevertheless, the survival of inside trading until 1961 does not mean that it was beneficial to investors. No firm has an incentive to suppress trading by its insiders on material information unless the private gains of doing so exceed the private costs. A good argument can be made that costs are very high, although they have recently fallen, and that the gains of forswearing cannot be completely captured by the firm. To see why, assume that inside trading is inefficient and ask when a firm would try to eliminate the practice.

For starters, it is hard to determine when inside trading occurs. It is necessary to distinguish trading on the basis of "material" information from other trading (which insiders may legitimately carry out for portfolio adjustment purposes or just to have more stock of their firm because they are more confident than the market of the management's abilities). It will be very costly to detect an insider's trades, because he can hide his trading activity. He can buy stock in street names or through nominees (including trusts and family members); he may route orders through a chain of brokers to make tracing difficult; the list of evasive devices is long. It will be costly, too, to determine which trades are based on prohibited "material" information. Even if it is in the interest of the firm and the employee to agree *ex ante* not to trade on inside information, the manager has both the interest and the ability to do otherwise *ex post.*

About the only thing a firm can do by itself to reduce the costs of enforcing compliance with a no-trading pledge is to prohibit all ownership of stock by its employees. This drastic response could not interdict managers' passing of tips to friends and family or secret trading through nominees. If a ban were enforceable, however, it could have costs far exceeding those of inside trading. Stock ownership is very useful in aligning managers' incentives with those of other investors. "Phantom stock" (the award of bonuses based on the appreciation of stock even though the employee owns no stock) is not a perfect substitute for the real thing. Managers who hold actual stock suffer capital losses when the firm does poorly, and they therefore seek to avoid such outcomes. Although phantom stock contracts could require payments from managers to their firms when the stock declines in price, it would be hard to enforce such contracts. The managers might have liquidity problems; worse, the required payments might exceed the managers' net wealth. Managers would have to bond their promises to make payments, and bonding is costly. Managers' ownership of real stock tackles the problem; the stock is the bond. Moreover, phantom stock deals do not allow managers to signal their abilities or to place extra bets on the firm when they are convinced that their talents are superior to the firm's or market's assessment. Real stock permits managers to place such bets.

Limits on managers' ownership of stock also could take the form of paying them in options that can be cashed only with the firm. Once more, though, the same problems occur. Better managers cannot distinguish themselves by buying more, and it is hard to arrange capital losses.

Compensation packages that do not include real stock also would inhibit competition for corporate control and the monitoring provided by such control contests. In any control fight, especially proxy contests and going-private transactions, one natural contestant is the current managerial group. Data show that these contests are beneficial to investors.[7] A compensation plan that eliminated managers' holdings of tradable shares would remove one of the potential contestants and reduce the returns to investors.

If we start from the premise that employees will (and should) hold actual shares of stock, a prohibition of insider trading will be very costly to enforce. The overwhelming majority of violations will go undetected. If the costs of policing a rule against trading on material information exceed the gains of the prohibition, firms rationally will not write contracts with such prohibitions.

The role of stock ownership is illuminated by the way lawyers, financial printers, and other specialists with access to inside information have treated their knowledge. These specialists need not be induced to hold residual claims in the firm. The quality of their performance can be measured, and they can be compensated, without regard to the firm's fortunes. Long before 1961, lawyers and printers agreed with the firms not to engage in trading on the basis of their inside information. These agreements were enforced in the least-cost way: law firms and financial printers absolutely prohibited their partners and employees from acquiring stock of clients or trading any existing stock. This enforcement device is available to these specialists at much lower cost than to the firms. Even so, enforcement has been very difficult; today both law firms and printers frequently are prosecuted for violating such pledges.

The costs of enforcing a prohibition also have changed over time. The best enforcement device may be to have the stock exchange itself search for "unusual" trades, that is, for instances of trading that are very large in relation to the ordinary volume, during the week or two before a firm's stock experiences a significant change in price. Powerful computers would be needed to record the price and trading patterns of each firm's stock and constantly search for deviations. The search would include recombining orders that arrive from different brokers (to thwart a detection-avoidance strategy of making many smaller transactions). Once the computer has flagged transactions as suspicious, the SEC, the exchange, or the firm could search to determine who traded and whether the trade was wrongful.

Computer-assisted search is the dominant enforcement method today. In 1950 it would have been impossible; indeed, the computing capacity necessary to reduce the detection costs to an acceptable level did not exist before the late 1960s, and the price of computation has fallen dramatically over time. This change in enforcement costs is a possible explanation of why firms did not try to stop insider trading before 1961 but now do not seek legislation to reverse the SEC's ban. It may explain both the survival and the decline of insider trading.

There remains a question about public enforcement. The use of computers to scan the entire market creates economies of scale in enforcement, but there are no public goods here. The stock exchanges can charge their member firms the costs of enforcement and exclude those who do not pay from access to information. The justification for public enforcement would be the improbability of detecting any given improper trade. When detection is rare, the penalty must be increased in order to create optimal deterrence. See Easterbrook (1983, 292–97) for a summary. When detection is highly unlikely, the optimal penalty may well exceed the net wealth of the offender. *Ex post* settling up along the lines of Fama (1980) will be impossible. Thus public enforcement, which can lead to imprisonment and other penalties firms cannot adopt for themselves, may be optimal.[8]

Carlton and Fischel (1983) have responded to this entire line of argument, which I made earlier in a different form (Easterbrook 1981, 333–35), by contending that because the costs of *writing* the prohibition into a contract are "minimal" (and were so even before computers), firms will draw up such contracts even if they do not plan to spend resources on enforcement. Then honest agents, at least, will refrain from inside trading, increasing the efficiency of some firms' operations. Carlton and Fischel infer from the absence of *any* contractual undertakings of this sort before 1961 that insiders' trading is efficient.

Whenever firms write contracts that they do not plan to (or cannot) enforce, however, they face a serious problem of adverse selection. Dishonest agents will find employment with the firm especially attractive. They will get their salaries and be able to engage in inside trades as well; they will be overcompensated. To avoid overcompensating the dishonest agents, the firm must reduce salaries across the board. Now the honest agents—those who do not trade on material inside information—will be underpaid and will leave. Bad agents drive out the good. The firm can increase the quality of its managers only by rescinding the "voluntary prohibition" of inside trading.

The difficulty of detecting who does and who does not comply with a prohibition on inside trading also makes it very hard for a firm to capture the gains of a prohibition, *even if the prohibition is both socially beneficial and perfectly enforced.* Suppose Firm A adopts and enforces a prohibition. It communicates the news to the market, and the price of its stock rises, reflecting the value of the new measures. Now Firm B copies the announcement but not the enforcement policy. The market will be uncertain whether Firm B in fact has abolished trading by its insiders. The price of B's stock will rise to reflect the benefits, discounted by the probability of enforcement. The more Firm B looks like Firm A to the market, the higher its price. Many B-type firms will try to take a free ride on the efforts of A-type firms. The stategy is more profitable to B than to A, because only A incurs enforcement costs. The more successful the B-types are in mimicking the appearance but not the reality of prohibition, the lower the price of A-type stock, because the market cannot trust A's representations. And if, because of the mimicry, the A-type firms cannot capture the full benefits of their enforced prohibition of trading, they too will find it most profitable to adopt strategy B.

This sequence, by which a socially beneficial strategy is unraveled, depends critically on the ability of B-type firms to mimic A-types or, equivalently, on the inability of A-type firms to distinguish themselves or "bond" their performance to their investors. Because inside trading is so hard to define and detect, mimicry should be easy. A successful A-type firm may have a hard time demonstrating how (or that) its measures work. If they deter violations, the A-type firm will have little visible evidence of its diligence. If the measures do not work, the violations may be undetected (or if detected, they may be interpreted as evidence that the firm is a B-type). B-type firms may adopt measures on paper and wink at violations. It is hard to imagine a method by which the firms could separate themselves with sufficient precision to permit true A-types to recover the costs of their efforts.

In a long-run equilibrium, only a firm's profits and real prospects influence the price of its stock. Beneficial programs of suppressing insiders' trades thus would increase price through their contribution to profits, whether or not the market believed the programs were being enforced. But we do not live in long-run equilibrium. If a firm can neither cover the costs of a program at the beginning (because it cannot distinguish itself properly) nor stop its employees from trading later on (because it cannot detect their trades), it also cannot convey the promise of future enforcement, and the market will discount the prospects of this firm more steeply than its raw profit data would suggest.

All of this leads to the gloomy conclusion that survival evidence is not very useful in evaluating trading. The historical pattern—trading until 1961, public enforcement thereafter—is consistent with a story that trading is efficient, but it is equally consistent with a story that public enforcers have a comparative advantage, aided by computers and the criminal law, in getting rid of an inefficient practice. We must look elsewhere for evidence.

Stock Market and Other Tests

Studies of the "profitability" of firms that do and do not try to control insider trading are unlikely to get us very far. Accounting data are not compiled to facilitate tests of such hypotheses. Accounting profit measures do not represent real economic profits. Moreover, because of the competition among firms to adopt efficient compensation and agency-cost-control devices, and the inflow of new capital to firms that reduce agency costs, the effects on profits of the rules about inside trading would be transitory and hard to detect. As a result, even if Manne is right that insider trading is a socially valuable form of compensation, we would not expect to see many traces in profit data.

It would be slightly more promising to look at the relation between insiders' trading and other forms of compensation. Manne's argument, together with the Carlton and Fischel elaboration, implies that, holding profits constant, the stated compensation (including bonuses, stock options, and other announced remuneration and benefits) of managers falls as average trading profits rise; indeed the stated compensation might fall faster than trading profits rise if this is an especially useful compensation device.

Some data are available on the total trades of some insiders. Certain managers and large stockholders must file reports under section 16(a) of the Securities Exchange Act of 1934. These reports may not be truthful, they do not distinguish trades on material nonpublic information from other trades, and many managers need not file. Nevertheless, they are at least a starting point for inquiry. Interpretation of the findings will present vexing tasks, though. If a study reveals a trade-off between stated compensation and trading profits, how are we to interpret this? None of the competing explanations of insider trading predicts the terms of this trade, so we have little basis for inference.

It might be more useful to search for substitution between insider trading and other agency-cost-control devices. The argument that insider trading aligns managers' interests well with those of investors implies that other (costly) devices for controlling agency costs would be employed less frequently, because they were less valuable at the margin, in firms with inside trading. This approach predicts that firms with more trading experience have fewer takeover and proxy contests, issue new stock less often (new issues trigger monitoring by investment bankers and investors), and have less debt (debtholders monitor through indenture trustees). There should be other substitutions as well. Managers' holding of stock is a way to reduce agency costs, so the efficiency thesis implies that firms with more trading by insiders have less of their stock owned by insiders. (This is not a paradox, because those who buy stock on inside information may sell the stock promptly after the market learns the information.) No one has conducted a test along these lines, and the availability of data may be a significant obstacle.

The best available tests of the benefits of insider trading would come from the stock market. If the market is reasonably efficient, stock prices reflect the benefits and detriments of insider trading. Using the methodology described in Schwert (1981), one could look for price changes at times of changes in approaches to insider trading. For example, what happened to stocks in 1961 when the SEC quite unexpectedly announced a ban on insider trading? When the courts agreed with the ban? When the New York Stock Exchange first put its computerized stock watch program into effect, making enforcement of the ban less costly? When courts began to increase the size of the penalties (substituting jail time for restitution of profits, as one example)? All of these changes should have left some traces.[9] Studies along these lines are hard to conduct because any change affects all firms simultaneously, but this problem has been handled for events as diverse as the enactment of the principal securities laws and the abolition of minimum commissions on the stock exchanges (see Jarrell 1984).

Just as we could use stock prices to look at effects on all listed firms, we also could concentrate on particular firms. What happens when insider trading is detected at a given firm and prosecuted? When a firm announces or implements a more effective program for detecting or inhibiting trading? When an investor brings (or wins, or loses) litigation, in the name of the corporation, to enforce the prohibition against a wayward manager? Again, Manne's analysis of insider trading suggests that as inside trades are penalized, the value of the firm's stock should fall, while other approaches suggest the opposite.

It would be foolish to put too much confidence in these tests. Much inside trading is undetected, and enforcement of the rules against the employees of Firm C may have an equal influence on Firm D's employees. Thus the effects of changes in inside trading rules may be too small to detect. Until such tests have been carried out, however, neither economist nor lawyer can offer a well-grounded opinion on whether insider trading is beneficial or not. The economics of agency cannot resolve this question without data, even with data the problem may be insoluble.

Legal Rules in the Face of Uncertainty

An economist can stop here in comfort. A lawyer cannot, for the law does not wait for scholars to resolve all uncertainties. Insider trading is either lawful or it is not; it cannot be 49 percent lawful.

One way the legal system can respond to the ambiguities is to invoke a presumption in favor of market outcomes and to conclude that the evidence in favor of restraining insider trading is too weak to support a legal rule. The evidence about the regulation of milk, barbers, and trucks suggests that many, perhaps most, legal rules would fail to pass any cost-benefit test. No cost-benefit analysis supports regulation of trading. The fact that most of the arguments I have discussed here support only an optional legal rule of prohibition (see note 8), if they support any rule at all, appears to strengthen the case for laissez-faire.

Yet there is no theoretical doubt about the propriety of legal intervention that requires firms to take account of the effects of their acts on third parties. This is the basis for environmental regulation and other rules that establish property rights in goods that might go unpriced. Other legal rules, including the "business judgment rule" and many of the doctrines of corporate law, rest on little more than theoretical reasoning. Until recently antitrust laws—the legal rules most beloved by economists—had nothing but theory behind them, and the theory has not gone unchallenged.

We ought to be suspicious of legal rules that are sought by, or appear to assist, small special-interest groups such as milk producers or barbers. There is no readily identifiable special-interest group of beneficiaries of insider trading regulation, however, and so a public-interest explanation of the rules is more plausible than otherwise. There are some reasons, which I have tried to spell out, for thinking that the market will not sustain an equilibrium in which some firms' insiders trade and others do not; it is so hard for a firm to identify itself as a nontrader that a process of unraveling could lead every firm to abandon all constraints, even if they are otherwise beneficial. The problems with private enforcement support public enforcement.

I said in 1981 that a continuation of the current legal rule appeared to be the best-supported of the many poorly supported alternatives. That still seems to me the appropriate conclusion, although I hold it with less confidence now than I did then. The difficulty of coming to any conclusion at all underscores the importance of the empirical work to which we must turn.

References

Alchian, Armen. 1950. "Uncertainty, Evolution, and Economic Theory." *Journal of Political Economy* 58:211.

Arrow, Kenneth W. 1985. "The Economics of Agency," in this volume.

Becker, Gary S. 1961. "Irrational Behavior and Economic Theory." *Journal of Political Economy*. Reprinted in *The Economic Approach to Human Behavior*, 153–68. Chicago: University of Chicago Press, 1976.

Berle, Adolph A., Jr., and Gardiner C. Means. 1932. *The Modern Corporation and Private Property*. New York: Harcourt.

Brudney, Victor. 1979. "Insiders, Outsiders, and Informational Advantages under the Federal Securities Laws." *Harvard Law Review* 93:322.

Carlton, Dennis W., and Daniel R. Fischel. 1983. "The Regulation of Insider Trading." *Stanford Law Review* 35:857.

DeAngelo, Harry, Linda DeAngelo, and Edward M. Rice. 1984. "Minority Freezeouts and Stockholder Wealth." *Journal of Law and Economics* 27:367.

Diamond, Douglas W., and Robert E. Verrecchia. 1982. "Optimal Managerial Contracts and Equilibrium Security Prices." *Journal of Finance* 37:275.

Dodd, Peter, and Jerold B. Warner. 1983. "On Corporate Governance: A Study of Proxy Contests." *Journal of Financial Economics* 11:401.

Dooley, Michael. 1980. "Enforcement of Insider Trading Restrictions." *Virginia Law Review* 66:1.

Dye, Ronald A. 1984. "Inside Trading and Incentives." *Journal of Business* 57:295.

Easterbrook, Frank H. 1981. "Insider Trading, Secret Agents, Evidentiary Privileges, and the Production of Information." *1981 Supreme Court Review* 309–65.

Easterbrook, Frank H. 1983. "Criminal Procedure as a Market System." *Journal of Legal Studies* 12:289.

Fama, Eugene F. 1980. "Agency Problems and the Theory of the Firm." *Journal of Political Economy* 88:288.

Fama, Eugene F., and Michael C. Jensen. 1983. "Agency Problems and Residual Claims." *Journal of Law and Economics* 26:327.

Friedman, Milton. 1953. "The Methodology of Positive Economics." In *Essays in Positive Economics*. Chicago: University of Chicago Press.

Gilson, Ronald J., and Reiner H. Kraakman. 1984. "The Mechanisms of Market Efficiency." *Virginia Law Review* 70:549.

Haft, Robert J. 1982. "The Effect of Insider Trading Rules on the Internal Efficiency of the Large Corporation." *Michigan Law Review* 80:1051.

Holmstrom, Bengt. 1983. "Managerial Incentive Problems—A Dynamic Perspective." Manuscript, March.

Jaffe, Jeffrey E. 1974. "The Effect of Regulation Changes on Insider Trading." *Bell Journal of Economics* 5:93.

Jarrell, Gregg A. 1984. "Change at the Exchange: Causes and Effects of Deregulation." *Journal of Law and Economics* 27:273.

Jensen, Michael C., and William Meckling. 1976. "Theory of the Firm: Managerial Behavior, Agency Costs and Ownership Structure." *Journal of Financial Economics* 3:305.

Jensen, Michael C., and Richard S. Ruback. 1983. "The Market for Corporate Control: The Scientific Evidence." *Journal of Financial Economics* 11:5.

Kitch, Edmund W. 1980. "The Law and Economics of Rights in Valuable Information." *Journal of Legal Studies* 9:683.

Leftwich, Richard W., and Robert E. Verrecchia. 1981. "Insider Trading and Managers' Choice Among Risky Projects," University of Chicago Center for Research in Security Prices Working Paper No. 63, revision July 1983.

Manne, Henry G. 1966. *Insider Trading and the Stock Market.* New York: Free Press.

Manne, Henry G. 1970. "Insider Trading and the Law Professors." *Vanderbilt Law Review* 23:547.

Manne, Henry G. 1974. "Economic Aspects of Required Disclosure under Federal Securities Laws." In Manne and Solomon, eds. *Wall Street in Transition,* New York: NYU Press.

Schumpeter, Joseph. 1934. *The Theory of Economic Development.* Cambridge: Harvard University Press.

Schwert, G. William. 1981. "Using Financial Data to Measure Effects of Regulation." *Journal of Law and Economics* 24:121.

Scott, Kenneth E. 1980. "Insider Trading: Rule 10b-5, Disclosure, and Corporate Privacy." *Journal of Legal Studies* 9:801.

Shavell, Steven. 1979. "Risk Sharing and Incentives in the Principal and Agent Relationship." *Bell Journal of Economics* 10:55.

Stigler, George J. 1983. "The Process and Progress of Economics." *Journal of Political Economy* 91:529.

Trueman, Brett. 1983. "Motivating Management to Release Inside Information." *Journal of Finance* 38:1253.

Chapter 5
Empirical Evidence of Incentive Problems and Their Mitigation in Oil and Gas Tax Shelter Programs

Mark A. Wolfson

Through the years, taxpayers have been remarkably responsive to legislative actions that affect their after-tax investment opportunities. The dramatic growth in tax-sheltered investments in the 1970s is one example. In 1981 alone, over $2 billion was invested in public oil and gas drilling programs (i.e., those registered with the Securities and Exchange Commission).[1] Tax-sheltered investments would undoubtedly attract still larger sums were investors not concerned about their inability to monitor the actions taken by those who manage the investments.

In 1972, the SEC and the Oil Investment Institute jointly proposed required registration of oil and gas programs together with "a comprehensive framework of substantive regulation rather than mere 'full disclosure' requirements." The alleged motivation was the SEC's finding that

> Many of the problems connected with oil programs derived from the structure of these programs "which is generally characterized by externalized management and separation of beneficial ownership from control." Thus, management of oil programs "virtually always involves self-dealing and other transactions and practices which may be unfair to investors."[2]

This paper discusses and empirically documents incentive problems that naturally arise in oil and gas limited partnerships, some of which are entirely induced by tax considerations. Some means to minimize these incentive problems are also discussed and subjected to empirical investigation. In some cases, the empirical tests are based upon rather sparse data. Accordingly, and with pun intended, the statistical analyses may be viewed as "crude" tests of the incentive problems and reputation effects that apparently characterize these agencies.

I will begin by sketching some relevant institutional details, including a brief discussion of the tax motivation for oil and gas drilling partnerships and a description of the two dimensions along which drilling programs differ most importantly: (1) the sharing of costs and revenues among general and limited partners, and (2) the type of drilling activity undertaken (i.e., exploratory, developmental, or a combination of the two). Then I will discuss incentive problems, together with means by which these problems might be controlled, and conduct empirical tests that basically document results consistent with the informal model. The final section of the paper offers some concluding remarks.

The Institutional Setting

The Tax Environment

The tax code encourages investments in oil and gas drilling projects in several ways. Most important is the immediate deductibility of intangible drilling and development costs, costs that would normally be capitalized initially and later deducted as depreciation or depletion.[3] Such costs typically amount to two-thirds of the total cost of drilling and completing a commercially successful well. Another feature unique to oil and gas drilling is the ability of independent producers and royalty owners to exclude from taxable income a percentage depletion allowance: 16 percent of gross income in 1983; 15 percent in 1984 and thereafter, up to half the taxable income from the property. The permitted depletion deduction may far exceed the capital investment incurred to bring the property to the point of production. A third favorable tax feature is the eligibility of oil and gas property dispositions for capital gains treatment, although much of the gain may be recaptured as ordinary income. A related advantage is the opportunity to exchange a partnership interest in a drilling program for common stock of certain corporations on a "tax-free" (actually, tax-deferred) basis. Finally, investment tax credits are available on some types of equipment that must be capitalized and depreciated; this provision, of course, is by no means unique to oil and gas drilling investments.[4]

The pervasive organizational form through which passive investors participate in oil and gas drilling programs is the limited partnership. Limited partnerships offer two main advantages. First, relatively large losses for tax purposes in the first year of operation are the hallmark of oil and gas tax shelters. The partnership form allows these losses to be passed through to the individual tax returns of the limited partners; this would not be possible if the venture were organized as a corporation.[5] In addition, it is possible to discriminate among partners in the allocation of costs and revenues, as long as these allocations have "substantial economic effect." For example, intangible drilling costs can be allocated to one class of partners (those who can most efficiently use the immediate tax deductions) and tangible drilling costs (which must be capitalized) to another. However, such an allocation requires that the partners literally bear these costs (i.e., their capital accounts must be affected directly).[6] This type of allocation is used in many but by no means all oil and gas limited partnerships. The motivation, of course, is to "sell" the benefits of tax deductions to the limited partners, to whom they are generally more valuable than they are to the manager/general partner. I turn next to a more complete discussion of the partnership sharing rules that are most commonly observed.

Program Structure: Sharing Arrangements

Sharing rules in oil and gas drilling programs can, with some simplification, be classified into four types: carried interest, functional allocation, promoted interest, and reversionary interest.[7] The most popular arrangement is the functional allocation (or tangible-intangible) structure. Programs with a functional allocation structure commanded 54.2 percent of the total amount invested in public drilling programs in 1980, 53.8 percent in 1981, and 53.8 percent in 1982.[8] Under this arrangement, the limited partners bear 100 percent of the cost associated with items that are immediately deductible for federal income tax purposes, and the manager/general partner bears 100 percent of the costs that must be capitalized for federal income tax purposes. It is not uncommon for 90 percent or more of limited partners' investment dollars to be tax deductible in the first year of operation.[9] By contrast, first-year limited partner write-offs under each of the other three program structures tend to be about 60 percent of the amount invested.

Table 1. Average Deal Terms across Program Structures (Percentages of Costs and Revenues Borne by the General Partner)

	Cost		Revenue	
	Before Payout	After Payout	Before Payout	After Payout
Carried interest	1	1	12.5	16
Functional allocation	tangible costs	tangible costs	40	40
Promoted interest	10	10	25	25
Reversionary interest	1	25	1	25

Source: Stanger (1982a, 69).
Note: Payout occurs when the limited partners have been distributed cash in an amount equal to 100 percent of their investment.

The functional allocation program structure is the only one that distinguishes between tangible and intangible drilling costs. With this exception, all programs are characterized by piecewise linear sharing of costs and revenues. Typical terms are shown in Table 1, which is taken from Stanger (1982a).

The promoted interest structure is the only one that is strictly linear in the sharing of costs and revenues. Typically, the general partner pays 10 percent of all costs in exchange for 25 percent of all revenues. The 15 percent difference between the cost and revenue sharing ratios is referred to as the general partner's "promoted" interest.

The carried interest structure is quite similar to the promoted interest structure, except that: (1) the general partner pays almost no costs, in exchange for a similar scaling down of the revenue-sharing percentage, and (2) there is often a slight nonlinearity in the revenue-sharing formula. The general partner's "promotion" typically increases by several percentage points once the program reaches full payout—i.e., once the limited partners have received cash equal to 100 pecent of their original investment.

In a reversionary interest structure, the nonlinearity in the sharing function is much more striking. The general partner pays essentially no costs and receives essentially no revenues until full payout is reached, at which point the general partner typically pays one-fourth of the costs and receives one-fourth of the revenues. Payout in a reversionary interest program may be defined on either a programwide basis or a prospect-by-prospect basis. The implications of this distinction are discussed later when incentive problems are considered.

Besides revenue and cost sharing, there is another element of uncertainty over which the risks could, in principle, be shared: tax audit by the Internal Revenue Service. Other types of tax-favored invest-ments, such as "tax-exempt" industrial revenue bonds, frequently of-fer some form of insurance against adverse tax treatment. Prospec-tuses for drilling programs, in contrast, generally include disclaimers on the tax treatment of certain items, although the sponsor's rhetoric typically implies that any adverse tax treatment is highly unlikely. Such a position would, of course, be more credible if backed by some sort of guarantee, for which investors would almost surely be willing to pay.

Perhaps the absence of risk sharing along this dimension reflects a desire to spread known risks rather than concentrate them in the hands of the sponsor. However, if the tax-treatment risk can be af-fected by the unobservable actions of the general partner or if the general partner has superior information about this risk, a guarantee becomes economically more sensible. In this regard, the Tax Equity and Fiscal Responsibility Act of 1982 may make tax guarantees much more desirable. To minimize audit costs, the Act permits the IRS for the first time to audit all partners simultaneously through the "tax matters partner" (typically the general partner), who acts as represen-tative for all partners. This raises an obvious incentive problem, as Dyco Petroleum discusses in its 1983 oil and gas program prospectus:

> Dyco, as the tax matter partner of the Programs, will have authority to settle or litigate Federal income and windfall profit tax controversies regarding the Program, which may be binding on Participants. Such authority may involve conflicts of interest as actions which may be beneficial to Dyco or to some or all Participants may be detrimental to other parties.[10]

Types of Drilling Activities

Drilling programs are routinely classified as primarily exploratory, primarily developmental, or balanced. Exploratory drilling is the risk-iest, because it entails drilling "in a relatively unproven area or to an unproven formation. Exploratory wells may be classified as follows: a) wildcat, drilled in an unproven area; b) semi-proven or controlled wildcat . . . drilled in an unproven area to extend the proven limits of an existing field; or c) deep test, drilled within a field area but to improve deeper zones."[11] Success rates for wildcat drilling are gener-ally below 30 percent. For semi-proven drilling, success rates are typi-cally between 30 percent and 60 percent.[12]

Developmental drilling is less risky; success rates generally exceed 60 percent.[13] Drilling is conducted "within the presently known or proved productive area of an oil and gas reservoir, as indicated by reasonable interpretation of subsurface data, and drilling to depth known to be productive."[14]

In practice, the type of program structure (sharing arrangement) chosen is not independent of the type of drilling conducted. This is no accident. I will argue that the dependence is related to incentive problems implicit in the program structures, an issue to which I now turn.

Incentive Problems and Their Mitigation

Potential Problems Common to All Program Structures

Public drilling programs must be registered with the SEC, and a prospectus must be filed. One is struck, in reading those prospectuses, by the prevalence of the sort of language economic theorists use to describe incentive problems and their mitigation. Each prospectus must contain a section describing "conflicts of interest" between the general and limited partners. As noted in a legal guide to tax shelter prospectuses, "Conflict of interest disclosures are definitely not in the 'boiler-plate' category, and the evaluation of such conflicts requires intensive analysis and cynical imagination by counsel."[15]

Several problems are commonly discussed in the prospectuses. First, the general partner may have an incentive to pursue a socially suboptimal drilling strategy in order to acquire information useful in decisions about other drilling prospects it owns in the same area. This is often called "proving up" the general partner's prospects with the limited partners' funds.

In addition, the general partner normally is involved in several drilling programs simultaneously. Because the general partner often does not have the same interest in each program, conflicts may arise regarding the general partner's allocation of time, drilling prospects, and other resources to the various partnerships. Even when the sharing rules are identical, nonlinearities may have a different impact on the general partner's effective interest in competing programs. Furthermore, the general partner often acquires limited partnership interests, and the amounts acquired may differ across programs.

Finally, the general partner or its affiiliates often provide goods or services to its partnerships for a fee. Obvious conflicts arise in setting the terms of exchange.

Program sponsors vary in the way they disclose these general problems and in the way they claim to deal with these conflicts. For example, with respect to proving up acreage controlled by the general partner, the 1981–82 Damson Development Drilling Program prospectus states:

> Should a Partnership acquire or lease or participate in drilling or producing operations on a Prospect in proximity to that of the General Partner or its Affiliates, the results of such activity by the Partnership may gratuitously benefit the General Partner or its Affiliates. . . . [This may] result in profits to the General Partner or its Affiliates, and any such profits will not be paid to the partnerships.[16]

Next, consider the following disclosure contained in the 1983 Dyco Petroleum Corporation Oil and Gas Programs prospectus:

> Dyco has taken certain steps to minimize, and in some instances, avoid conflicts. For example, Dyco does not acquire undeveloped acreage for the purpose of developing it for its personal account in competition with drilling programs it sponsors. Dyco may never profit by drilling in contravention of its fiduciary obligations to the Program and Participants. Neither Dyco nor any affiliate will retain undeveloped acreage adjoining a Drilling Program prospect in order to use Drilling Program funds to "prove up" the acreage owned for its own account.[17]

Apache Petroleum's 1983 prospectus provides a general promise not to prove up general partner acreage. Apart from reputation considerations, which are discussed below, such an assurance is hardly credible. Apache then goes on to discuss the problem more specifically and realistically.

> Under no circumstances will Apache cause a Partnership to drill a well for the purpose of proving up a Prospect owned by Apache or any other partnership managed by Apache.

> If a partnership carries out drilling activity on a Prospect it owns that results in production of oil or gas in commercial quantities, then the partnership will have the right to acquire any adjoining acreage held in Apache's inventory within a minimum of one spacing unit in all directions from the Productive Well. If the Partnership is unable to purchase the adjoining acreage because its capital contributions have been expended or committed and alternative methods of financing are unavailable or inadvisable, the decision whether it is prudent to borrow for the purpose of acquiring such additional property from Apache will be made by Apache as the General Partner. . . .

> If a Partnership carries out some drilling activity on a Prospect which it owns that does not result in production of oil and gas in commercial quantities then, notwithstanding the results of the drilling activity (including any favorable implications for adjoining acreage), the Partnership will have no right to acquire any adjoining acreage held in Apache's inventory if the Partnership has spent or committed 90% of its public offering proceeds.

Thus, Investors should be aware that a Partnership's drilling activity may develop favorable information regarding adjoining acreage which it has no right to acquire and, in this situation, the Partnership may receive no benefit for having incidentally provided this information despite the expenditures it has made.[18]

With respect to terms of trade between the general partner and the limited partners, the 1982 prospectus for Mission Resources Drilling Program states:

> Neither the General Partner nor its affiliates may render to the limited partnerships any oil field equipage or drilling services, act as operator of prospects developed by the limited partnerships, or sell or lease to the partnerships any equipment or related supplies, except pursuant to the following conditions: the prices charged for such services, supplies or equipment must be competitive with those charged by other persons engaged in the business of rendering comparable services or supplying comparable equipment and supplies, or, if the seller, operator, or lessor is not in such business, equal to the costs of such services, equipment or supplies or at competitive prices, whichever is less, and further, that any drilling services be billed on either a per foot, per day, or per hour rate, or some combination thereof.[19]

The general partner in such a program could largely avoid the non-arm's-length transactions conflict by contracting out all work that it (or its affiliates) now performs. Of course, this would not necessarily be efficient. One must trade off the incentive cost of not dealing at arm's length against the benefits of internal organization (i.e., economies of scope). The desirability to the partnership of having the general partner (or its affiliates) perform many of the services increases if the general partner is concerned about establishing or maintaining a reputation as a skillful operator. I argue later that such economic forces are indeed present. Note also that the notion of "competitive prices," discussed in the prospectus, is ambiguous in the face of economies of scope.

Finally, the 1982 Hilliard Fund prospectus contains the following statement concerning transactions between related parties:

> Prospects may . . . be transferred to the Partnership by an Affiliated Partnership on terms established by Hilliard. If such transactions do occur, the Managing General Partner will retain an independent expert to review the fairness of the transfer, including the retention of an interest in the Prospects by the transferring partnership and all other terms and provisions of the transfer.[20]

Clearly, given the cost of retaining an independent expert, a "first-best" optimal (i.e., full information) solution to the general partner/limited partner contracting problem is not possible.

Tax-Induced Incentive Problem Distinctive to Functional Allocation Program Structures

The functional allocation program structure is designed to maximize the value of the tax benefits "sold" by the general partner to the limited partners. But this optimization along the tax dimension creates a potentially serious incentive problem. Consider the sequence of events diagrammed below:

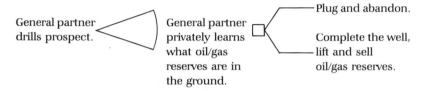

The general partner decides whether to complete the well on the basis of information not available to the limited partners. At this point, conflict of interest can give rise to a "noncompletion problem."

To understand how completion decisions are made, let $E(R_i) = K(D_i + C_i)$ for all prospects i, where E = expectation operator; R = net (of lifting and marketing costs) revenues from sale of oil/gas reserves; K = constant > 1; D = drilling cost; and C = completion cost. K should be interpreted as the general partner's skill parameter. I further assume that investors are risk neutral and that all gambles are timeless and infinitely divisible. Finally, I impose an investment constraint of I partnership dollars on the managing general partner:

$$\sum_{i=1}^{\infty} \alpha_i D_i + \beta_i C_i \leq I,$$

where $\alpha_i = 1$ if the general partner chooses to drill a hole on prospect i; otherwise $\alpha_i = 0$. Similarly $\beta_i = 1$ if the general partner completes a well on prospect i; otherwise $\beta_i = 0$.

Note that $K > 1$ is in no way inconsistent with a market equilibrium since there exists an upper bound on the amount of drilling and completing an operator can feasibly undertake. This investment constraint can arise for at least two reasons: (1) explicit limitations on borrowing of funds in the partnership agreement (such contractual provisions are often observed); (2) technological constraints on the level of activity that can be undertaken by a manager. Since the investment constraint will generally be binding, each dollar spent by the general partner on drilling or completion of any particular well represents a foregone opportunity to invest in another well. In fact, K represents the social opportunity cost per dollar of drilling or completion expenditure.

A "noncompletion incentive problem" arises at the time the general partner decides whether to complete the well for which it has privately learned the extent of oil and gas reserves. From the perspective of the partnership, the socially optimal decision rule, assuming no tax distortion, is to complete a well if and only if $R_i > KC_i$.[21] But the general partner's privately optimal decision rule is different.

In the typical functional allocation program, the limited partners pay essentially all of the drilling costs, and the general partner is responsible primarily for the well completion costs. Hence, the general partner's decision rule is to complete if and only if $sR_i > KC_i$, where s is the contractually specified share of net revenues allocated to the general partner. In most functional allocation programs, s is a constant 40 percent; it is always well below 100 percent.

An immediate implication of this simple model is that the general partner will complete fewer wells than if the drilling activity were free of incentive problems (e.g., if the activity were organized as a sole proprietorship). A socially costly noncompletion decision will be rendered whenever $R_i > KC_i > sR_i$.

Prospectuses are surprisingly candid in recognizing this problem. For example, Dyco Petroleum Corporation acknowledges:

> All drilling program structures involve conflicts of interest. Functional Allocation of costs creates conflicts at the time of well completion, where completion of a commercial but non-profitable well might prove to be in the best interest of the Participants, though not of Dyco. The feasibility of any such completion, as well as the selection of any Leases to be acquired by the Drilling Programs, will be determined solely by Dyco . . . [D]ecisions with respect to completion or continued operation, although consistent with industry practice and based on Dyco's best judgment of the well's potential for profit, may not necessarily be in the best interests of Participants.[22]

The Hilliard Fund provides a similar description of the incentive problem, but adds a promise, of questionable credibility, not to take actions against the best interests of the limited partners:

> A situation may arise in which the completion of an Initial Well (the majority of the costs of which are Capitalized Costs) on a Prospect would be more advantageous to the Limited Partners than to the General Partners. The situation would arise where a completion attempt on an Initial Well, the majority of the costs of which are paid by the General Partners, could

apparently result in a marginal well which would return some but not all of the completion cost incurred by the General Partners but would return revenue to the Limited Partners. In order to mitigate this potential conflict of interest, the Managing General partner commits that it will complete all wells drilled by the Partnership which in the exercise of good business practice should be completed, taking into account the best interests of the partnership.[23]

A Templeton oil and gas drilling program essentially promises to complete all wells for which $R_i > KC_i$, i.e., the socially optimal decision rule:

> It may be beneficial to TMPL (the General Partner) to elect to plug and abandon a marginal well (although the Limited Partners might prefer completion) . . . The Managing Venturer will determine the feasibility of completion attempts in accordance with industry practice and will complete all wells which, in its judgment, would be completed by a *prudent operator drilling for his own account* [emphasis added].[24]

There are several ways in which the "undercompletion" incentive problem can be mitigated. For example, one could directly monitor the general partner's decision. This is generally not done, however, presumably because the cost of monitoring would exceed the expected benefits.[25] Alternatively, one could overcome the incentive problem by defining the general partner's share of revenues as $\hat{s}R + (1 - \hat{s})C$, rather than simply sR, where $\hat{s} < s$. In other words, s would be adjusted downward and cost recovery would be permitted on a fraction (equal to $1 - \hat{s}$) of the completion cost. This would render the general partner's overall share of revenues and costs equal to:

$$\hat{s}R + (1 - \hat{s})C - C = \hat{s}(R - C).$$

Under such a sharing arrangement, the general partner would fully internalize the externality a completed well would provide to the limited partners. The reason we do not observe this arrangement, however, is that it would not satisfy the IRS "substantial economic effect" requirements for the cost allocation to be recognized for tax purposes. That is, the IRS does not permit such sleight-of-hand transformations of functional allocation arrangements into contracts in which there is an incomplete allocation of risk bearing along functional lines.

Still another way to minimize the undercompletion incentive cost is to choose prospects in which it is least likely that a socially costly decision will be rendered—that is, to minimize the probability that ($R_i > KC_i > sR_i$). This could be accomplished by drilling primarily exploratory rather than development wells. Exploratory wells are characterized by a high probability of $(C_i > R_i)$ and a low probability of R_i much greater than C_i. Unless s is very small (recall that the typical value is 0.4), the probability of $(R_i > KC_i > sR_i)$ is relatively low.

Prospectuses routinely predict the allocation of funds to exploratory and development drilling. Later, empirical evidence will be provided that supports the hypothesis that functional allocation program dollars are largely devoted to exploratory drilling in an attempt to minimize the social undercompletion loss.

A fourth method for the mitigation of incentive costs involves the general partner's economic incentives to build a reputation as a skilled driller/operator/manager (a high K parameter). It is widely held that skill is an important factor of production in this industry. Of course, skill is not directly observable by outsiders. However, performance measures, such as the value of proven oil and gas reserves or cash distributed to limited partners, will generally be correlated with the general partner's skill level.

A striking feature of oil and gas limited partnerships is that the general partner typically forms new partnerships each year. An audited statement of past performance ("prior activities") is a required disclosure in each prospectus, information that represents the building blocks of a sponsor's reputation. Clearly, limited partners will be willing to pay a premium to participate in a program if, other things equal, the general partner's past performance suggests above-average success in finding oil. Prospective investors will naturally use track records to forecast future performance when skill is an important factor of production. Hence the general partner may well have an incentive to take actions that increase overall partnership payoffs, even if such actions reduce the general partner's profits in the present partnership. The actions of the general partner are unobservable to current and prospective limited partners. Hence a partnership subsidy provided by the general partner will lead investors to make a more favorable assessment of the general partner's skill level. This inference is completely rational despite the fact that it would be unwarranted if the general partner's actions were observable. The general partner is thereby able to recoup the current period "loss" through improved sharing arrangements in future partnerships.[26]

Whether reputation effects are present is an empirically testable proposition. If they are, then track records should be "priced" in the sense that a premium can be charged for the right to buy into a partnership operated by a general partner with a good reputation. Of course, industry experts are generally aware of the importance of these considerations. For example, Haft asserts that a "crucial factor in all tax shelters is the ability, reputation, and past experience of the sponsor-manager of the program. It is one of the underpinnings of the business and economic feasibility of the program."[27] Stanger states that the "most important information is the drilling company's past record of performance."[28] And Apache's prospectus packaging bills the firm as "oil and gas finders with a track record."

To test for reputation effects I need proxies for both the price charged to buy into a partnership and the track record of the general partner in finding and marketing oil and gas. To capture price, I use the so-called net return rating (NRR) supplied in the *Stanger Register.* This number measures "the effect of deal terms on the limited partner's share of future revenues based on a *uniform* oil and gas finding success rate."[29] Of course, general partners' *actual* oil and gas finding success rate will vary considerably even if the rates are uniform *ex ante;* but even the *ex ante* rates will differ when skill is an important factor of production. Hence, assuming rational pricing on the part of general partners, the NRR captures cross-sectional differences in expected oil and gas finding success rates: the higher the net return rating, the lower the expected success rate of the general partner, assuming rational pricing of contract terms.

As measures of the general partner's track record, I use two variables: (1) weighted average total expected return ratio and (2) number of years in the business. The "total expected return ratio," a measure of past performance, is defined by Stanger as "cash distributions, plus undiscounted escalated future net revenues and partnership net working capital (less long term debt) as of December 31, 1981, divided by the total investment (original investment plus assessments)." Despite obvious weaknesses (e.g., inattention to the timing of cash flows), "the total expected return ratio (ERR) is the traditional measure [of performance] used by the drilling fund industry."[30] For each sponsor/ general partner, I take an average of the ERRs for each drilling partnership formed during the 1977–80 period, weighted by the number of limited partner dollars invested in each partnership.

For the twenty-seven sponsors for which I have both NRR data and weighted average ERR data, the number of prior partnerships used to establish the track record variable ranges from two (in only one case) to thirty-seven. The data used to calculate the weighted average ERR observations are all taken from *Stanger's Drilling Fund Yearbook 1982.*

The data on NRR and the number of years in the business are taken from the April 1983 issue of the *Stanger Register* and the July 1982 issue of the *Stanger Report*.

There are two reasons for using length of time in the business as a second track record variable. First, the weighted average ERR is likely to suffer from nontrivial measurement error.[31] In addition, using the longevity variable allows me to increase my sample size from twenty-seven to thirty-nine, which in principle could increase the power of my tests. In fact, I find that both explanatory variables provide statistically significant support, in an ordinary least squares regression model, for the hypothesis that reputation effects (i.e., track records) are priced, as seen in Table 2. My hypothesis is that a general partner with a good reputation can command a price premium—that is, there will be a negative relationship between the net return rating and the track record variable. I find that the null hypothesis of no linear dependence can be rejected at conventional levels of significance in favor of a negative relationship.

Analysis of residuals suggests that the assumptions underlying the tests are well specified. As a check for specification error, the regression model was also estimated with four additional explanatory variables: the percentage of funds devoted to exploratory drilling; the percentage of limited partner contributions that are tax deductible in

Table 2. Test for Reputation Effects (Ordinary Least Squares Regression Models)

(1) $\text{NRR}^a = 2.612 - 0.058 \times \text{weighted average ERR}^b$
$$(T = -2.009)^c$$
   Adjusted $R^2 = 0.105$

(2) $\text{NRR}^a = 2.621 - 0.006 \times \text{years in business}$
$$(T = -1.893)^d$$
   Adjusted $R^2 = 0.064$

Sample means

Weighted average ERR:	2.143
Number of years in business	9.462
NRR (in model 1)	2.487
NRR (in model 2)	2.561

[a] NRR = Net Return Rating. It should be interpreted as a standardized price charged for the right to buy into a partnership. The higher the NRR, the lower the price.

[b] ERR = Expected Return Rating. It is an *ex post* performance measure, despite the term *expected*.

[c] Significant at <0.03 with 27 observations.

[d] Significant at <0.05 with 39 observations.

the first tax year of operation; a dummy variable for functional allocation program structure; and a dummy variable for reversionary interest program structure. None of the four variables was statistically
significant (individually or jointly) at even the 20 percent level (two-
tailed probabilities). The track record variable remained significant but
at a less extreme level (<10 percent), in part because of the loss in
degrees of freedom when four additional parameters are estimated.

Having introduced the NRR variable as a proxy for expected oil and
gas finding rates, I can now proceed to a limited test of whether
incentive problems are eliminated by reputation effects or other economic forces such as monitoring. Using the April 1983 issue of the
Stanger Register, fourteen functional allocation programs were
identified, along with their net return ratings and type of drilling activity (primarily exploratory, primarily developmental, or "balanced").
Table 3 provides the details.

Although sample sizes were small, significant results were obtained.
The average net return ratings are 2.36 for exploratory, 2.55 for balanced, and 2.70 for developmental programs, suggesting high expected success rates, relative to the norm, in exploratory programs as
compared with the less risky programs. As noted earlier, the undercompletion problem in functional allocation programs is most severe

Table 3.   Net Return Ratings for Functional Allocation Programs by Type
of Drilling

	Exploratory	*Balanced*	*Developmental*
	2.28	2.38	2.59
	2.36	2.53	2.59
	2.43	2.53	2.68
		2.55	2.92
		2.59	
		2.61	
		2.68	
Mean	2.357	2.553	2.695

Significance levels from the Mann-Whitney U Test
    Exploratory vs. balanced = 0.017
    Exploratory vs. developmental = 0.028
    Balanced vs. developmental ≈ 0.07
Overall significance level from the Jonckheere test for ordered alternatives
    <0.005

Source: *Stanger Register,* April 1983.

in developmental drilling programs and least severe in exploratory drilling programs. Thus this finding is entirely consistent with the undercompletion incentive problems being priced. The Mann-Whitney U statistic shows the following significance levels: exploratory vs. balanced (1.7 percent); exploratory vs. developmental (2.8 percent); balanced vs. developmental (≈7 percent). The Jonckheere Test for Ordered Alternatives shows an overall significance level of less than 0.5 percent. Hence although reputation effects are (statistically significantly) "priced," naturally mitigating incentive problems, the phenomenon is not so strong as to eliminate incentive problems entirely. Rather, the incentive problems that persist are sufficiently prominent that they are (statistically significantly) "priced" as well. In this respect, my results are more consistent with the positive implications of the labor market reputation model of Holmström (1983) than with those of Fama (1980).

To avoid drawing unwarranted inferences, I checked to determine whether any of the differences documented in Table 3 could have been the result of differences in expected first-year tax write-offs. In fact, if anything, the differences are understated when the effect of tax write-offs is considered, since estimated average first-year write-offs are 80 percent, 84 percent, and 87 percent, respectively, for the exploratory, balanced, and developmental programs. If the tax write-off effect is rationally priced, this would depress the net return ratings for developmental programs relative to the other programs.

Nor can differences in experience (number of years offering programs) explain the differences in net return ratings. The averages are twelve years, twelve years, and thirteen years, respectively, for exploratory, balanced, and developmental programs. Again, if anything, the differences in Table 3 are understated when differences in experience are factored in.

Only functional allocation program structures appear to show differences in NRR as a function of type of drilling. For example, consider promoted interest program structures, where there does not appear to be any incentive problem related to the riskiness of the drilling program. The average net return ratings are 2.49 for three exploratory programs, 2.54 for two balanced programs, and 2.41 for six developmental drilling programs. No pattern is discernible, even upon closer inspection.

Before moving on to a consideration of problems specific to reversionary interest program structures, I wish to mention briefly another potential incentive problem distinct to functional allocation programs: the "excessive leasing problem." The Woods 1983 Drilling Program prospectus sums it up nicely (p. 47): "The Functional Allocation formula makes it desirable from Woods' standpoint . . . to structure the arrangement in a manner which will create greater deductible items as opposed to nondeductible items." In recognition of the fact that there is an incentive to lease rather than buy equipment, even if leasing is more costly to the partnership overall, the contract states that if "equipment is leased rather than purchased, such rental costs, though a deductible expense, will be charged as a Capital Cost."[32]

The Completion Problem in Reversionary Interest Program Structures

For reasons I do not understand, industry experts view reversionary interest program structures as providing good incentives to general partners. Furthermore, they argue that there exists an incentive to *over*complete marginal wells, in contrast to functional allocation programs. Haft notes:

> A method more advantageous [than the promoted interest structure] is to give management a reversionary working interest in which management obtains a share of profit after investors have received their money back. The "payback" to investors can be calculated on a per well basis or on an overall program basis. Obviously the payback to investors of the overall program amount prior to profit participation by management is more favorable to investors.[33]

And Stanger writes, "In one widely used program structure called 'reversionary interest,' the investor pays the completion costs as well as the intangible drilling costs. A low quality drilling company might complete a number of marginally economic wells with investor dollars."[34]

I wish to discuss three points made in these statements that are misleading at best and incorrect at worst:

1. Reversionary interest programs provide better incentives than carried interest and promoted interest structures.
2. Reversion on a programwide basis is more favorable to investors than reversion on a prospect-by-prospect basis.
3. The general partner has an incentive to complete *more* marginal wells than investors would prefer.

I argue that unless the general partner is risk averse, reversionary interest program structures provide the *least* efficient sharing arrangements.[35] Let me begin by establishing why reversion on a prospect-by-prospect basis may be better than reversion on a programwide basis. The simple reason is that when the general partner is simultaneously managing more than one partnership, as is typically the case, conflicts arise in the allocation of properties and time to the various partnerships when some are above payout and others are below payout. The prospectus for the 1982 Mission Drilling Program, which reveals a programwide reversionary interest structure, recognizes this problem:

> The General Partnership has previously formed limited partnerships for the exploration and development of oil and gas and will form additional limited partnerships in the future to engage in such activities. These activities involve a conflict of interest in that the time and resources of the General Partner and its affiliates will be devoted to activities other than the business of the limited partnerships formed hereunder, or because the compensation payable to the General Partner from other limited partnerships may be greater than the compensation payable to it by the limited partnerships formed hereunder. . . . In transactions involving farmouts or joint ventures of interests among different limited partnerships . . . the General Partner will represent and make decisions for each of the parties, and may benefit from cost savings and reduction of risk.[36]

Reversion on a programwide basis provides the general partner with an incentive to "overinvest" in geological surveys and other information that make possible a judicious assignment of prospects among partnerships. Reversion on a prospect-by-prospect basis overcomes such conflicts. However, it introduces a complication of its own, the completion problem.[37] Contrary to Stanger's assertion that there exists an overcompletion problem, there is actually an undercompletion problem, as in functional allocation programs, but for different reasons.

Using the same notation as when functional allocation programs were considered, the payoffs to the general partner under a reversionary interest contract can be stated as follows:

Payoff	*Contingency*
$s_1 R$	$R < D + C$
$s_1 R + (s_2 - s_1)(R - D - C)$	$R > D + C$

Here s_1 and s_2 represent parameters of the piecewise linear contract. Table 1 indicates that typical values are 0.01 for s_1 and 0.25 for s_2; s_1 is always less than s_2.

As before, let $E(R_i) = K(D_i + C_i)$ for all i, where K is the general partner's skill parameter. I continue to assume that investors are risk neutral, that all gambles are timeless and infinitely divisible, and that an investment constraint of I dollars is imposed on the managing general partner, which means that K also represents the social opportunity cost per dollar spent drilling or completing any given well. Consider first the case in which, following drilling at cost D_i, the general partner privately observes $R_i < KC_i$. In this case, the net revenues available in the ground fall short of the social opportunity cost to complete the well. The general partner could invest C_i in a new hole j instead, in exchange for which the partnership would get $E(R_j) = K(C_j + D_j) = K(C_i) > R_i$. Clearly, it is socially desirable to abandon prospect i.

The general partner will also find it privately optimal to abandon prospect i. Note that the general partner gets $s_i R_i$ if he completes well i. The alternative is to drill hole j. Also note that since $s_2 > s_1 > 0$, the expected payment to the general partner is strictly increasing in $\sigma(R_j)$, the "spread" of the R_j distribution.[38] Consider the least favorable case for the general partner, that is, $\sigma(R_j) = 0$. Then abandoning hole i provides a payoff of:

$$
\begin{aligned}
&s_1 R_j + (s_2 - s_1)(R_j - C_j - D_j) \\
&= s_1 K(C_j + D_j) + (s_2 - s_1)(K - 1)(C_j + D_j) \\
&= s_1 KC_i + (s_2 - s_1)(K - 1)C_i \\
&> s_1 R_i + (s_2 - s_1)(K - 1) C_i > s_1 R_i.
\end{aligned}
$$

Hence the general partner will abandon hole i. With $\sigma(R_j) > 0$, he will also abandon hole i, *a fortiori*.

Now consider the case of the marginal well, where after an expenditure of drilling cost D_i the general partner privately observes $R_i = KC_i + X < D_i + C_i$, where $X > 0$ is defined as the excess of revenues over the social opportunity cost to complete the well. Since the alternative to completion provides expected revenues $R_j = K(C_j + D_j) = KC_i$ (which is less than the $KC_i + X$ from completing well i), it is socially desirable to complete well i. If completion takes place, the general partner will receive $s_1(KC_i + X)$. This must be compared with what he expects from abandoning. As before, we consider the least favorable case first, where $\sigma(R_j) = 0$, in which case the general partner gets

$$
\begin{aligned}
&s_1 C_i + s_2(K - 1)C_i \\
&= s_1 KC_i + (s_2 - s_1)(K - 1)C_i.
\end{aligned}
$$

The general partner will abandon hole i whenever $(s_2 - s_1)(K - 1)C_i$ exceeds $s_1 X$. From Table 1, we know that the typical value for s_1 is essentially zero (more precisely, 1 percent, versus 25 percent for s_2). Hence abandonment will (almost) always take place in this case, even though it is socially desirable to complete. The undercompletion problem becomes even more severe when $\sigma(R_j) > 0$.

To illustrate, suppose:

D_i = \$2 million
C_i = \$1 million (D_i is commonly roughly twice C_i)
K = 1.2 (20 percent expected rate of return)
X = \$1 million (completion provides a return of \$1 million above the expected return from abandoning)
s_1 = 0.01
s_2 = 0.25
$R_i = KC_i + X$ = \$2.2 million

Completion provides a return to the general partner of $s_1 R_i$ = \$22,000. Abandonment provides a return (for the case of $\sigma(R_j)$ = 0, that is, $R_j = KC_i$ = \$1.2 million with certainty) of $s_1 C_i + s_2(R_j - C_i)$ or \$60,000. Hence, the general partner will be nearly three times better off if he abandons hole i despite the fact that hole i provides \$1 million more (an increase of over 80 percent) for the partnership to share. Of course, with $\sigma(R_j) > 0$, the difference would be even more dramatic in favor of abandoning.[39]

For the case of s_1 = 0, the general partner will never complete a marginal well whenever $(D + C > R > KC)$, although it is always socially optimal to do so.[40] As in the case of functional allocation sharing arrangements, the incentive problem is least significant when there is a small probability of drilling marginal wells. Hence if the undercompletion incentive cost is important, we would expect to observe general partners announcing plans to conduct more risky drilling, on average, in reversionary interest programs (just as we expected for functional allocation programs) than in the other program structures, where the noncompletion problem is absent (promoted interest programs) or relatively minor (carried interest programs).[41]

Table 4 provides striking confirmation of this prediction. Here we tabulate the number of limited partner dollars allocated to each of twelve types of programs (four types of sharing rules times three types of drilling) for all programs reported in *Stanger's Drilling Fund Yearbook 1982*, which covers the period 1970–80. Roughly two-thirds of the

Table 4.   Allocation of Limited Partner Dollars to Various Program
Configurations ($000s) 1970–80

	199 *Exploratory* *Programs*	*160* *Balanced* *Programs*	*237* *Developmental* *Programs*	*Total*
Functional allocation	$978,220	$464,063	$ 68,291	$1,510,574
(267 programs)	(65%)	(31%)	(5%)	
Reversionary interest	$336,886	$ 90,755	$ 81,558	$ 509,199
(97 programs)	(66%)	(18%)	(16%)	
Promoted interest	$ 43,799	$153,483	$255,360	$ 452,642
(81 programs)	(10%)	(34%)	(56%)	
Carried interest	$ 7,259	$172,227	$234,017	$ 413 553
(151 programs)	(2%)	(42%)	(57%)	

Source: *Stanger's Drilling Fund Yearbook 1982.*
Note: Figures in parentheses are percentages of row totals; because of rounding they
may not add to 100 percent.

dollars going into functional allocation and reversionary interest programs are for exploratory drilling activity, whereas over half of all
dollars invested in carried interest and promoted interest programs
are for developmental drilling. A formal chi-square test of the data in
Table 4 could be misleading because of the obvious violation of the
independence assumption across dollars of investment. Hence, a formal statistical test is omitted. Still, the results are clearly economically
significant.

A more direct test of whether reversionary interest program structures give rise to an undercompletion problem is provided by comparing completion rates on fourteen exploratory reversionary interest
programs offered by Apache Oil & Gas between 1970 and 1978 and
sixteen exploratory functional allocation programs offered by Apache
over the period 1977 to 1980. The reversionary interest programs provide for reversion on a prospect-by-prospect basis, as indicated in
Apache's 1978 prospectus.

Apache's 1983 prospectus includes a table entitled "Gross and Net
Wells Statistics," which provides statistics on the number of wells
completed successfully in each of the thirty prior programs referenced
above. Although the prospectus does not indicate what the program
structures or types of drilling were, *Stanger's Drilling Fund Yearbook
1982* does. Table 5 provides a summary for all net wells drilled.[42] The
two programs are not significantly different in terms of the percentage

Table 5.   Completion Statistics: Apache Oil & Gas

A.   Successful Completion Statistics across Program Structures

	Total Net Wells Drilled	Productive	Percentage Productive
Reversionary interest programs ($N = 14$)	203	97	47.78
Functional allocation programs ($N = 16$)	103	51	49.51

B.   Successful Completions for First Wells

	Total Net Wells Drilled	Productive	Percentage Productive
Reversionary interest programs ($N = 14$)	111	22	19.81
Functional allocation programs ($N = 16$)	51	10	19.61

Sources: Prospectus for Apache Oil & Gas Program, 1978 and 1983; *Stanger's Drilling Fund Yearbook 1982.*

of successfully completed wells. If anything, relatively more wells are completed successfully in the functional allocation programs.

If attention is restricted to the first wells drilled on any prospect, the riskiest type of drilling, there is still no difference between the two program structures in terms of performance. Hence if results for the functional allocation programs reflect an incentive to abandon marginally commercially productive wells, it appears that the reversionary interest program structure provides similar incentives.

One caveat is in order here. Implicit in the tests for similarities in Apache's incentives across program structures is the assumption that a valid comparison of success rates has been made. In other words, I have assumed that the pool of prospects from which drilling was conducted was identical, *ex ante*, for each of the program sharing arrangements. Although all drilling was classified as "primarily exploratory," this may not be sufficient.

A final test of sharing-rule-induced differences in behavior across programs is to compare variability of *ex post* returns to limited partners, controlling for nominal differences in drilling risk. In particular, I compare *ex post* returns for eleven developmental functional allocation programs, twenty developmental reversionary interest programs, sixty-two developmental carried interest programs, and nineteen developmental promoted interest programs. This represents all programs listed in *Stanger's Drilling Fund Yearbook 1982* formed in the years 1977–80. Although all programs involve developmental drilling, my earlier discussion suggests that there is an incentive for functional

Table 6.   Sample Standard Deviations of *Ex Post* Returns (Stanger "Expected Return Ratings") for Developmental Drilling Programs across Program Structures

Program Structure	Number of Programs	Sample Standard Deviation
Functional allocation (FU)	11	2.789
Reversionary interest (RE)	20	1.310
Carried interest (CI)	62	1.189
Promoted interest (PI)	19	0.927

F-Statistics for Pairwise Comparisons
(Significance Levels if 0.100 or less)

	FU	RE	CI
RE	4.737 (0.005)		
CI	5.952 (0.001)	1.257	
PI	9.441 (0.001)	1.993 (0.100)	1.586

allocation and prospect-by-prospect reversionary interest programs to select riskier projects. This is also true, but to a minor extent, for carried interest programs. However, it is not true for promoted interest programs. Hence, my prediction is: σ(functional allocation) > σ(reversionary interest) > σ(carried interest) > σ(promoted interest).[43]

Table 6 provides strong evidence consistent with these predictions. The rankings of the sample standard deviations are exactly as predicted, and the sample standard deviation of expected return ratings for the functional allocation programs is statistically significantly higher than for each of the other three types of programs. In addition, the sample standard deviation for the reversionary interest programs is statistically significantly higher than for the promoted interest programs.

Over time, one would expect to see the amounts invested in reversionary interest sharing arrangements dwindle.[44] Like functional allocation arrangements (and unlike promoted interest and carried interest arrangements), reversionary interest programs present an incentive problem with respect to well completion, but without the offsetting tax benefit of functional allocation programs, where first-year tax write-offs are, on average, more than one-third higher than in all other program structures.[45]

Programwide reversionary arrangements also pose an incentive problem in terms of allocation among competing partnerships of resources in general and drilling prospects in particular. Indeed, rever-

Table 7. Distribution of Investments by Drilling Program Structure
1979–82

| | (Percent of Total) | | | |
	1979	1980	1981	1982
Reversionary interest	16.5	15.1	12.9	10.6
Promoted interest and carried interest	24.1	30.7	33.3	35.6

Source: *Investor's Tax Shelter Report*, January-February 1983, 14.

sionary interest arrangements have been attracting relatively fewer investor dollars over time, as shown in Table 7. In a study covering five hundred partnerships formed before 1981, Arthur Jerrold King (president and founder of Investment Search, Inc.) found that, "surprisingly, the carried interest structure (which includes both carried interest and promoted interest arrangements) turned out to be more favorable for investors than the reversionary interest structure."[46] I do not find this surprising at all.

Concluding Remarks

Tax-sheltered investments are notorious for their incentive problems. This is true of tax-motivated investments in real estate, equipment leasing, research and development, movies, cattle breeding, cattle feeding, art masters, and on and on. I have focused on problems specific to oil and gas drilling partnerships, because the cross-sectional heterogeneity is sufficiently well contained that experimental control could be achieved, and hence empirical tests could be conducted.

The incentives literature to date contains little or no rigorous empirical testing of proposed theories. In this study, I have attempted to demonstrate that these theories are far from lacking in testable implications. In particular, I argued that functional allocation and reversionary interest sharing arrangements introduce incentive problems that are less prevalent or absent in carried interest and promoted interest sharing arrangements. Several empirical tests confirmed the arguments. Incentive problems can be mitigated in several ways, and empirical tests confirmed that such forces as reputation effects are at work in the market. Indeed, without such countervailing forces, the tax-sheltered limited partnership would surely not have survived as an organizational form.

References

Fama, E. 1980. "Agency Problems and the Theory of the Firm." *Journal of Political Economy*, April.

Haft, R. 1973. *Tax Sheltered Investments*, Security Law Series, vol. 4. New York: Clark Boardman Company, Ltd.

Harris, M., and B. Holmström. 1982. "A Theory of Wage Dynamics." *Review of Economic Studies*, July.

Holmström, B. 1982. "Managerial Incentive Problems—A Dynamic Perspective." In *Essays in Economics and Management in Honour of Lars Wahlbeck*. Helsinki: Swedish School of Economics.

Investor's Tax Shelter Report, January-February 1983.

Kreps, D., and R. Wilson. 1982. "Reputation and Imperfect Information." *Journal of Economic Theory*, August.

Milgrom, P., and J. Roberts. 1982. "Predation, Reputation, and Entry Deterrence." *Journal of Economic Theory*, August.

Stanger, R. 1982a. *Tax Shelters: The Bottom Line*. Fair Haven, N.J.: Robert A. Stanger & Co.

———. 1982b. *Stanger's Drilling Fund Yearbook 1982*. Fair Haven, N.J.: Robert A. Stanger & Co.

Stanger Register, April 1983.

Chapter 6
Agency Costs, Employment Contracts, and Labor Unions

Richard A. Epstein

The division of labor is a common feature of modern social institutions. By coordinated activities, transacting parties can realize gains that exceed those obtained first by working independently and then by trading finished products in discrete market transactions. The inexorable voluntary movement to complex organizations is itself powerful evidence of the substantial anticipated gains. But even if the emergence of large organizations may be regarded as socially inevitable, their precise form is not, for a great deal of freedom remains in structuring their internal operation with a view to minimizing the relevant costs.

This paper examines one kind of costs: the agency costs that arise because firms must operate through individuals who act as agents for others, rather than on their own account.[1] Its central focus is labor markets. By way of background, the first section of the paper offers some brief introductory remarks about the problem of agency costs as applied to other contracting contexts. Thereafter the agency cost question is examined in three separate labor market environments: first, unregulated markets without any coordinated behavior between workers; second, unregulated markets in which coordination between workers is both allowed and feasible; and third, markets under the National Labor Relations Act, with its system of collective bargaining through exclusive union agents.

The first section of the paper reviews the agency literature and indicates why private contracts over a broad range of subject areas typically do not call for "full expectation damages," that is, damages designed to leave the innocent party to a contract as well off as if the contract had been properly performed by the other side.

The second section explains the widespread voluntary use of the contract at will, that is, contracts that allow parties to terminate arrangements for good reason, bad reason, or no reason at all. Notwithstanding their fragile appearance, these arrangements often prove very durable in the long run and allow each side to monitor the performance of the other, thereby limiting the possibility of opportunistic behavior. This section also briefly explores those situations in which private parties might choose more complex contracting arrangements, such as contracts for a term or those terminable only for cause.

The third section of the paper shows that the use of the at-will arrangement is inconsistent with any form of unionization, since the complex internal structures of unions can only survive in an environment that protects the union from the employer's unilateral decision to fire all key union operatives. It is most unlikely therefore that union firms could be competitive with nonunion firms in unregulated markets. Thus the National Labor Relations Act, which prohibits at-will contracts with respect to union activities, imposes efficiency losses in the operation of the economic system.

The Agency Problem in Law and Business

In ordinary legal usage, an agent is simply any person who undertakes some business on behalf of another person—perhaps a single transaction, perhaps the control over an entire business. While transacting firm business, any employee is an agent for the firm, as are certain outside parties, such as independent contractors, including lawyers hired to represent the firm. In dealing with the legal rules that regulate the agency relationship, lawyers customarily distinguish between (1) the way in which the principal is bound to third parties for the acts of his agents within the scope of the employment, and (2) the rights and duties between the principal and the agent.

The first aspect of the problem is by far the simpler, as the principal has long been held strictly accountable for any acts undertaken by the agent within the scope of his apparent authority (as measured by the perceptions of the third party).[2] The liabilities so created are categorical in nature. The employer is allowed to defend himself on the ground that the acts were not performed by the agent as agent; for example, the firm cannot be charged for the nonpayment of the employee's home mortgage. But once the agent is on firm business, the employer is quite literally shorn of all defenses against third-party suits, no matter how great the employee's breach of a duty to the employer. Thus the employer is liable for employee actions that the employer had expressly forbidden; nor can the employer show it exercised all possible care (however measured) in selecting and supervising its employees. The firm's liability is called vicarious because the wrong of the employee is imputed to the employer, without regard to its own wrongful conduct.

The rationales for this austere legal regime are many and diverse, and no single one of them will account for the current doctrine in full.[3] But at least two factors help explain the durability of the rule. First, the rule makes no attempt to fine-tune the system. Its clear and categorical form makes it easy to apply the law to the myriad transactions in which the agency problem arises. Second, the rule has powerful implications for the internal organization of the firm. All errors in the operation of the firm are now charged to the firm itself. The outsider need not peer into the black box of firm operations. That is a task for the employer alone. In fact, the firm's position here is a familiar one, for many actions of employees affect the firm's profitability without entailing legal liability to the outside world: the deal not closed because of an internal misunderstanding may prove more costly to the firm than the unfavorable contract made by an employee acting outside the scope of his authority. Vicarious liability only ensures that the firm's need for internal control is the same for both potential litigation and foregone profits.

In considering the internal control of the agency problem, it is important to recall that the agency relationship is born of contract. The firm must control its employees to prevent them from diverting firm resources to private gain.[4] The most obvious form of diversion is simple theft, but the problem can manifest itself in many other forms. Employees may do other work on firm time, or exert minimal efforts on the job, or even channel the firm's prospective customers to their own side businesses (as when a junior architect does a small job on the side for a firm client). Such employee misbehavior constitutes a breach of the employment contract that costs the employer, if not property itself, then time, labor, or prospective advantage. From a social point of view, this employee misbehavior creates a divergence between private and social costs, for as the productivity of the worker goes down the firm will have to increase its prices and lower its output from the levels it could reach without employee breach. Correction of the abuse is in the interest of both the firm and the society at large.

The costs of the agency relationship do not show any fatal defect of firm organization, given its other and greater benefits. Like other costs, they only raise the question of what steps the firm should take to minimize these many forms of misbehavior. Sadly for lawyers, litigation is only one weapon in the employer's arsenal, and an expensive and cumbersome one at that. Alternatively, the principal can give notice to the world of the limits of its agent's authority (as by publication or direct communication) so as to make it unreasonable for any third party to rely on the agent's apparent authority. Internally, the firm can hire some individuals to supervise the work of others; it can monitor the performance of its workers by day-to-day quality control or comprehensive year-end review; it can set the terms of payment, promotion, and transfer so as to instill faithful performance; and in extreme cases it can use its power to hire and to fire.

All of these methods of control cost money, and no firm will attempt to eliminate all abuse by its agents. As with any kind of cost, it pays to reduce agency costs only to the point at which the marginal gains equal the costs of additional control. In a world with diminishing returns, an exclusive reliance on any one form of control is highly unlikely to be desirable. The appropriate mix depends on the internal configuration of the firm, the composition of its labor force, the asymmetry of information between employer and employee, the impact of reputational effects, and the like. But because the agency relationship arises from contract, strong incentives are at work in the well-functioning firm to choose the proper mix of controls at the outset, and to adjust levels of employee compensation to take into account the residual risks of error.

But how does one know whether the firm is functioning well, or whether its management is well informed? If the firm is a sole proprietorship, the bottom line creates a powerful incentive to see that the appropriate steps will be taken. But what happens in a publicly held corporation? Here the universal use of shares has two great advantages. First, shares allow each individual to have an undivided interest in all the assets of the corporation, an interest exactly fungible with those of other shareholders. Second, shares allow individuals to diversify their investments across firms and industries. Where more complex divisions of risk and return are desired, different classes of equity (including warrants) and debt (secured and unsecured) can be introduced.

The shareholders face an agency problem of their own, of course, as it is highly unlikely that any single small shareholder will supervise the firm managers—his agents—when the gains from that supervision must be shared with all the other shareholders, none of whom contribute to the costs of supervision. Various legal devices, chiefly derivative suits, have been employed with indifferent success to give isolated shareholders the proper incentives to monitor firm management, but these are difficult to organize and to maintain even in the best of circumstances.[5]

The sale of shares to another party is, however, an alternative that obviates many of the problems of litigation. If the new shareholders remain as disorganized as the old ones, then the transfer will not overcome the free-riding problem. But if the shares are sold in response to a tender offer by another corporation or other organized group, the problem of controlling management behavior takes on a new dimension. If the tender offeror acquires full ownership, it will be rid of the free-rider and coordination problems that plague individual shareholders; in a partial takeover of control, these problems will be reduced proportionately. A successful tender offeror does not need litigation to discipline management. The acquisition of other firm assets (whose relative value is fixed) enables the new owner to change management on demand. Such a change will not restore the assets or profits lost by old management, but it will make it possible to redeploy the firm assets in order to increase the overall return. Because the purchaser could command the control denied to isolated shareholders, the threat of sale gives the current owners some control over present management. With a price set somewhere between the current market value and the promised market value, shareholders and outsiders can enter into mutually beneficial transactions to oust old management, unless the management is given legal rights to upset or frustrate that bargain.[6]

As shareholders can discipline managers, managers can discipline lower-level employees, and so on down the line. The entire mechanism of control depends upon real and threatened contractual moves. Even if the threat is acted upon only infrequently, it can ensure a high level of performance through the system, so long as it can be acted upon at low cost. Of course there will be slippages in the system when the span of control must be exercised through many levels. But these do not constitute an indictment of the system of voluntary controls unless one can find some coercive system that will better discipline the behavior of agents. The sorry performance of centralized planning should dash any such hopes. Takeover bids are not a device to increase the value of capital as such, but rather are a means of controlling the labor that directs its use.

How Capital and Labor Differ

Two main features enhance the efficiency of capital markets. The first is the institution of corporate stock, which makes it easy to transfer individual interests by creating a common coinage in the firm's assets. The second is the ability of individuals to diversify their risk by taking holdings in a large number of different corporations. The stockholder whose eggs are in many baskets worries less about the fortunes of a single company, and more about the tendency of legal rules and institutional arrangements to maximize the size of the investment pie as a whole. Thus, in the limit, a person who holds an index fund will have an interest in both the acquiring and the acquired corporation in any takeover transaction, and will therefore tend to support the rule that maximizes the sum of both his investments.

The employment relationship differs on both points. First, there is no common coin of the realm. All the shares of General Motors common may be fungible, but not so all its workers. Each has a unique blend of reliability, intelligence, loyalty, strength, health, and the like. While the buyer of common stock does not care from whom he buys, the employer is not indifferent to the choice of employees. Promotion and training, hiring and firing, whether of household help or department heads, are always highly tricky and individuated tasks.

Capital and labor markets also differ with regard to the diversification of risk. While investors can buy the market to protect themselves, employers are always limited by the number and type of positions that have to be filled, which in turn depend upon the size and the internal organization of the business. A firm can always gain by weeding out weak employees and promoting abler ones. But the measurement of individual productivity is at best a chancy process. Poor workers may seek to conceal their weaknesses. Able workers have strong incentives to reveal their talents, but they are always on the lookout for employment elsewhere at higher wages. The employer therefore is under enormous pressures to maintain and improve the quality of its work force, and must make ceaseless marginal adjustments in order to operate at peak efficiency.

Employees too encounter difficulties in the employment relationship, as they are also generally unable to diversify risks effectively. Most workers can have only one full-time job at one time, and whenever they take a second, they jeopardize the first. Because employees must put all their eggs in one basket, they have to watch the basket with great care. In short, the employment relationship is often troubled because there are enormous difficulties of information and diversification on both sides. Modern economics makes a powerful distinction between search and experience goods, that is, between those goods that can be examined before purchase and those whose properties can only be discovered through use. Each side of the employment relationship contains elements of each, for there is much about jobs and workers that can be learned only after the employment relationship is formed.[7]

Although these problems may arise with special intensity in the employment situation, they are by no means unique to labor markets. Contracts of sale, for example, can present problems of under-diversification, especially when economies of scale dictate that large orders for a standard item be placed with a single supplier. Likewise the temporal dimension can raise special problems for both buyer and seller. If goods are sold under warranty, there is always the question of whether product malfunction results from some defect in the original goods or from their misuse. If the sale is made on credit, the question arises whether the seller should rely on the buyer's general credit, demand a third-party guarantee, or obtain a lien on the particular goods that survives the buyer's bankruptcy. Indeed, the difference between labor and sales transactions is often blurred at the margin, especially when the original seller makes custom goods to the buyer's order or obliges himself to repair or maintain the good originally sold.

As in the straight employment situation, the question of contract theory is what mix of remedies, legal and nonlegal, should be adopted to control the transactional risks. One approach is to assume a measure of perfect compensation, so-called expectation damages, requiring the party that breaks the contract to pay the innocent party enough money to put him in the position that he would have enjoyed if the contract had been fully performed.[8] But actual cases and contracts tell a very different story that reflects a greater sensitivity to the economic function of legal rules than to the demands of legal formalism. Most nineteenth-century decisions, written in an age in which freedom of contract was an accepted principle, are filled with sharp limitations upon the recovery of damages. A central theme of these cases was that damages were not recoverable merely because they were foreseeable but only because they had been contractually assumed by the breaching party.[9] When the seller failed to deliver goods, the measure of damages was the difference between the contract and market price, without reference to any additional losses borne by the buyer.[10] The seller of land who was unable to make good title to his buyer was obliged to refund the original deposit, but not to pay damages that would give the buyer the benefit of the bargain.[11] Lost profits were denied to the owner of a mill when the carrier misdelivered a millshaft entrusted to it for shipment.[12]

The damages below expectation were also commonplace, especially in the earlier twentieth century. Telegraph companies routinely exempted themselves from consequential damages for misdirected or mistaken messages, but did allow the sender to have the message read back for an additional sum.[13] Contracts often stipulated that the purchaser of defective goods could not recover consequential damages (e.g., plant down time or lost profits) attributable to the breach, an issue that has been the subject of frequent litigation in recent years.[14] Instead the seller was under an obligation to repair or replace, often at his own option. A film supplier who sold a defective roll of film assumed responsibility only for the cost of a new roll of film, not the value of the finished picture.[15] Finally, many employment contracts provided damages for work-related injuries that fell far short of complete protection for pain and suffering, lost earnings, and medical expenses.[16]

A different pattern emerges in the more recent twentieth-century cases, in which the cardinal assumption is that the parties do not have freedom to contract over the remedial provisions of a contract.[17] In many ways the limitation on contractual freedom is made explicit by legislative provision, as for example by the language of the Uniform Commercial Code, which blends the old and new legal orders in uneasy harmony. "Consequential damages may be limited or excluded unless the limitation or exclusion is unconscionable. Limitation of consequential damages for injury to the person in the case of consumer goods is prima facie unconscionable but limitation of damages where the loss is commercial is not."[18]

The contrast between the voluntary rules and the regulatory system is quite striking. The externally imposed rules all hew quite closely to the ideal of expectation damages. In contrast, the voluntary damage rules that dominated the nineteenth century have several distinguishing features. First, the measure of damages is calculated by some simple formula that does not depend upon the idiosyncratic responses of either side to the relationship. Second, the compensation is set deliberately below the actual level of loss, in large measure to induce the innocent party to mitigate the consequences of breach. In effect the contracting parties build in certain forms of abstract injustices at the front end that are cured by their joint consent.

Because labor contracts are subject to the same information and agency problems that emerge elsewhere, it should not be surprising that they adopt many of the same features—ease of administration, remedies below actual costs—that are found in voluntary markets for other goods and services. The explanation of this pattern of behavior leads us back to the basic problem: what institutional practices can minimize the adverse impact of agency costs and information problems? Here the clear answer seems to be those that are structured to enable each side to obtain information about the other, without hampering mobility and diversification. In principle this argues for a thoroughgoing regime of freedom of contract, as the parties themselves can best figure out how to minimize the various risks in an effort to increase their joint output. On this point both the common law and the contractual practice has historically given rise to a powerful, indeed inflexible, presumption that all contracts were at will unless otherwise specified.[19] Thus even if the parties specified that a contract of employment was "permanent" or for an "indefinite" period of time, the general (and proper) response was to construe it as if either party could terminate the arrangement at any time, without having to give any reasons for termination, and without being subject to a suit for damages.

Variations to this basic theme are observed, but these are consistent with the general pattern of behavior. Sometimes the employer or the employee may have obligated himself to give the other side notice of the intention to terminate. Similarly, where the employee is dismissed without notice, the contract or the firm practice may provide some *fixed* severance pay. But in both cases damages are computed on a simple formula, and no effort is made to award damages equal to the asserted loss of the other side, who is given the strongest possible incentives to mitigate losses. Contracts at will cannot eliminate all suits arising out of the employment relationship. Wages certainly may be recovered for work already done; obligations not to disclose trade secrets survive the termination of employment; and suits for prior work-related injuries may also be a distinct possibility. But at every point steps are taken to ease the redeployment of both capital and labor.

It has been estimated that 60–65 percent of the employment contracts in the United States are at will.[20] This figure is subject to a number of ambiguities. First, should agreements that call for notice or severance pay be considered contracts at will, as I believe? Second, how should we classify the plans of many large corporations that call for the arbitration or mediation of dismissal or other grievances? It is not clear whether they govern as a matter of uniform practice or of legal right. Nor is it clear how many of these plans would remain in place if employers did not (for example) perceive the need to adopt formal procedures to protect themselves against suits for racial or sexual discrimination. In any case, at-will contracts constitute a very common form of employment contract. Senior officers of large corporations often serve at the pleasure of their board of directors. Indeed, the 60–65 percent figure noted above is even more impressive than it seems at first blush, since the denominator includes union, certain charitable, and government contracts, where collective agreements, the peculiar internal structure of nonprofit organizations, or civil service arrangements preclude the at-will arrangement.[21]

The widespread use of the contract at will, I believe, is due to the advantages it offers in allowing the parties to respond to the dual problems of agency costs and imperfect information. The contract at will fosters the mobility and diversification of labor, thereby allowing labor markets, within limits, to imitate the desirable features of capital markets. Thus the contract at will permits the employee to diversify his risk over time and is therefore attractive even to risk-averse employees, notwithstanding their apparently precarious position. In contrast, a contract for a specific term requires a greater employee commitment to the employer even though the employee may harbor substantial doubts whether the relationship will work out well. To be sure, an employee might desire the best of both worlds, the right to a term employment and the option to leave at will, but employers will reject such arrangements because of their need to control employee misbehavior. Strong employees are likely to command higher wages under a contract at will than one for a term, for employers know the probability of poor performance and perhaps termination will be reduced under the incentive structure of the at-will contract. And once the proper incentive structure is in place, any needed adjustments can be made in the wage rate.

At-will contracts have certain advantages over contracts terminable only "for cause." The for-cause contract necessarily interferes with the ceaseless marginal adjustments required in the employment context. The powerful incentives for employee misbehavior will be more difficult to check, and the employee will be in a position to resist by litigation any changes in ancillary terms, which normally are made without any permanent disruption in the employment relationship. In contrast the at-will contract allows the contracting parties simultaneously to counter the tendency to cheat and to correct for original contracting errors, whether in the perceived value of employee services or in the overall market rate for labor changes. The ability under at-will contracts to make adjustments in the subsidiary terms also reduces the pressure to make explicit and continuous adjustments in the wage rate, which as a practical matter may be very difficult to reverse. Thus small adjustments on other terms (employer to employee: go home early to watch the Little League game; employee to employer: don't worry, I'll lock up the store if you have to go to the doctor; and so on) may help stabilize the arrangement without continually broaching the delicate question of wages.[22]

One great strength of the contract at will is that litigation will never be the preferred means to redress a grievance. Instead the parties will be able to exercise their power to fire or to quit, or the lesser included powers of renegotiation, without fear of legal complications. While legally permissible, capricious firings and resignations are not likely to prove a significant problem. Quitting often places the employee at risk, and may result in the loss of certain firm-specific skills not transferable to another job. Firing an employee may be risky. The employee must be prevented from doing acts that are harmful to the business. A replacement must be found and trained. Other employees must be reassured that their positions are secure. At the very least the employer may have to increase the wage rate in order to prevent the unwanted departure of the best employees, especially if the dismissal is perceived as unjust.

These strong and ever-present business constraints therefore caution against the use of an absolute power in an arbitrary way: for even if absolute power may corrupt the sovereign, its use in private contexts is sharply limited.[23] The at-will contract does not guarantee that employers and employees will make sound decisions, but it does help stabilize the situation by creating the proper level of threats. The losses from severing the relationship will be greater for the party who misbehaves, so that the innocent party has the better threats because the guilty party has more to lose. (Who cares if he is fired by an employer who cheats him regularly?) If the threat mechanism works very well, then the at-will contract permits labor markets to incorporate to a lesser degree the features that enable financial markets to operate smoothly.

The argument does not imply, however, that all private contracts will be negotiated on an at-will basis. Indeed, it helps identify the situations in which more complex arrangements are appropriate. Here a central question is whether the size and the temporal duration of the expected gain are sufficient to justify more complex contractual arrangements. That might often be the case, for example, with entertainers and athletes, for in such situations the difference between the contract wage and the market value of the services can be very large. More complex contracts could emerge when one party to the employment relationship has to make a very substantial capital outlay at the outset, which he can only recoup over a period of years, as might have been the case in the colonial period with indentured servants. Finally, the internal demands of complex organizations may well require the adoption of internal grievance procedures or arbitration.

Once the contract at will is abandoned, however, the parties will then have to draft other provisions to ensure the right level of service and protection for both sides. Athletic contracts may well have performance clauses; indentured servants' contracts must have provisions that prevent the employer from overworking servants or putting them out into an improper trade; arbitration agreements must specify internal procedures and cost-sharing devices. All of these refinements cost money, thereby reducing their attractiveness relative to the contract at will. We should expect these arrangements to exist, but they require very substantial gains to make them worthwhile.

This account of the contract at will rests on familiar classical economic assumptions. It assumes individual self-interest, and demand and supply curves that are well behaved—negatively sloping demand, positively sloping supply. In addition, it assumes that the parties have imperfect information and contract as they do because *they know that they do not know*, that is, because they are aware of the common pitfalls lurking in employment relations. By identifying the dangers that the contract is designed to overcome, the argument here offers an explanation of why at-will contracts generally operate to the mutual benefit of both parties. If this argument is correct, then the contract at will should be welcomed both as a manifestation of the joint intentions of the parties and as a simple and effective response to the problem of contracting in the employment context.

Nonetheless the arrangement is often attacked in legal circles on the ground that individual workers or employers misperceive their own private interest, or that high information costs prevent them from insisting upon some alternative contractual arrangement, typically of the for-cause variety.[24] But this argument proves too much, for if high transaction costs block two-party negotiations, then virtually every voluntary transaction must be suspect. Indeed ignorance is far less likely in the employment context than in the consumer context, because the employment relationship tends to extend over time and involves a very substantial proportion of the resources of both parties. In many cases the at-will term is the product of explicit negotiations, and where it is not, it is often the result of an implicit understanding. Why then assume that the standard arrangements are ill suited to the cases of silence, especially when there is no alternative term that can be implied in a consistent or systematic fashion?

In evaluating the soundness of the contract at will, moreover, it is a great mistake to concentrate too closely on the particulars of the litigated cases. There will always be breakdowns in the process, as some employers will make unwise use of their power to fire at will. In the litigated cases, a few courts have adopted a position that reads into every contract an implied term that dismissal from employment must be made only "in good faith."[25] But occasional abuses do not indict a widespread contractual arrangement. The basic question is what rule of employment will tend to minimize the sum of errors in the hiring and firing context.

There is no evidence that the rule of "good faith" will produce less error than the at-will standard. Under the good-faith standard, employees who are manifestly incompetent may be able to persuade a jury that they were fired because they resisted illicit demands for social or sexual favors. In addition, the administrative costs of the good-faith contract are substantial, as every employee termination becomes a potentially triable lawsuit. Good faith is sufficiently open-ended that any plaintiff may be able to conduct an extensive pretrial investigation in search of the employer's elusive improper motive as the "sole," "dominant," "primary," "substantial," "observable," or "inferrable" motive for the firing. The great danger of the good-faith standard, then, is that an employee who is justly dismissed will litigate in the courts, where he can impose heavy costs upon the employer under the current legal rules that govern not only the trial itself, but the discovery process before trial.

At-will contracting poses its own distinctive kind of risk, of course: some employees may be wrongfully dismissed. But the potential for harm in that error is generally far less than in the litigation under the good-faith rule. When one employee is wrongfully discharged, another will typically be hired in his place, so that the personal hardship of one is offset by the benefits that are conferred upon another. The displaced employee may suffer serious emotional or reputational losses, but there are gains along both these dimensions by the employee hired as a replacement. Thus employees *as a class* may be better off with a rule that facilitates mobility than with one that creates some form of contingent property right in individual employment. Because every employee necessarily shares in the benefits of the at-will contract, it should not be evaluated through the eyes of an aggrieved employee seeking damages after the fact. The proper focus is that of all prospective employees before the contract is formed, a class that includes many who have enjoyed durable and successful arrangements under the at-will rule.

In addition, the costs of erroneous dismissal are often small and largely self-correcting. Able employees usually will be able to find another job. Even if they cannot rely upon the references of the previous employer, they can still marshall other information to persuade an employer to hire them: other employees may vouch for their efficiency; samples of previous work can be furnished; previous employers consulted. The task is all the easier if the second job is offered on an at-will basis. At the same time the firm has strong incentives to avoid firing good employees. Erroneous dismissals will reduce productivity, and consequently market share and influence, as firms with superior personnel policies prosper in comparison. Why launch upon a path of legal intervention to handle a problem that is already subject to heavy self-regulation?

More serious difficulties can arise under the good-faith standard. Employee suits may cripple the operation of the firm and may deter the removal of inefficient employees, thereby blocking the promotion and employment of other workers, including those unwisely dismissed by other employers. Nor is there any reason to believe that a successful suit can restore the employee's reputation. Potential employers will take into account the error rate of the underlying litigation and may shy away from hiring a person who is obviously prepared to sue his employer. In addition, a for-cause rule would influence the firm's original hiring decision, making it more reluctant to take on risky workers because of the greater implicit cost of dismissal.

A defense of at-will contracting does not depend upon its being an errorless arrangement. In the best of circumstances, the employment relationship is conducive to substantial levels of error. It is therefore pertinent, and probably sufficient, to note that the cost of trying to correct the occasional error in a world with contracts at will is the disruption of the entire system of informal checks and balances adopted by trial and error over the years. The contract at will persists in private markets because it offers a sensible response to difficulties in forecasting the future, and to the persistent risks of misbehavior that run on both sides. From the perspective of either individual liberty or economic efficiency, the contract at will should be welcomed, not banned.

Contracts at Will and Collective Action

Thus far the examination of the employment relationship has implicitly ruled out any cooperative efforts among employees. The analysis, however, becomes more complex if individual employees can band together against their common employer. Now it is necessary to consider two variations on the basic theme. In the first instance, assume (contrary to the current legal position) that there are no restrictions on any types of contracts that emerge from the process of voluntary negotiations. While employees may seek to form a united front, employers may also strive (with the so-called yellow dog contract)[26] to make nonmembership in a union a condition of employment. The second situation is the present system of collective bargaining: a majority of the workers within a defined unit can determine whether a union shall represent all workers within the unit and if so, which union it shall be. Let us take the cases in order.

Voluntary Unions

If only voluntary unions are allowed, it is very difficult to determine what kind of contractual arrangements will eventually emerge. Yet the key role of at-will contracts suggests that unionization would be an infrequent phenomenon. At-will contracts have very powerful efficiency properties, but they are also compatible only with nonunion firms. Unionization in voluntary markets suffers the comparative disadvantage that it cannot be married with contracts at will. Thus assume that a union is in place and certain terms and conditions of employment have been agreed upon for the workers. Can the employer be allowed to trump the rest of the contract by exercising his power to fire at will? The employer could fire a few key union agents, and then demand instant renegotiation of all terms by the simple expedient of firing the remaining workers, who then might be offered work on new and less favorable terms. For its part, the union could simply call its members out on strike at any time to force a favorable renegotiation of the agreement. Yet these abrupt transitions would completely eliminate any return from the very substantial costs incurred by both sides to reach an agreement that is necessarily far more detailed and complex than the at-will contract.

Unionization requires some degree of institutional stability over the long haul. Here the examination of union-negotiated employment contracts is somewhat theoretical, given the present extensive web of government regulation. Still it seems likely that even in an unregulated environment most union contracts would be for extended terms, usually a period of several years. Even this figure tends to understate the contract duration if the additional terms impose obligations to negotiate (perhaps in "good faith") an extension of the original term. Workers will enter into these long-term contracts only if they offer better terms than are available in a spot market. To obtain gains from union membership, however, workers must rely less upon the exit right, and more upon direct expenditures in the current jobs, which take on the form of capital assets under long-term contracts. In addition, litigation will displace mobility as the chief device to control against the possible abuses by both sides.

One of the most heavily litigated subjects concerns the grounds for dismissal. Most union contracts incorporate some form of for-cause requirement. As a term of art, *for cause* is defined largely by its opposition to the at-will contract; yet definition by opposition does not invest the term with a unique and distinctive meaning. Instead it takes on enormous coloration both from the contract language and from the firm practice, informal and formal, that surrounds its use. But even here its precise meaning may differ from firm to firm, and union to union, thereby increasing the litigation costs on both sides.

The tensions that call forth the for-cause agreement are easily identified. The employer cannot abandon all right to fire and still hope to maintain any acceptable levels of production. Indeed at some point the union itself cannot support a rule that promises the bankruptcy of the firm on which the livelihood of its members depends. In other words, the union must find some way to prevent free-riding by some of its members to the detriment of the others. Yet the union cannot allow its key operatives to be fired at will. The for-cause language represents in general form a compromise between the two extremes that gives both sides something of what they want without undermining the collective form of the labor agreement.

Still substantial strains remain. Thus the restriction upon employer freedom will never suffice if employer discretion is allowed for all decisions short of hiring and firing. Under such a regime the employer could, for example, lower the wage (in the limit, to zero), forcing the employee to seek work elsewhere. Similarly, the employer could demote or transfer the employee, or deny him various kinds of fringe benefits until he is induced to quit. To eliminate the last vestiges of the at-will regime, the for-cause requirement must extend to all close substitutes for hiring and firing: promotion, layoffs, seniority, transfer, vacation, fringe benefits, and all other rewards and punishments. Clyde Summers, a leading supporter of the for-cause rule has written, "The statute [on unjust dismissals] must reach all forms of disciplinary action related to an employee's job, including demotion, reduction in pay, reduction in seniority, assignment to undesirable work, and forced resignation."[27]

Nor do the control devices stop here. Broad categorical rules, establishing rigid job classifications, may be used in order to prevent favoritism and abuse, as a general nondiscrimination provision makes it more difficult for either employer or union to impose differential penalties on unwanted individual workers. But these contractual devices have rigidities that prevent employers from responding to changes in the demand for jobs or in the performance levels of individual workers. The problem of setting wages and assigning tasks to employees exists in any market. But under unionization the additional need to preserve the collective agreement limits the ability of the firm to respond to it.

The required institutional adjustments do not end with the formation of the collective agreement. When a dispute arises, what rights do various parties have to participate in its resolution?[28] It is quite clear that the firm must be entitled to participate as well as the individual worker whose grievance is manifest. Even in unregulated labor markets, the union must also have some voice in the process, for the resolution of any particular dispute has ramifications for the other workers, even if it has no binding precedential effect. Yet the worker might well resist having the union as his sole representative, because what is good for the individual worker may not be good for the rest of the unit, even in the absence of powerful intraunion rivalries.

Generally speaking, successful unionization must simultaneously address two separate agency problems. The firm has to worry about the abuses by its agents, the employees, while the employees have to worry about the abuses of their agents, the union representatives. If, moreover, some portion of the wage gains of the individual workers represents monopoly profits (including quasi-rents), the dangers of abuse by union leaders are even greater, since they have the constant opportunity of diverting some portion of the surplus (in payment for services rendered, as it were) without driving union members down to a competitive wage.

It is not surprising that other institutions develop to respond to the demands that union contracts create. Summers has thus noted how the judicious use of arbitration can ease many of the difficulties of policing the employment arrangement.[29] But what should be made of the point? Arbitrators are hired to reduce the errors that will be made once the basic commitment has been made to collective agreements. But the proper question is, even with arbitration available, are collective agreements superior to a network of at-will contracts, which would largely dispense with the need for arbitration in the first place? The relative simplicity of the at-will arrangement is one of its greatest virtues.

How then can unions survive in voluntary markets, given the enormous costs of collective decision making? In principle, the answer must be that the union itself provides various benefits to the parties that justify its costs, including the abandonment of at-will contracts. But what form do these benefits assume? One possible explanation is that the union provides a mix of personnel services that the firm itself (perhaps because of its adversary relationship to the worker) is unable to duplicate. Yet large nonunion firms devote a substantial amount of time to personnel relationships, even where the formal contract provides for termination at will. Many firms prepare lengthy handbooks of personnel policy that greatly influence life inside the firm, even if all parties understand that they are not legally binding.

Nor do any of the obvious sources of market failure explain how unions help increase the overall productivity. To be sure, one could argue that employers—perhaps because their managers are only agents of the shareholders—either systematically fail to recognize the true interests of the firm or use negotiations with workers to divert part of the firm profit to their own benefit.[30] There are, however, insuperable problems with both of these possible explanations. Even though the firm faces the agency problem, it does not disappear because a union represents the workers. Instead a second agency problem is added to the original one. Indeed the complex legal structure can only increase the delegated authority of the firm's agents (for how else can they handle the greater uncertainty that now arises?), whose work is ever more difficult to monitor. With or without unions, firms themselves have incentives to overcome the misconduct of their own managers, and it is mistaken to believe that the occasional ignorance of individual managers and employees could lead to the widespread emergence of voluntary unions. Those firms that cannot effectively limit the abuses by their employees will be driven out of business. They will not be rehabilitated by unionization.

Unionization under Protective Regulation

The discussion of the previous section rested on the premise that the markets for employment were unregulated. In fact, there has been an extensive federal presence in labor markets since the mid 1930s. The Norris-LaGuardia Act (1932) made the traditional yellow-dog contract void and against public policy, thereby preventing firms from suing unions for inducing various workers to join unions without giving up their jobs, as they were often required to do by contract.[31] Even after Norris-LaGuardia the employer could still terminate an employee at will if he engaged in union activities, even if it could not sue the union directly. The National Labor Relations Act in 1935 made it an "unfair labor practice" for the employer to dismiss workers for engaging in protected union activities.[32] The statute in effect engrafted a for-cause requirement into all employment contracts. To be sure, the statute allows an employer to dismiss a worker for no reason at all, or for bad reasons unrelated to union activities. But unless the employer can put forward a strong economic justification for the dismissal, courts have often inferred that it was in fact covertly motivated by an antiunion animus.[33] Thus under the current legal order, litigation for discharge is a live possibility whenever a union or a prospective union is involved—a far cry from the dominant common law approach.

Unions need the statutory protection in order to compete with nonunion competitors. Before (and sometimes after) the statute, unionization was accompanied by frequent violence (as in efforts to keep nonunion labor away from the workplace) and fraud (as in the continuation of work in the conscious knowledge that it was in breach of contract).[34] In the modern context, the use of violence has been limited by the passage of the national labor legislation, even though charges of fraud on both sides abound in union recognition elections. Nonetheless the situation is far removed from a voluntary market, as private coercion has been replaced by a set of government-imposed rules on union organization that are themselves antithetical to voluntary agreements. Thus the statutes specify that the majority of workers within a "bargaining unit" have the right to determine whether they will be represented by a union, and if so which union it will be. The question of what constitutes a proper bargaining unit generally rests upon the historical composition and distribution of the work force, and voting eligibility is administratively determined under the sketchiest of Congressional guidance.[35] The election that follows can therefore take into account only the preferences of the workers on the job and in the unit as defined. All potential employees are excluded from the process. The net effect of the institutional arrangement is to reinforce the tendency to substitute litigation for migration as the preferred means of handling employment disputes.

The current labor law also exacerbates the various conflicts of interest that form the nub of the agency problem. When collective organizations form voluntarily, we can generally expect that appropriate steps will be taken to reduce conflicts to a tolerable level. To some extent, individual workers can protect themselves by contract when the group is formed if they believe that their interests are at variance with those of the group at large. Key workers can demand that certain organic changes in the operation of the union be approved by a supermajority vote, or that positions on a governing board be held by members of certain trades. Finally, the power of individual workers to withdraw also acts as a check against abuse. Negotiations over membership tend to reduce the variance in tastes among the group members; the explicit agreement tends to reduce both uncertainty and the dangers of coalition and intrigue; and the power to withdraw is still a further check against abuse.

When consensual modes of formation are abandoned, however, the new combination of administrative decision and majority vote may well produce a group whose membership differs sharply in tastes and demands. As the labor statutes themselves are not drafted with the detail of written constitutions, coalitions and factions can more easily obtain a very powerful influence over internal union affairs. Similarly, as a union is certified it represents both members and nonmembers, notwithstanding the obvious conflicts of interest between them, and it remains in power even after there are substantial shifts in either the composition or sentiment of the workers within the bargaining unit. Continuous incremental adjustments are frustrated on every front. The problems of voluntary unions are necessarily intensified under the current legal regime.

One possible legal response is simply to acquiesce in whatever outcomes are dictated by internal union procedures. Most courts, however, have intervened to impose duties of "fair" representation to protect minority groups from the union abuses,[36] most obviously in cases of race and sex. Notwithstanding strenuous judicial efforts, no satisfactory formula has yet been found to control other alleged breaches of fiduciary duty by union officials.[37] Nor has any academic commentator been able to develop a workable set of rules to control the problem. The reason why this ambiguity is tolerated should be clear. The organizational difficulties of collective bargaining are the price that union workers pay in order to extract monopoly profits, or at least firm-specific rents, from their employers and through them the consuming public at large.[38] The workers who do not find the price worth paying cease to be members of the unit and cease to have their preferences counted. The increased homogeneity in turn increases the success of the union, even if the costs it imposes upon former members and potential members are carefully hidden from view.

It is now possible to draw the analysis full circle. As discussed earlier, agency costs are in principle best regulated by contract. In many employment situations contracts at-will turn out to be the preferred solution for all concerned. When labor unions are introduced, the contract at will is no longer a viable option, as the dictates of union structure require some insulation against the counterstrategies of employers and excessive power by union officials. Yet displacing the contract at will requires complex institutional arrangements in their stead, with more players and more rules. Each additional layer makes it more costly to control the twin problems of agency costs and imperfect information. Within the existing framework, firms and individuals will take steps to reduce the costs that are imposed: unions are not self-destructive, employers are not fools. But the optimal social solution will be achieved here, as in so many other areas, only when the regulatory barriers to private contract are removed from the legal and economic system.

Part Three
Agency in Organizations

Chapter 7
Transfer Pricing as a Problem of Agency

Robert G. Eccles

Introduction

A common problem for firms organized into a number of divisions is how to establish transfer prices for goods exchanged between those divisions.[1] Although this problem emerged more than sixty years ago with the invention of the multidivisional structure (Chandler 1962), its management is still not well understood (Vancil 1978; Kaplan 1982). From the efficiency perspective of economic theory, the preferred ways of setting transfer prices hinge on marginal cost, its accounting near-equivalent of variable cost, and mathematical programming. In practice, however, only the simplest instances of the transfer pricing problem can be resolved through such approaches. Surveys show these techniques are rarely used (Vancil 1978; Tang 1979).[2]

The transfer pricing problem can be considered as a problem of agency. Jensen and Meckling (1976, 308) defined an agency relationship as "a contract under which one or more persons (the principal[s]) engage another person (the agent) to perform some service on their behalf which involves delegating some decision-making authority to the agent." Although much of the agency literature focuses on the problems of the separation of ownership and control (Jensen and Meckling 1976; Fama and Jensen 1983a, b) or on explaining various organizational forms (Fama and Jensen 1984), the concept of agency can also illuminate relationships within organizations. Although "the nature of the contractual obligations and rights of the parties are much more varied and generally not as well specified in explicit contractual arrangements" between individuals at different hierarchical levels in an organization, Jensen and Meckling (1976, 309) felt that "extensions of our analysis . . . show promise of producing insights into a viable theory of organization." Baiman (1982), for example, has

151

surveyed the research in agency theory that has implications for managerial accounting. Accounting systems play an important role in specifying the nexus of contracts or the network of contractual relationships between principals and agents.[3] Transfer pricing is one of the areas in which accounting systems play an important role.

In the multidivisional firm, the president or chief executive officer (CEO) is the principal and the division general managers (DGMs) are his or her agents.[4] The CEO delegates some decision-making authority to the DGMs over resources committed to businesses based on particular products and markets. Jensen (1983, 325) refers to this as "the system for partitioning and assigning decision rights among participants in the organization." The two decisions relevant to the transfer pricing problem are (1) the choice of a division's suppliers and customers, and (2) the setting of a transfer price for internal transactions. The agency relationships between the CEO and DGMs determine who will make these decisions and how the agent's performance will be measured, evaluated, and rewarded or punished. Profitability, return on investment, and other financial criteria are nearly always included as performance measures. Evaluations of performance are based on budget objectives, past performance, and the performance of external competitors and other divisions within the company. Rewards include bonuses, salary increases, and promotions. Punishments include the absence of rewards, demotions, and dismissals. Nonpecuniary criteria are also used in measuring and evaluating performance, along with more symbolic forms of reward and punishment.

This paper presents a positive theory of transfer pricing using both the concept of agency and empirical evidence collected in a field research project. Data were collected in thirteen companies and included interviews with 150 managers (one-third general managers, including several CEOs, one-third financial managers, and one-third managers from other functions), internal documents such as memoranda and special studies, and publicly available information. These companies were in four industries: chemicals, electronics, heavy machinery, and machinery components.

Fairness in Agency Relationships

The problem of fairness—never considered in the literature on agency relationships—was frequently mentioned by the managers as an essential aspect of such relationships. Fairness is especially important to the agent.

The difficulty of defining the concept may help explain why this largely technical literature has ignored the issue of fairness. In a contractual context, fairness refers to the parties' perceptions of the extent to which the contract has been fulfilled. Difficulties emerge because real-life agency relationships are formed in conditions of uncertainty, are incompletely specified, and evolve over time as conditions change. In contrast, most models of agency employ simplified concepts of uncertainty, are completely specified, and apply only to a single period. The literature focuses on specifying contracts that maximize objectives of the principal, such as total firm profits, under the assumption that agents pursue only their self-interest. The challenge is to establish incentives such that agents, in pursuing their self-interest, achieve the objectives of the principal. In addition the principal may incur monitoring and bonding expenditures in an effort to limit the divergence of the agent's interests from that of the principal (Jensen and Meckling 1976).

The conditions in which fairness exists can be described in terms of the partitioning of decision rights, the performance measurement and evaluation system, and the reward and punishment system. Perceived fairness exists when principal and agent agree on the criteria for measuring and evaluating performance; the agent has the necessary authority, through decision rights, to affect the outcomes on which he or she will be judged; the parties agree on the relationship between performance and rewards or punishments, and on how performance actually is measured and evaluated; and actual rewards and punishments conform to expectations, given the achieved performance. Because fairness is something perceived by both the principal and the agent, disagreement is always possible.

Complaints of unfairness have many sources. The agent may feel he or she has insufficient authority to influence the objectives on which performance is measured (the well-known problem of responsibility exceeding authority). Principal and agent may disagree about what criteria should be used for performance evaluation, how performance should be measured for agreed-upon criteria, what rewards are appropriate for given performance levels, how the agency contract should be adjusted when conditions differ from those assumed at its establishment, or what should be done when one party fails to fulfill his obligations (i.e., reneges on the contract). The problem of achieving fairness in relationships is part of the fabric of everyday social and economic life.

The problem is complicated by the fact that principals often have more than one agent. The CEO may have several DGMs, for example. Each agent evaluates the fairness of his or her contract with the principal partly in terms of how it compares with the contracts held by others. Most of the literature, however, treats the agency relationship as a two-person problem. Transfer pricing is at minimum a three-person problem involving one principal and two agents. Baiman (1982, 177) noted that "the results from a two-person analysis may not necessarily extend to a larger firm for several reasons."[5] When multiple agents exist, the individual principal-agent contracts may or may not contain specifications about agent-agent relationships. The principal's concern is how his relationships with his agents are affected by their relationships with each other.

Fairness has a significant bearing on the efficiency objectives of the principal. If agents believe they are being treated unfairly, their incentive may be reduced and they may even work against the interests of the principal. Agency costs may then rise, either because of residual loss or because of monitoring and bonding expenditures incurred to guard against such loss. Alternatively, agents may receive rewards greater than necessary for certain levels of performance, which is unfair from the principal's perspective. The extent to which an agency contract fulfills fairness and efficiency objectives depends on how difficult it is to implement a particular contract in a particular social structure. This question of practical viability is too often ignored in agency theory.

The Need for Positive Theory

Because theory and practice in accounting have diverged so significantly, some researchers have called for a "positive theory of accounting" to contribute to the "development of a body of theory to explain why organizations take the form they do and why they behave as they do" (Jensen 1983, 319). Christenson (1976, 646) expressed this divergence between mathematical solutions to problems and what is actually done in practice as a question: "Why don't practicing managers pay more attention to what we have to offer?" Focusing on this question, he noted, has led to a healthy increase in the attention paid to behavioral factors. He further suggested that the development of theories relevant to practice must begin by establishing what current practice actually is. Jensen (1983) agreed that institutional evidence should not be ignored simply because it is difficult to express in quantitative terms. Christenson (1976, 646–47) goes even further in arguing that "In those sciences which have been successful in enabling us to explain, predict, and control phenomena, theories or formalized languages have been found initially in the informal practitioner languages, and not in the analysis of observational data."

In the spirit advocated by Christenson, Zimmerman (1979) used agency theory to explain the prevalence of cost allocations in practice. He noted that "accounting researchers typically ignore the positive question of why firms persist in allocating costs in spite of the continual admonitions by educators against doing so" (p. 505). Zimmerman recognized that cost allocations have important behavioral effects, arguing that they are a way of reducing "the agency costs associated with consumption by inducing the subordinate to act as a monitor of his superior" (p. 509). However, he did not take the further step of asking managers why they allocated costs.[6]

Transfer pricing is another area in which theory and practice diverge widely. As Kaplan (1982, 497) observed, "under conditions that make decentralization worthwhile—that is, an uncertain environment with private information possessed by local managers—we do not know a great deal about optimal transfer pricing policies." Even Vancil (1978, 142), who studied the use of transfer prices in 247 companies, felt that he was "unable to say anything definitive—or even mildly useful—on the subject of transfer prices," and concluded that "the issue remains as a perennial puzzle for academicians, while practitioners continue to cope."

For Kaplan the conflict between resource allocation decisions and divisional performance is "the essence of the transfer pricing conundrum" (p. 498). This conflict is based on a theory about the role of transfer prices that is not supported by the role of transfer prices in practice.

A Positive Theory of Transfer Pricing

In practice, the transfer pricing problem has two key elements: the sourcing decision (are internal transactions mandated or can the divisions choose between internal and external transactions?) and the pricing decision (are internal transactions valued at full cost or at a transfer price intended to give the selling division a profit margin on its costs?).[7] Of the few surveys that have been conducted on transfer pricing, none explicitly examined the sourcing decision. As for pricing, survey evidence suggests that 25 to 30 percent of internal transfers are on a full-cost basis and the rest are valued by some method intended to include a profit on the transferred good. These methods include market price defined in various ways (e.g., list price, bid price, and competitors' prices); market price less discounts (sometimes given to reflect presumably lower transaction costs on internal exchanges); cost plus profit markups (e.g., average corporate return on sales, average corporate return on investment, and a fixed percentage of full cost); and negotiation between DGMs and other managers in the divisions (using whatever cost and market information they choose to submit).

Kaplan (1982, 500), reviewing Vancil's survey results, noted that 42 percent of companies used either a full-cost scheme or full cost plus a profit markup—methods "for which we have no theoretical justification other than simplicity and objectivity." "Justification" in this sense would be based on the traditional economic definition of the transfer pricing problem: what price will induce the DGMs of the selling and buying divisions to set output levels for the intermediate and final good, respectively, in such a way as to maximize corporate profits?[8] Various marginal-cost and mathematical programming methods have been devised that could be used to determine such an "optimal" transfer price. But setting prices this way would often interfere with the measurement of the selling division's performance as a profit center. Hence the divergence between theory and practice.

To understand why actual transfer pricing practices are chosen, one needs a somewhat broader frame of reference. Managers are faced with two decisions. First, does an explicit vertical integration strategy exist for the intermediate and final good? Second, is the entire production of the intermediate good viewed as a distinct business, or only the proportion sold outside? In the latter case capacity devoted to internal transfers is viewed as a manufacturing unit for the buying division. The transfer pricing problem must be defined in terms of strategy, not profit maximization. While profitability is always a concern in developing strategy, other objectives such as certainty of profits, growth, and market share are also important and often involve tradeoffs with profitability.[9]

A strategy of vertical integration between the intermediate and final good is based on mandated transactions between the selling and buying divisions. When it does not exist, external transactions can be substituted for internal ones. Although "vertical integration has never been a well-understood phenomenon" (Carlton 1979, 189), the question of whether or not a vertical integration strategy exists has meaning to managers. There are many reasons for using such a strategy, such as obtaining low-cost raw materials, ensuring supply of the intermediate good, and becoming familiar with its product and process technology.[10] Some of these are intended to improve short-term profitability whereas others have longer-term advantages.

When a company pursues a strategy of vertical integration, the intermediate good can be viewed either as a business in its own right or as an input to the final good. The latter is the typical practice when the entire output of the intermediate good is used in the production of the final good. The supplying division is then defined as a cost center, and its performance is measured and evaluated by comparing actual costs to standard costs for given volume levels.[11] If all of the intermediate good is sold externally, the supplying division is defined as a profit center, and its performance is measured by subtracting costs from revenues and evaluating this profit calculation in terms of objectives, past performance, or competitors' performance. In this case the intermediate good is a business in its own right.

The problem is more complex when the intermediate good is traded both internally and externally, since management has a choice in how it defines internal transfers. They can be viewed as manufactured components valued at full cost, just as outputs of the buying divisions' manufacturing unit are valued. Alternatively, internal transfers can be seen as sales to a customer, valued at market price, just as sales to external customers are valued. The first approach, it is often argued, makes it possible to price the final good lower than competitors' products, which can help the buying division build market share. The counterargument is that competitors who source the intermediate good externally must pay market price and so should the buying division.

Whether the price of the intermediate good affects corporate profitability is a complex question in practice. The answer depends on several factors, including industry structure (extent of backward vertical integration by competitors in the final good) and product pricing practices. Although my study showed that transfer prices sometimes affect resource allocation decisions, this was not the dominant concern of managers. Instead, they were most concerned about how transfer prices define the roles of divisions and allocate profits between trading divisions.

When full-cost transfer prices are used, the selling division assumes a profit center role in its external transactions and a cost center role in its internal transactions. The performance measures for the buying and selling divisions then are not directly comparable, since the profits on the internally transferred intermediate good are reported in the buying division. Market price transfers, in contrast, define the entire selling division as a profit center. In this case the buying and selling divisions are both profit centers, and their performance can be compared.

In a company following a vertical integration strategy, the issues of transfer pricing and divisional role definition are interrelated: the transfer pricing method defines the roles, and definitions of roles establish the appropriate transfer pricing method. Thus, an understanding of transfer pricing should contribute to a problem identified by Jensen (1983, 324):

> Consider, for example, the use of profit centers vs. cost centers as the basis for defining divisions of an organization. Although economists and accountants have analyzed both of these organizational devices, no satisfactory theory exists that will predict when an activity within an organization will be organized as a cost center and when as a profit center.

A satisfactory answer to this question must take account of the fact that in practice divisions are not simply cost centers or profit centers. As Vancil (1978, 141) noted, "the term 'profit center' is too broad, covering wide variations in the authority and autonomy of profit center managers." Many gradations between these two extremes are possible when goods are transferred between divisions: the transfer pricing method determines how much of a cost center and how much of a profit center the selling division is. Vancil suggested using the proportions of internal and external transactions as a way of developing a taxonomy of profit centers. Mandated internal transactions limit the autonomy of DGMs; the significance of this restriction increases with the proportion of total output sold internally. Thus transfer pricing is a central issue in developing a taxonomy of profit centers, since it affects both the autonomy of DGMs and how their performance is measured and evaluated.

Four Agency Configurations

In examining transfer pricing practices in the thirteen companies I studied, I found a variety of arrangements, which can be usefully described in terms of four agency configurations, each involving one principal and two agents. This typology is based on two characteristics: whether a vertical integration strategy exists, and whether the intermediate good is considered a business in its own right. In each configuration, the principal seeks to establish three elements of the agency contract: (1) the decision rights and responsibilities of the agents, (2) how their performance is measured and evaluated, and (3) the rewards and punishments for performance (Jensen 1983), so as to achieve both efficiency and fairness objectives.

In the first configuration, which I term *market agency*, internal transactions are not mandated, and DGMs can choose external transactions if they are more attractive. This configuration is diagrammed in Figure 1A. Two variations are possible: (1) The principal has no involvement in setting the transfer price, which is established by the agents themselves. This is by definition a market price, since it is established between divisions in a market context, because the principal exercises no hierarchical authority. (2) The principal establishes some guidelines on the transfer price, such as lowest price to an outside customer, but lets DGMs use this price to determine whether to trade with each other.[12] Market agency is used when there is no vertical integration strategy, and so internal transfers are small in amount.

The *hierarchical agency* configuration occurs when internal transactions are mandated and valued at full cost (Figure 1B). The selling division is considered as a distinct business only on external sales. In *conflict agency* (Figure 1C), internal sales are mandated and valued at a market price since the entire selling division is considered to be a distinct business.

Finally, *compromise agency* involves two prices (Figure 1D). The buying division pays full cost (or very occasionally variable cost) and the selling division receives a market price. The double counting of profits is eliminated at a higher level when the books are closed. Internal transactions may or may not be mandated.

Market Agency

In the market agency configuration, relationships between the principal and the agents and between the agents themselves resemble relationships in the market. The relationships between principal and agents bear similarities to that between investors and the firm; agent-

Figure 1
Four Agency Configurations for Transfer Pricing

A. Market Agency

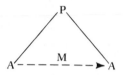

B. Hierarchical Agency

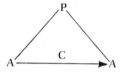

C. Conflict Agency

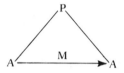

D. Compromise Agency

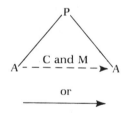

or

⟶

P = Principal
A = Agent
---➤ = Nonmandated transaction
⟶ = Mandated transaction
C = Full-cost transfer price
M = Market transfer price

agent relationships bear similarities to those between suppliers and customers. This configuration can be described more precisely in terms of Jensen's three components of agency.

DGMs have substantial decision rights and responsibilities. They control nearly all of the resources needed to manufacture and sell their products and have autonomy in choosing markets and suppliers, including the choice between internal and external ones. Performance is evaluated largely in terms of financial criteria such as profitability and return on investment, measured against budget objectives or the performance of competitors or other internal divisions. Rewards and punishments for DGMs are based on the performance of the division, not the company as a whole. On the continuum between cost and profit centers, divisions in this configuration are very much profit centers.

Market agency contracts are generally perceived as fair by the agents. Because performance evaluation is based on financial outcomes, DGMs must have the resources and decision-making responsibility necessary for achieving these outcomes. At the same time, rewards must be based on financial outcomes of their division alone, since DGMs have no responsibility for the outcomes of other divisions.

Market agency is often found in diversified companies where the interdependencies between divisions are very low; conglomerates and holding companies are extreme examples. The principal cannot have detailed knowledge and understanding of the many diverse businesses in which the firm is engaged. Operating responsibilities and most decisions are delegated to the agents. The principal invests money in a division on the basis of expectations about its potential, both in absolute terms and in relation to other divisions. The principal's role is similar to that of a banker or investor. As long as divisional interdependencies are low, the danger that DGMs will optimize their performance at the expense of the company overall—the classic concern in the transfer pricing literature—is small.

Among the companies I studied, Bacon & Bentham, Inc., an electronics firm, is a good example of the market agency configuration. A highly decentralized company, largely built upon acquisitions, Bacon & Bentham, had twenty-four divisions organized into six groups. DGMs were described by one manager as "kings in their little fiefdoms" and had substantial operating autonomy. The controller remarked, "At Bacon & Bentham we have attempted to become as decentralized as we safely can. We delegate as far down as possible while retaining control. The CEO has full control and delegates authority to officers and line management through the use of policy bulletins."

The primary performance measures were sales, profits, and average return on equity. A large portion of a DGM's salary was based on incentive compensation, tied to these performance measures, which could amount to 25 to 40 percent of base salary. Performance was evaluated against objectives described as "achievable but tough" and against the performance of the top one-third of the companies competing against the division. If a DGM failed to achieve these objectives two years in a row, he or she was taken out of that position and made a consultant or placed on special assignment in a staff position.

In market agency the principal does not require trading between his agents. Exchanges will occur only if the terms of the trade are mutually acceptable, as is the case in most external transactions.[13] If the transfer price, in conjunction with other terms such as warranties, deliveries, and service, is acceptable to both the selling and buying division, an internal transaction takes place. If not, external transactions will be chosen.

When the principal plays no part in determining transfer prices—as is most consistent with market agency—the selling division essentially faces the classic industrial marketing problem, which includes the issue of product pricing, while the buying division confronts the industrial purchasing problem, which includes the issue of vendor selection.[14] Corey (1976, 1978) identified three ways in which prices are set for industrial exchanges. Cost plus markup pricing is used when a buyer selects a vendor to manufacture a unique product. Market bidding is used for commodity products for which market prices exist. Competitive bidding, a method intermediate between the other two, is used for products that are differentiated according to vendor, but are neither unique nor commodity goods.

This transfer pricing policy will produce maximum corporate profits only when the intermediate good is traded in a perfectly competitive market. Many industrial goods, however, are sold in imperfectly competitive markets. Corporate profits may suffer if buying divisions source externally when spare capacity exists in the selling division, if divisions selling the final good forego business that would be profitable for the company as a whole, or if divisions do not coordinate product development efforts using proprietary technology that could yield competitive advantages.

Whether the choice between external and internal sources or customers is economically inefficient cannot always be easily determined in practice. For example, if internal prices for an intermediate good are higher than market prices, a decision to source internally may amount to subsidizing an inefficient production process; on the other hand, sourcing from the lower-priced outside supplier may carry the risk of missed deliveries or even vendor bankruptcy. In market agency the complex vendor selection and product pricing decisions are left to the DGMs. Individual decisions may or may not optimize divisional and corporate performance, but the principal feels that on balance this configuration will best meet his or her objectives. When technological and demand interdependencies between the divisions are small, any economic inefficiencies will be small as well.

At Bacon & Bentham the selection of external transactions over internal ones both contributed to and detracted from economic efficiency. Two divisions of the company manufactured semiconductors, but internal transactions for this product were small. Internal customers characteristically wanted to purchase small volumes of custom chips, but the manufacturing operations of the semiconductor divisions were not set up for the efficient manufacture of orders of this type and size. External suppliers who specialized in small custom runs, however, found this business attractive. Mandating internal purchases would have resulted in a less efficient use of resources, especially if the semiconductor divisions had to forego profitable external business. The semiconductors produced by the internal selling divisions and those required by internal buying divisions were in a strict sense different products.

While reliance on external suppliers may have led to the most efficient use of resources in the short run, it prevented the internal buying divisions from learning about some products of the semiconductor division that could have been designed into their products. These internal sales would have been as profitable as external sales for the semiconductor division. Thus closer cooperation might have led to the development of proprietary semiconductor chips that would have provided a competitive advantage and increased profitability.

Even when buying divisions were willing to purchase chips internally, they were not given any special consideration. As a manager in a selling division put it:

> We can be hard-nosed. We have a $100 million backlog and are not looking for business. We don't give many discounts, even on the outside. Right now

we have limited capacity and are asking for $70 million to increase our capacity. We tell internal customers that if they're willing to pay the price, we'll put them in the backlog and they can wait their turn.

I observed a similar pattern at Milton, Inc., another company that used market agency relationships. One semiconductor division made commodity chips, but the buying divisions needed primarily specialty products that could not be efficiently manufactured internally. Another semiconductor division that made very advanced products found internal customers too technologically unsophisticated to understand and make use of these chips. Because of this mismatch between internal needs and internal supplies, most semiconductors were sourced externally. DGMs in both selling and buying divisions recognized the advantages of external sources even when internal transactions were possible. The DGM of one semiconductor division had even recommended against pursuing an opportunity to replace Intel as a supplier to an internal customer. Accepting this business would have increased his volume by $4 to $6 million. But he argued that, "As long as Intel's product line is more comfortable and they will jump through hoops to give you good quality, it is in the corporation's interest to stay with them."

In practice, vendor selection decisions are significantly influenced by factors such as service and breadth of product line carried by the supplier. Milton Electronics managers saw that few rewards were given for maximizing internal business; rather, they were based almost exclusively on divisional financial performance. Thus both buyers and sellers had strong incentives to obtain the most favorable exchanges possible, which usually favored external transactions.

An irony of market agency is that there may be disincentives to internal transactions, even if they are favorably priced. The problem is that internal transactions occur within a hierarchy. A Bacon & Bentham manager explained the preference of buying divisions for external vendors rather graphically: "Sister divisions suck hind tit. I've seen it happen here."[15] A staff vice president at Milton presented the same view from the perspective of selling divisions: "If they sell inside, they are only doing what they are supposed to do. If they screw up, they get in trouble." And the group general manager in charge of the semiconductor divisions at Bacon & Bentham explained, "It is more difficult to work inside than externally. In the smallest impasse a guy can go up the line. Nobody wants to have his boss coming and telling him he's not cooperating. It is always difficult so you need a financial incentive or something else such as recognition for being a good corporate citizen."

Complaining to top management about problems with internal transactions is a double-edged sword.[16] Doing so draws the attention of the principal to the agent's operations, over which he or she has been given substantial decision-making autonomy. Frequent complaints that require the involvement of the principal may ultimately reduce the agent's autonomy, or raise questions about his or her ability to fulfill the contract. The so-called prisoner's dilemma applies: If neither DGM complains about a problem and they work it out between themselves, they can both avoid the potential negative effects of involvement by the principal. However, if either DGM complains, the other will appear to be the guilty party unless he also complains. Furthermore, there may be advantages in complaining first, especially if the principal accepts the DGM's argument and decides in his favor or if the other DGM does not complain. One way out of this dilemma is simply not to engage in internal transactions. Particularly when internal transactions are small in amount, their potential problems may outweigh any advantages.

The gravity of this problem depends on how strongly financial performance is emphasized and what mechanisms exist for negotiating settlements. The more favorable the terms (price, quality, service, etc.) one DGM can negotiate, the better his performance will be, at the expense of the other. As a manager at Milton stated: "In my experience sister divisions are more antagonistic to each other than they are to outsiders. Basically this is because of competition as to who is the best performer. There is the suspicion that other divisions are doing something to get more than their share."

This competition between profit centers, which also exists in interfirm transactions, increases with the importance of internal comparisons of divisional profitability. Comparisons with sister divisions may have consequences for both the DGM's short-term financial rewards and his or her longer-term career prospects. On interfirm transactions, advantages accruing from long-term relationships help to keep the competition over short-term results from becoming detrimental to longer-term performance. Similar incentives on intrafirm transactions exist only to the extent there is a mutual desire for a longer-term relationship, and the "prisoner's dilemma" constrains this desire.

If the principal feels that these problems are hurting corporate performance, he may decide to dictate the transfer price. Ordinarily some reference is made to the market when transfer prices are established by hierarchical authority. Common solutions are to use the lowest outside market price or the market price less some discount to reflect lower internal transactions costs (e.g., no credit risk, no marketing expenses, no accounts receivable).[17] The principal's objective is to establish a transfer price sufficiently favorable to induce the buying division to source internally. While this may solve some problems, such as external sourcing when internal supplies are available, it may create others, such as internal purchases of an inferior intermediate good that hurts the performance of the final good over the long term. Such effects are especially likely if the buying division general manager is under strong pressure to achieve short-term financial objectives, as is often the case in market agency.

When the principal sets the transfer price, the selling division general manager may raise the issue of fairness if he feels that the price is too low, especially if he is required to accept internal business, in which case his customer selection autonomy is violated as well. These restrictions in autonomy may cause DGMs to feel that they have insufficient authority for the performance measures on which they will be evaluated and rewarded. Conscious of these problems, Bacon & Bentham's top management determined there would be no corporate involvement in the sourcing and pricing decisions. As one manager put it, "Everybody has his own transfer pricing method, which depends on his management philosophy. If we interfere with the management of profit incentives, we have to reimburse them. Once we interfere with their day-to-day operations, they can complain to us." Such a policy reflects a view that problems resulting from perceived unfairness will lead to greater inefficiencies than will decisions that optimize divisional performance at the expense of corporate objectives.

The principal's exercise of hierarchical authority, which violates the contract of market agency, may create as many problems as it is intended to solve. A better approach may be to make internal transactions as similar to external ones as possible. For example, internal purchases are often made as bookkeeping entries at the end of the month, which prevents the buying division from withholding payment if it is dissatisfied with the exchange. It would be inconsistent to enable the buying division to withhold payment if the transfer price has been set below market because the selling division presumably need not incur accounts receivables expenses—but such a change would make the transaction more similar to an external purchase, and might be preferred by the buying division general manager.[18]

Managers in both buying and selling divisions at Bacon & Bentham admitted that better cooperation would increase internal sales in a way beneficial to all involved. They suggested that it might be useful for buyers to make an effort to educate sellers on their needs, and for sellers to let buyers know more about their products and their capabilities; in addition, they saw a need for closer coordination of new product development. Several managers suggested that these objectives could be achieved by assigning salesmen specifically to internal accounts. One semiconductor division had already taken this step when it found that internal divisions were buying its products from distributors rather than directly from it.

When market agency is used in principal-agent contracts, agent-agent relationships resemble those between firms engaged in marketplace transactions, but are complicated by the fact that they occur within a hierarchy. Either agent can appeal to the principal if he does not like the result of an internal transaction. Although such an appeal to hierarchical authority is easier than litigation, the recourse of contracting parties in the external market, it can impose costs by undermining the decision-making autonomy of the agents. Often the easiest way to resolve this tension is simply to forego internal transactions. No simple generalization can be made about the effects of such a decision on corporate performance.

Hierarchical Agency

In hierarchical agency relationships between the principal and the agents, and between the agents, are based on the authority hierarchy and task specialization in the organization. The principal can order the agents to take certain actions, in particular to trade with each other.

The restriction of agents' decision-making autonomy limits the extent to which their performance can be measured and evaluated solely on the basis of divisional financial outcomes. Hierarchical agency is a form of "team production," discussed by Alchian and Demsetz (1972). They noted that in this situation "it is impossible to determine each person's marginal productivity" (p. 779) and emphasized the need to measure productivity by observing the behavior of those supplying the individual inputs. Performance measurement and evaluation are more subjective than in market agency. Rewards are based on joint outcomes and compliance with the principal's directives rather than strictly on divisional financial results.

In hierarchical agency transfer prices are full cost, either actual or standard. Just as mandated internal transactions reinforce the hierarchical authority of the principal, full-cost transfers reinforce the distinctive organizational roles of the selling and buying divisions. The selling division functions as a cost center in mandated internal transactions, and performance is evaluated in terms of manufacturing efficiency, not profitability. Its role is identical to that of a manufacturing unit in the buying division. The buying division, in contrast, is evaluated as a profit center.

In external transactions, the selling division's role is that of a profit center, since it has more autonomy in selecting external customers and receives revenues from which costs can be subtracted to calculate profitability. The buying and selling divisions can be compared on their external sales. But since profits on internal transactions are all reported in the buying division, total financial results of the two divisions are not comparable. The more balanced the proportion of internal and external sales, the greater the difficulty faced by the principal in establishing an agency contract with the selling division general manager that is based on a combination of the cost and profit center roles.

Fairness in this configuration depends on the principal's ability to demonstrate an understanding of the agents' contribution beyond reported financial results, particularly that of the selling division general manager. It is also important that the selling DGM accept the cost center role of his division on internal transfers. If he gives priority to external customers as a way of maximizing the profitability of sales, for example, the performance of the buying division may be hurt without any impact on the performance measures of the selling division in either its cost center or its profit center role. In comparison with market agency, the principal needs to have more information and to be more actively involved in the activities of both divisions in order to determine if either one is optimizing its performance measures at the expense of the other.

Hierarchical agency is often found in vertically integrated companies in which a substantial percentage of the intermediate good is transferred internally. Because a vertical integration strategy typically requires substantial capital investment, such companies participate in a narrower range of businesses than those using market agency. For this reason and because the intermediate goods have a common raw material base, the principal is better able to understand each of the businesses in some detail. The large capital investment also requires mandated internal transactions to prevent divisions from optimizing their performance at the expense of the total company. For example, when demand for the intermediate good is high, the selling division could improve its profitability by increasing external sales rather than supplying internal customers, who must then be forced to pay especially high spot market prices for raw materials.

Among the companies I studied, Rousseau Corporation was one that used hierarchical agency. A highly vertically integrated chemical company whose end products were based on a few basic chemicals, Rousseau was located in a small town. Nearly all of its managers were chemists and chemical engineers who had been recruited right out of college and promoted within the company, and few outside managers were hired. These managers knew each other well and had an intimate understanding of the company's businesses and corporate strategy, which had been constant for many years.

Managers were evaluated on the basis of their overall contribution to the company, not just the profitability of their divisions. One manager explained, "They are measured on profit before taxes, but we evaluate them more on the basis of the quality of their effort. It is largely subjective judgment and includes a poll of their colleagues." The substantial interdivisional dependencies made it impossible to rely solely on measures of financial outcomes. Top management's subjective judgment was complemented by a poll of the DGM's colleagues, so that he would have less incentive to boost his own division's performance at the expense of others. Since all managers shared a common understanding of the company's technologies and businesses, DGMs perceived these evaluations to be fair. Bonuses were based on total corporate performance and an individual's performance appraisal, not on formulas based upon divisional results.

Interdependence between divisions is emphasized and nonfinancial measures of performance are most important when actual full cost is used as a transfer price. Actual full costs are calculated by dividing all fixed and variable expenses for a period (usually one month) by the number of units produced. The higher the volume, the lower the unit costs. And since all of the selling division's costs are charged to the units produced, the cost of a given number of units can vary from month to month as total divisional output fluctuates. Thus, if external or other internal sales are different from the previous month, the cost to the buying division for a fixed volume will also change. Costs to the buying division will depend both on manufacturing efficiencies and inefficiencies for which the selling division is responsible and on volume effects that may or may not be beyond the control of the selling division.

Aquinas Chemical Company, like Rousseau, was a highly vertically integrated company. Although a very sophisticated financial control system was in place, Aquinas used actual full-cost transfer prices. Top management even determined the plant from which buying divisions would obtain their product, for many products were made in more than one plant. In making these sourcing assignments, top management tried to minimize transportation costs and balance plant loadings for manufacturing efficiency. Trade-offs between these two objectives made the problem very complex. Although not all managers were happy with this method of transfer pricing, since costs of a product varied with the plant that produced it, there was little sentiment to change to a standard-cost or market price approach. The company's controller explained: "The alternatives, such as using market-based pricing or keeping track of who gets favorable and unfavorable variances, are worse than what we have. Financial information is important but it doesn't provide yes or no decisions for managers. We still pay them to run the business."

Because this transfer pricing method had a recognized impact on divisional financial results, subjective judgment played a large role in evaluating a DGM's performance. Bonuses for individual managers were based on company, divisional, and personal performance. In evaluating personal performance, the most heavily weighted of the three factors, an important consideration was actions that helped or hindered other divisions. When the principal establishes the criteria for measuring, evaluating, and rewarding performance, it is important to recognize the effect of decisions made by other divisions, or by the principal, that the agent cannot influence. The agent will not consider it fair to be held strictly responsible for outcomes that are affected by actions of others beyond his or her control. To base evaluation and rewards purely on unadjusted financial measures would be clearly perceived as unfair if actual-cost transfer prices are used.

The use of actual full-cost transfer prices also has potential inefficiencies. A common complaint is that the buying division will optimize its profits by producing at a volume lower than that which would optimize corporate profits.[19] This criticism assumes that the buying division general manager has the autonomy to decide on output levels for the final good and does so under a profit-maximizing objective. However, in hierarchical agency the principal can have substantial involvement in output level decisions. Furthermore, if profitability in the buying division is decreased by setting output levels of the intermediate good that maximize corporate profits, profit objectives can also be reduced. And, as has been noted, measures of financial outcomes are not the sole basis of performance evaluation and reward.

Another efficiency complaint raised against full-cost transfers is that the final good will be uncompetitively priced when the buying division adds a markup for overhead and profit to full costs. This problem is especially complicated with actual full-cost transfers, since the buying division does not know the total costs until the period is closed. If the final good is priced as a fixed markup on cost, its price will fluctuate as unit costs fluctuate on the intermediate good. The seriousness of this problem depends upon the extent to which simple cost-plus product pricing is used. In general, this is not a recommended practice.[20]

My field study found little evidence that managers were much concerned about the possible problems of suboptimal output in the buying division or uncompetitively priced final goods. When such concerns were expressed it was generally in relation to a system that used market-based prices for internal transfers; in this situation managers interviewed tended to call for the use of full cost.

Rousseau Corporation used standard full-cost transfer prices, although buying divisions were not charged for negative volume variances, which remained in the selling division. Managers expressed no concern about resource allocation inefficiencies, either on a short-term basis (as in the determination of output levels) or on a long-term basis (as in capital investment decisions). Transfer prices were considered irrelevant to investment decisions, since capacity addition decisions were based on special studies that looked at all stages of the production process. The numbers generated in these studies were not dependent upon transfer prices, and were not the sole basis of the decision in any case. One manager explained, "We don't have a hurdle rate that we pursue. Instead, we ask does it make strategic sense? A lot of economic studies are garbage anyway since they are sensitive to price and volume. We look at the strategic position of a business more than the numbers. This has worked for us." Rousseau's strong financial results over the last ten years suggest that the use of subjective judgment in making resource allocation decisions has not hurt the company's performance.

Because standard full costs were used for transfer prices, financial measures for Rousseau's buying divisions were not affected by the actions of other buying divisions and selling divisions. But this company put little emphasis on divisional results. One manager explained, "Our attitude is that we are not a conglomerate. We do better when we try to operate as a single unit, as a coordinated system. The corporate organization coordinates the global strategy for all products. This is a very difficult way to operate, but that's our mentality."

This attitude was so prevalent, and top management was so familiar with divisional operations, that managers felt confident they would be rewarded for making decisions that were in the best interests of the company as a whole. "Our objective is total corporate profits," one explained. "I can make a decision that costs my division money but if it makes the company money I'll be okay. It's an inherent philosophical and intellectual thing. We react to overall optimization." At Rousseau Corporation, hierarchical agency produced principal-agent relationships that were perceived as fair, resulted in agent-agent cooperation, and did not appear to have negative economic consequences.

At Locke Chemical Company, hierarchical agency was not nearly as well accepted by the agents. A shift from market-based transfer prices to standard full cost had been associated with a company reorganization that created a basic chemicals division. This new division was expected to centralize manufacturing expertise in running large-scale, capital-intensive operations on seven major intermediate chemicals that were the basis of nearly all of the company's end products. The reorganization was seen as a means of achieving "step-change" or nonincremental improvements in process technology that would significantly reduce manufacturing costs.

Difficulties arose as a result of disagreements about the decision rights of this new division and the methods by which its performance would be measured and evaluated. Conflict was much greater than at either Rousseau or Aquinas Chemicals, even though Locke made much greater efforts to allocate variances from standard costs to those responsible for them. In fact, these efforts at precise measurement and pinpointing of responsibility were to a large extent a result of the conflict.

Between 30 percent and 90 percent of the output of the seven building-block chemicals was transferred internally. The Basic Chemicals Division was given responsibility to sell what was left over to the external market after meeting internal requirements. Some managers in buying divisions felt they should not have been given this responsibility. Managers in the Basic Chemicals Division were disturbed that the word "marketing" was not in their charter. The department that performed this function was called the "commercial department."

Before the reorganization, all transfers had been on a market price basis, and all divisions were profit centers. Top management realized that if this policy were continued, the new Basic Chemicals Division would report a vast majority of the company's profits. This was thought to be undesirable since the company had positioned itself to investors as an end-product specialty chemical company, not a producer of basic chemicals. As a result it was decided to adopt a standard full-cost policy for the seven building-block chemicals. The decision was implemented hastily, in order to be able to prepare the next year's budget. The company's chief financial officer admitted, "When we were designing the new structure I'd have to say candidly that there was little attention given to how we would move products between the divisions. It was one of those restructurings done by a few people at a very senior level. The transfer pricing issue was overlooked." Basic Chemicals became the only Locke division that was not a pure profit center, but instead had both cost center and profit center roles.

On the day the Basic Chemicals Division was formed, its first DGM announced to his managers that he considered profitability a key measure of divisional performance. He was also known to believe that positive variances were good for motivational purposes. A very senior manager, he had more influence and status than many of the buying DGMs; as a result, he was able to keep cost information from them and avoid involving them or the corporate controller in setting standard costs.

A number of problems in agent-agent relationships arose. Buying division DGMs felt that performance measures of their divisions were distorted, which in some cases had cost them bonus money. They believed that standard costs were consciously set too high because the selling division general manager wanted to be able to show a positive variance—a measure formally equivalent to profit as the difference between revenues (standard costs) and costs (actual costs). When the actual costs of raw materials and utilities purchased by the Basic Chemicals Division, were greater than expected, the negative variances were shared among the buying divisions; positive variances on these inputs, however, were retained by the selling division as "profits."

Unlike Rousseau Corporation, Locke tried to hold buying divisions responsible for negative volume variances. To prevent them from requesting more product than they really needed as a way of ensuring that they got enough supplies, a "take or pay" provision required them to pay for what they requested even if they actually took less. In some cases, after such charges had been made, the selling division was able to find external buyers; in effect it was paid twice for the same product. To avoid such excess charges, buying divisions might be tempted to request less product than they expected to need. To discourage this practice, Locke required them to pay spot market prices for any amount greater than requested. Since spot prices were higher than standard full costs, Basic Chemicals earned a profit on these transactions too. It is no surprise that buying division general managers felt that they were in a "lose/lose situation."

Another subject of conflict was a surcharge included in the calculation of standard full costs, which was intended to cover start-up, obsolescence, marketing, administrative, and technical expenses. Buying divisions argued that this charge was inappropriate because Basic Chemicals did not incur marketing expenses on internal sales. They also felt they received less technical support than they were paying for.

The various rules for transfer pricing all had the effect of producing positive variances and profits in the Basic Chemicals Division, further confusing the nature of the hierarchical agency contract. While few complaints were made about poor resource allocation decisions, many managers in both divisions felt that the situation was unfair. Even though profit expectations for buying divisions reflected the standard costs used in transfer prices, DGMs' sense of what these intermediate goods "should" cost affected their perception of the fairness of the arrangement. And budgeted financial objectives did not account for the problems of allocating variances, the take-or-pay provision, or spot market price payments for demand in excess of projections.

Ironically, it was impossible to determine whether Locke's reorganization had achieved the one objective on which everybody agreed: significant cost reductions through process technology improvements. Soon after the Basic Chemicals Division was created, oil shortages drove up raw material prices sharply. Thus it became difficult to compare current and historical costs as a way of determining if significant cost reductions had been achieved.

Eventually Locke reorganized the problem away by dissolving the Basic Chemicals Division and returning to a policy of market price transfers. Its experience is a good example of how difficult it is to implement a purely financially oriented approach to performance measurement, evaluation, and reward when interdependencies are mandated and selling divisions must assume split roles. No matter how careful and precise the measures, there can always be disagreement about how accurately they measure the contributions of the separate divisions. To resolve fairness issues, one must incorporate subjective judgment into the agency relationship.

Conflict Agency

Conflict agency relationships attempt to overcome some of the difficulties associated with hierarchical agency by substituting market-based prices (including cost plus profit markup) for full cost as a transfer price.

In hierarchical agency the selling division functions as a cost center in its internal transactions. One problem with this arrangement is that in many organizations cost center managers have less prestige than profit center managers, who are responsible for the bottom line. And because the manufacturing unit in a division is under the authority of the DGM, there is also an implied subservience in the relation of the cost center to a profit center. Moreover, even if agents feel that their contributions are clear to the principal, they may be less sure that they are recognized by others in the organization who rely more upon financial information. If the principal should be replaced, records of financial performance could become the primary source of information for evaluating agents.[21]

In addition to these natural human concerns, which may or may not affect efficiency, critics of full-cost transfers argue that an insufficient markup for overhead and profit is often placed on the final good. These critics reason that since competitors purchase raw materials from external suppliers at market price, the division selling the final good can price lower as a way of increasing volume or obtaining the same volume with less work. In either case, profits to the company are less than they would be if the same percentage markup were placed on a higher cost base resulting from market price transfers of the intermediate good.

If market prices are used for mandated internal transfers, the selling division can be evaluated as a profit center. There may be adverse consequences for decision making, however. In effect the intermediate good is marked up twice—but competitors may be paying less than market price, for example, if they are vertically integrated and transfer on a cost basis. Kaplan (1982, 483) called this conflict between the performance evaluation and output level decision-making roles the "essence of the transfer-pricing conundrum."

A conflict agency configuration is used when the entire output of the selling division is regarded as a distinct business. Even though a substantial share of output may be devoted to internal sales, the proportion is often less than when full-cost transfers are used. Decision rights, criteria for performance measurement and evaluation, and the allocation of rewards and punishments are very similar to those of hierarchical agency. In particular, because of restrictions on the agents' decision-making autonomy, the principal's subjective judgment is important in measuring, evaluating, and rewarding performance.

When market-based transfer prices are used for mandated transactions, conflict is inevitable. Since both buying and selling divisions are being evaluated on the profitability of their total output, transfer prices significantly affect performance measures. Even when both agents feel that the principal recognizes their contributions, they may be concerned with other parties' judgments of reported figures. Competition between agents is likely, since each can calculate the percent of total corporate profits being earned by his division.

It is often very difficult to determine the "true market price" for a transaction, particularly for very large-volume transactions, products differentiated for internal use, and proprietary products manufactured only for internal use. Because external transactions cannot be substituted for internal ones, it is not possible to use the market to establish a price. Conflict arises as the DGMs attempt to determine the transfer price using whatever information they think is relevant.

Highly vertically integrated industries are usually oligopolistic. The selling division may be one of just a few producers of an intermediate good; there may be no external supplier with the available capacity to satisfy the buying division. There is then no way to determine what the market price would be if the transaction were an external one. To solve this problem, companies often attempt to obtain information on comparable external transactions, to find out about transfer prices used in other companies, and to estimate what volume discounts should be. The last issue is a never-ending source of dispute on large-volume internal transfers. Since the size of any discount can substantially affect divisional profitability, however, each DGM has an incentive to collect information that will support his or her case, and this information can be useful to top management in assessing the competitiveness of the selling division. Both DGMs will also have reason to collect information on prices of comparable external transactions, including those between external suppliers and customers, and on competitors' transfer prices. Of course, these prices will be regarded as a valid comparison only to the extent that they are for transactions similar in terms of volume, longevity of the relationship, quality, and so on. Establishing transaction comparability is very difficult.

For differentiated and proprietary products, the transfer pricing problem is especially complex. No equivalent external transactions exist. The company may attempt to get prices by obtaining outside bids. But if outside suppliers know they are only being used to obtain a price and have little chance of actually getting any business, they may quote especially high prices as a way of signaling that they are not interested in this business or in playing this game. If they do feel they have a chance, they may submit especially low bids as a way of getting a foot in the door, after which they plan to raise their prices.

An alternative approach to determining a market price is to calculate gross margins for similar products sold to external competitors and add these to the product costs for internal transfers. The buying division general manager is unlikely to accept this approach unless he has access to the selling division's costs and profit margins on external sales. This introduces an element of control into the selling division's operations.

The conflict inherent in mandated market-based transfers is useful in two ways: it generates information for the principal, and it prompts each agent to monitor the other for inefficiencies. In attempting to determine a "fair market price," the agents collect information on other transactions, which may be made available to the principal if they involve him in their dispute. This information can be used to assess the competitiveness of either division. Even if the principal is not involved in the conflict, the agents use this information as a way of monitoring each other. Buying division general managers watch the costs of the selling division, whose manager in turn monitors their pricing practices.

These monitoring roles are similar to the one identified by Zimmerman (1979) in his explanation of why cost allocations were used in spite of the theoretical objections to this procedure. But while he focused on the monitoring of the superior by the subordinate, in the transfer pricing situation it is the agents who monitor each other. This monitoring can occur in full-cost transfers as well, as demonstrated by the Locke Chemical Company example. Monitoring incentives are especially strong when both agents are in charge of profit centers, however, since their financial performance is then directly comparable.

The information and agent-agent monitoring produced by the conflict agency configuration are not without their costs. To ensure that the disadvantages do not outweigh the advantages, the principal must make certain that principal-agent relations are regarded as fair (although perceived unfairness in agent-agent relations is the cause of the conflict). The principal must also prevent the conflict from becoming destructive, as when the agents actually try to undermine each other. This can occur when transfer prices provide the substantive excuse for conducting an interpersonal dispute that involves emotional issues. Conflict can also get out of hand when either division is suffering performance problems, as when demand is down and competition is especially severe. In such a situation, a change in the transfer price is often sought as the easiest way to show performance improvements.

Agents' attitudes toward conflict influence its efficiency and fairness consequences. If they are uncomfortable with conflict, some of the positive effects of monitoring on efficiency may be lost. However, they can also use conflict as a means of optimizing divisional performance at the expense of total company performance. To keep conflict at the proper level, the principal must evaluate its effect when measuring and rewarding performance.

An example of conflict agency existed at Paine Chemical Company, which had a particular transfer involving one selling division, reporting to a group general manager, and two buying divisions, reporting to a different group general manager. These three divisions were very important to total company performance, and the recently elected president had previously run all three of them for a number of years and understood them well. The three DGMs had been placed in their jobs by the president in a reorganization he implemented soon after taking over the presidency. One of his objectives in the reorganization was to put younger, more aggressive managers in charge of the businesses, which had formerly been managed by older managers who were near retirement. These older managers were made group general managers, as a graceful way to remove them from having direct responsibility over these businesses. Transfer prices of market price less a 5 percent discount were set by the selling DGM.

Because the buying divisions were the two largest customers of the selling division, their general managers argued that they should receive volume discounts. The selling division general manager argued they should not, since outside customers did not receive volume discounts. The buying division general managers claimed that volume discounts *were* given, however.

It was difficult to resolve this issue, since external contracts had been written at various points in time, under different market conditions. Arguments about cost differentials were complex, particularly since both internal users took a product different from what was sold externally. The larger buying division took the product in a less finished form than was sold externally, which the DGM felt warranted a larger price reduction than he currently received.

The selling division general manager objected to the 5 percent discount, claiming that his marketing expenses were not this high. Because of these many complexities, the DGM with the largest internal purchases felt that no agreement could be reached using external prices as a basis for determining a transfer price. He advocated a cost plus markup approach based upon average gross margins for products sold externally to comparable markets.

This conflict had raged for more than two years, during which time many studies were made and memos written by both sides. The president was sent copies of many of these documents, which contained a wealth of information on external markets, prices to customers in these markets, prices received by competitors from other suppliers (obtained in some complex ways), cost data on the selling division, technical and marketing expenses in the selling division, and so forth.

The conflict escalated when the selling division announced a large price increase on both internal and external sales. The external market refused to accept most of this increase, however, and actual sales were made below list prices. Comparable reductions in transfer prices were not made, and the buying division general managers felt that their profits were understated as a result. This was especially troublesome to the large internal user, since that division was in an industry experiencing low profitability because of severe overcapacity.

Although all three DGMs were dissatisfied with the situation, none thought the president was evaluating and rewarding them unfairly. They all felt he recognized their contribution to the company, since his intimate familiarity with the businesses enabled him to evaluate performance in spite of reported financial results. The DGMs were less sure that others in the company were able to do this. Thus, in their quarterly presentations to the board of directors, the general managers of the buying divisions reported their results using both market price and full cost transfer prices. These managers were also concerned about the perceptions of corporate financial and planning staff. The DGM of the division with poor profitability was especially concerned because he felt that others in the company blamed his division for hurting total company performance. He also felt that low profits reported by his division hurt the morale of his managers. Finally, a certain amount of personal animosity existed between him and the selling division general manager, which was exacerbated by the selling DGM's authority to set transfer prices unilaterally.

All the time of my study, Paine had recently hired a new controller, who was planning to take the transfer pricing decision away from the DGMs. He said, "We will get guys to agree on a pricing system and then we will take it away from them. I would be very nervous letting division general managers calculate price. And whatever we do, not everybody is going to be happy. We're going to keep score. We'll get senior management to approve this. Then the division general managers can get as mad at us as they want." It seemd unlikely, however, that the controller would get this authority. The president said, "I'm not going to step into this thing. They're negotiating about what the true market price ought to be. It is best to let the division general managers decide. I don't think controllers have the knowledge of the market place to set prices. The customer regulates the selling price. The vice president of marketing is in a better position to adjudicate, but he's too smart to get involved in this."

The president was willing to tolerate the amount of time the DGMs spent on this conflict and did not seem to fear that it would be harmful to company performance, though the three divisions represented a substantial portion of total company assets and sales. He was recognized as a manager comfortable with conflict, but also as a strong CEO who was not afraid to step into issues that needed resolution. During the time of this conflict, he had been emphasizing increased DGM responsibility for divisional performance and had increased their decision-making autonomy. Too much involvement in this dispute would have been inconsistent with his desire to give younger managers experience in running profit centers. Conflict agency proved a good solution. The interdivisional conflicts caused the DGMs to monitor each other and provided the president with detailed information on these businesses.

Compromise Agency

Compromise agency seeks to resolve some of the problems between agents that may be hurting company performance. This agency form, which is much less common than the other three, involves two transfer prices. The selling division receives a market price (perhaps with some adjustments) and the buying division pays full cost (or perhaps variable cost in a very limited number of cases). The double counting of profits is taken as a higher-level elimination when the books are closed. Internal transactions may or may not be mandated.

Compromise agency can be used for all internal transfers (as is typically the case when the goal is to overcome the problems of market agency) or for specific products only (as when compromise agency replaces conflict agency). Although it would seem to offer something to everybody, this form has its own efficiency and fairness problems. It cannot be used for all internal transfers when they are large in amount, since the double counting of profits would make the whole much less than the sum of the parts. This would obscure performance measures and lead to profitability figures that would seem artificial to managers.

As discussed earlier, market agency can create disincentives to trade internally, even if such transactions would contribute to corporate performance. Both Bacon & Bentham and Milton attempted to deal with this problem by using compromise agency for all transactions. At Bacon & Bentham, where some internal transactions were mandated, compromise agency compensated the buying divisions for this restriction in their sourcing autonomy by giving them the intermediate good at lower than market price. At Milton internal transactions were not mandated, but it was hoped that the low prices of the intermediate goods would be a sufficient incentive for buying divisions to source internally.

The implementation of compromise agency at Bacon & Bentham had been precipitated by the acquisition of a small computer company whose product was new and still had technical problems. It was losing money when acquired. Bacon & Bentham's Controls Division has been sourcing computers for its products from a competitor of the new Computer Division and continued to do so after the acquisition. The chairman of the company was concerned about the impact on the Computer Division if its customers found out that the Controls Division preferred competitors' products. He also wanted to increase the volume of the Computer Division in order to reduce costs. In addition, he felt that internal customers could help identify and solve technical problems. He implemented a "dual pricing" policy that involved two transfer prices—cost to the buying division and market price to the selling division.[22] The chairman determined the market price for these internal transfers.

The Controls Division was unhappy with this arrangement. Although lower prices might enable it to price its products more competitively, managers did not feel that advantage justified the risk of using an unknown product without a reputation for quality and reliability. After several years the dual pricing policy was dropped, except for products purchased as capital assets. This change was prompted by a higher than expected elimination at the corporate level one year—a danger inherent in this agency form. When either division is having difficulty meeting its profit objectives, one solution is to increase internal sales or internal purchases. This is especially likely when both divisions are having financial difficulties. Buying divisions may choose to use products that are available internally at below-market prices, even if they are not the best for their needs. Since they are only paying full cost they have little incentive to bargain vigorously over the market price portion of the transfer. The monitoring advantages in conflict agency are largely lost. For similar reasons selling divisions will want to increase their internal sales.

When internal transfers exceed the expected level, there will be a higher than expected elimination of the double-counted profits. At Bacon & Bentham, this greater than expected elimination occurred when both divisions were suffering poor performance as a result of a general recession—that is, when the company could least afford it. Company profits fell more than anticipated.

In discussing the return to market agency, the controller explained, "there was too much flexibility. We've matured and outgrown this now that we know how to transfer products inside and the benefits of doing so." The transfers between the Computer and Controls divisions persisted, for Controls' products were now designed to include the company's computer, and switching to another supplier would have been difficult.

Milton also used a dual pricing scheme for several years, but then returned to market agency for some of the same reasons as had Bacon & Bentham. As one manager explained, "The bookkeeping system didn't have the ability to handle it. It didn't work out too well since it was difficult to administer. But it did get more transfers going so it was the right move at the right time. Dual pricing sort of died of its own complexity and conflict. There were some situations where divisions could get something internally that didn't exactly fit their needs but went ahead and did it since cost was so much less than market price." While all managers agreed that dual pricing had been complex and subject to a number of problems, not all agreed that it had had any positive long-term consequences.

Milton experienced another problem that can emerge with compromise agency. While it is assumed that market price is greater than full cost, and thus the two prices provide the right incentives for both divisions, this is not always the case. The company had priced its externally sold semiconductors on the basis of average cost of production over the entire product life cycle. Because of significant learning curve effects, average costs are less than costs at the beginning of the product life cycle. In the early life of the product market, market price is actually less than full cost. There would have been no incentive to source semiconductors internally had the company not made an exception to the dual pricing policy.

At Hobbes Instrument Company, where conflict agency was prevalent, compromise agency solved a problem that had emerged with a battery that was used in several products and sold in the replacement market through the Parts Division. As a result of a complex set of technological and market changes, the Parts Division felt that it was losing market share in the replacement market because it was expected to get a certain gross profit margin on top of the market price at which it acquired the battery. A dual pricing policy (the term used at

Hobbes Instrument Company) was implemented so that the Parts Division could get its customary margin while pricing more competitively. Both efficiency and fairness objectives were met, since everyone was satisfied with this arrangement. However, the battery was the only product in the company being transferred on this basis.

In some circumstances transfer prices seem to affect the price of the final product, its profitability, and its market share—and in some cases they do not. If prices of the final good are determined by the market, the transfer price will affect profitability. If products are priced through markups on cost, which of course depends on transfer prices, the division selling the final good may lose market share if it attempts to get its customary margin while competitors are willing to accept a lower profit or have lower costs.

This begs the question of why the division expects to get its customary margin. If the goal is simply to meet profit objectives, the principal could lower these objectives so that the final good could be more competitively priced. The information the principal needs to implement a dual pricing policy is the same information needed to lower profit objectives. It is unclear why the former course would be preferred to the latter.

Some Remaining Questions

The transfer pricing problem illustrates the kind of empirical issue that needs to be addressed in a theory of agency extended to two agents. On the basis of an extensive field research project, four basic transfer pricing policies were identified, each associated with an agency configuration with distinctive decision rights and responsibilities, criteria for measuring and evaluating performance, and rules for allocating rewards and punishments. In each case the critical issues are whether the firm has an explicit strategy of vertical integration and whether the selling division is considered as a business in its own right for both internal and external sales. All four configurations present efficiency and fairness problems that must be actively managed.

A number of questions remain open to further research. Answers to these questions would increase our understanding of each of the agency forms as well as test the validity of this typology. If this typology proves useful, it could be applied to other more general problems, such as how resources are distributed in the firm (organizational design), whether agents are charged for resources not under their direct authority, and what cost allocation methods are used when they are charged. These questions were at the heart of Vancil's (1978) decentralization study.

The following questions strike me as particularly interesting and relevant:

1. What is the relationship between transfer pricing and final product pricing in each configuration?
2. What is the relationship between transfer pricing and objective setting?
3. When a strategy of vertical integration exists, is there a relationship between amount of the intermediate good transferred internally and the transfer pricing method used?
4. Have any companies used dual pricing for all internal transfers for a number of years, especially when the amount of internal transfers is high?
5. In what situations for each configuration will efficiency problems be greatest?
6. In what situations for each configuration will fairness problems be greatest?
7. How do principals balance efficiency and fairness objectives?

References

Abdel-khalik, A. Rashad, and Edward J. Lusk. 1974. "Transfer Pricing: A Synthesis." *Accounting Review* 49 (January): 8–23.

Alchian, Armen A., and Harold Demsetz. 1972. "Production, Information Costs, and Economic Organization." *American Economic Review* 62 (5): 777–95.

Baiman, Stanley. 1982. "Agency Research in Managerial Accounting: A Survey." *Journal of Accounting Literature* 1:154–213.

Carlton, Dennis W. 1979. "Vertical Integration in Competitive Markets Under Uncertainty." *Journal of Industrial Economics* 27 (3): 189–209.

Chandler, Alfred D., Jr. 1962. *Strategy and Structure: Chapters in the History of the Industrial Enterprise.* Cambridge: M.I.T. Press.

Christenson, Charles. 1976. "Proposals for a Program of Empirical Research into the Properties of Triangles." *Decision Sciences* 7 (October): 631–48.

Corey, E. Raymond, 1976. *Industrial Marketing: Cases and Concepts,* 2nd ed. Englewood Cliffs, N.J.: Prentice-Hall.

———. 1978. *Procurement Management: Strategy, Organization, and Decision-Making.* Boston: CBI Publishing Company.

Fama, Eugene F., and Michael C. Jensen. 1983a. "Separation of Ownership and Control." *Journal of Law & Economics* 26 (June): 301–25.

———. 1983b. "Agency Problems and Residual Claims." *Journal of Law and Economics* 26 (June): 327–49.

————. 1984. "Organizational Forms and Investment Decisions." Working Paper No. MERC 84-02, Graduate School of Management, University of Rochester.

Hirshleifer, Jack. 1956. "On the Economics of Transfer Pricing." *Journal of Business* 29 (July): 172–84.

Jensen, Michael C. 1983. "Organization Theory and Methodology." *Accounting Review* 58 (April): 319–39.

Jensen, Michael C., and William H. Meckling. 1976. "Theory of the Firm: Managerial Behavior, Agency Costs and Ownership Structure." *Journal of Financial Economics* 3:305–60.

Kaplan, Robert S. 1982. *Advanced Management Accounting.* Englewood Cliffs, N.J.: Prentice-Hall.

Mautz, R. K. 1968. *Financial Reporting by Diversified Companies.* New York: Financial Executives Research Foundation.

Oxenfeldt, Alfred R. 1975. *Pricing Strategies.* New York: AMACOM.

Porter, Michael E. 1980. *Competitive Strategy: Techniques for Analyzing Industries and Competitors.* New York: Free Press.

Reece, James S., and William R. Cool. 1978. "Measuring Investment Center Performance," *Harvard Business Review* 56 (May-June): 28–49.

Tang, Robert Y. W. 1979. *Transfer Pricing Practices in the United States and Japan.* New York: Praeger Publishers.

Vancil, Richard F. 1978. *Decentralization: Managerial Ambiguity by Design.* Homewood, Ill.: Dow Jones-Irwin.

Verlage, H. C. 1975. *Transfer Pricing for Multinational Enterprises.* Westmead, Farnborough, Hampshire, England: Gower Publishing Co.

Webster, Frederick E., Jr. 1979. *Industrial Marketing Strategy.* New York: John Wiley & Sons.

Zimmerman, Jerold L. 1979. "The Costs and Benefits of Cost Allocations." *Accounting Review* 54 (July): 504–21.

Chapter 8
Agency as Control

Harrison C. White

Agency is an ancient device for getting business done, which remains fresh and in common use. It is intensely social in its mechanism, since it gets one person to do something for another vis-à-vis a third person, but only with heavy reliance on the lay of the social landscape. Opportunism and flexibility, in both the short and the long term, are the key to agency's perennial robustness.

Control remains the purpose of agency, as I hope to show by presenting a spectrum of examples from a variety of settings and periods. I shall pay particular attention to examples from industry, finance, and business in general. As a sociologist I have had an exciting time studying developments and new directions in clinical and case research among colleagues at the Business School, for they appear to have some resonance with classical sociology as well as recent comparative work on formal organization. But some things that they take for granted I find puzzling and interesting. As an outsider I feel more comfortable beginning naively with some definitions and parsing of terms.

"There are two ways of getting the work of distribution of one's products attended to: one is by means of agents, and the other is through sale to independent dealers." This opening sentence from Nathan Isaacs's (1924–25) *Harvard Business Review* article "On Agents and 'Agencies' " opens up some of the difficult general issues of control and agency in organization. Neither agents nor dealers are perfectly satisfactory as distributors, Isaac notes. "The seller becomes involved by the law of warranty in a legal relation with the purchaser when he sells through an agent. . . . On the other hand, in selling to a dealer, one loses control over resale prices and limits his power of control over sales policies and concurrent activities, such as the handling of competing lines." Tactical and strategic trade-offs are apparent, and the rich texture of Isaacs's accounts suggests the wide variety of agency ties as well as the broad range of structural context. He pours scorn on the readiness of the law to impose sharp antitheses on what is really a spectrum of relations of agency. "The manufacturer or wholesaler may find it advisable to lend a hand in financing the ultimate consumer of his product by organizing such a banking institution as the General Motors Acceptance Corporation or making some arrangement with existing banks so that the flow of his product will not be checked by the limited power of the dealers to extend credit to consumers" (p. 267). Isaacs would agree that agency as control is the central issue.

But agency is not just a matter of merchant networks; agency permeates the running of large corporations as well. Richard F. Vancil (1983, 1) has observed that a key feature of large, decentralized business corporations in this country is that "the group of managers in each firm is self-selected and self-perpetuating." The sociologist is immediately alerted to possible analogues to kinship systems, to established churches, and more directly to guild systems and their modern variant, professions.

Writing on "Agency" in the 1930 edition of the *Encyclopedia of the Social Sciences*, the institutionalist lawyer Karl Llewellyn points out that agency "was once a, if not the, major way of organizing a mercantile enterprise. . . . It still remains the major building material, even in the corporate structure." He goes on in what I shall argue is a highly prescient way: "Finally with growing specialization, agency takes on another aspect . . . the specialized purveyor . . . moves largely out of the control of his principal, becomes an independent unit and may gather sufficient financial power to finance and even control his scattered 'principals' (so the textile factors and import bankers). . . . In all such cases of independence of the 'agent' the tendency is strong for the one-time agency to be swallowed up in contract, as between two independent dealers." Llewellyn goes further to cast agency in the most general terms: "every member in being hired, fired, or promoted is for the moment an outsider with reference to the unit, and deals as an outsider with some representative."

Although economists may speak of "the agency problem," agency is in fact a solution, a neat kind of social plumbing. The problem is the ancient and ineluctable one of how to attain and maintain control in order to carry out definite, yet varying, purposes.

The great thing about agency is its flexible and intermediate scope as social plumbing. Agency is intermediate between formal organization or hierarchy, on the one hand, and market, on the other. Hierarchy tries to insist on a whole planned structure consisting of chains of ties overseeing all particular actions; market tries to ignore any further connections beyond a single-step transaction at the market interface. But agency has some depth of tie beyond the immediate principal-agent transaction—for example, control of resale price as noted by Isaacs—without at all implying a whole architecture of ties.

Control means assuring that the principal's actions and work get done among and by some people. Formulation and implementation *both* are required in effective control; that's the rub. Or on a bigger scale the two faces of control can be described as strategic and operational. This combination is what makes actual control in real time, tangible control, so hard to achieve. Hierarchy can at least outline how to insist on operational control, but those organization charts get in the way of the attentiveness and flexibility needed to keep strategy alive, relevant. On the other side, fleeting contacts with a series of partners in an ideal market is an insufficient basis for operational consistency of control, but can be an effective context for strategizing.[1]

Agency is more than a tie: it is a context for ties that cast shadows of commitment. First consider the variable nature of a tie used toward a practical end. At one extreme is the relation of *shaliach*, the Old Testament prototype for plenipotentiary tie. The *shaliach* was sent "not only 'in the name' but 'in the person' of his principal, so that the envoy's action unalterably committed the principal . . . in the presence of his principal the *shaliach* has no function and virtually no existence as such" (Dix 1946, 228, 230). At the other extreme is the minimal tie of mutual acknowledgment of civil existence needed for relations in a market. Somewhere in the middle of what can be seen as a whole scale would come the agency tie of our times, as Llewellyn laid it out.[2] It is in the middle in many ways simultaneously: the length of time continued, the degree of transitivity, and so on. Moving toward *shaliach*, we would encounter the employee tie; an employee has less say than an agent in the content of action carried out and receives a more fixed reward (see "Agency and Compensation" below). Toward market would be subcontracting and "putting out," as discussed in the section "Small-Time Control."

Decentralization and Procurement

Let me introduce immediately two prototypes from modern business practice that exemplify management recognition of the advantages of agency for control. The first example is the increasing use of profit centers as a form of management decentralization, which represents the introduction of agency relations within a formal corporate hierarchy. I need only quote from a recent survey by Vancil (1979, 129–31):

> The definition of the business responsibility of a profit center manager . . . is his mandate to act as an agent of change. The scope of his charter defines the arena within which he is to act more or less autonomously in adapting his products to meet the current and future needs of his customers. . . . Dynamically, the life of a profit center manager in a decentralized firm is . . . in two separate tempos. . . . One tempo beats to the rhythm of the corporate evolution of leadership, strategy, and structure. . . . A second important dynamic . . . is the current operating performance of each profit center. From one year to the next . . . a particular profit center manager's autonomy may change significantly.

Although effective, the intrusion into corporate structure of an agency mechanism sits uncomfortably: "The ambiguous role of a profit center manager is rarely acknowledged as such in the parlance of business executives" (p. 61). Attending to two conflicting faces of control, strategic and operational, is difficult. Agency introduced into the formal structure helps give flexibility to ease the difficulty. Definiteness and predictability and thus operational control are essential to gaining scope for the action, yet they limit the responsiveness and flexibility of control, the strategic aspect. The tension and difficulty are reflected in the intense ambivalence of managers in acknowledging just how they are introducing agency through the decentralized profit centers.

My second prototype from current American business practice runs the other direction: pulling agency relations into apparently impersonal market situations. In *Procurement Management: Strategy, Organization, and Decision Making,* E. Raymond Corey vividly illustrates the extraordinary intrusions of buyer firms into supposedly distinct producer firms on the other side of markets. Chevrolet is an extreme case but not unique in its insistence that the books and factories of its suppliers be open both to its engineers, to help with development and quality control, and to its accountants, to verify costing figures used to justify prices. Procurement costs typically run about half of a manufacturing company's final sales, so it is no wonder that such long-term, multistep, and intense agency relations are intruded into market sites of procurement. Strategic as well as operational control is involved. "A critical dimension of sourcing strategy is the *composition* of the vendor complex," notes Corey (1978, 34). The most basic strategic aspect is the scope of products and product lines to be covered in the procurement relation. Critical to these strategic aspects is "the nature of the supplier-customer interface. Considerable technical development work and engineering interchange would argue for one or two suppliers at the most. Such relationships require enormous amounts of time and energy, security control, and individuals on both sides who relate well to each other" (p. 35).

Several implications can be drawn from these two initial examples. First, control does not fit well within neat boundaries. Moreover, control is not easy to achieve within a fixed layout of positions in an organizational machine. The very concept that plays so crucial a role in exerting pressure for control, namely profit, is necessarily somewhat elusive. "Profit" should be seen as a running target for a shifting set of actors, rather than as a tidy level to which an identified pitcher is filled.

In the subsequent sections I shall start with historical examples, and there certainly is no shortage of them here either. Both the introduction of agency into formal structure and its use to "thicken" market relations can be traced in de Roover's exposition of *The Rise and Decline of the Medici Bank 1397–1494*. "Major or strategic decisions, such as the establishment of a new branch or the renewal of a partnership contract," he notes, "were always made in consultation with the general manager, who was very powerful, although he had only a minor share in capital and profits. . . . One of the general manager's main tasks was the supervision of the branch managers in order to prevent their making undue commitments or unwise investments" (de Roover 1966, 76). Time and again, the Medicis would reach into an existing local banking arrangement and by use of partnerships achieve overlapping control of financial business in a new area of Europe. The senior Medicis used many relatives in setting up branches, but they were, after some early experiences, careful about operational control: each relative was set up on a decentralized basis with recompense dependent upon net outcomes.

Control must be both flexibly strategic and reliably operational, and both on the same turf. This turf itself is better seen as part of existing networks of formal and informal relations: just that part which needs to be brought into focus at a given time. Control must be crafted continually out of what are residuals as seen by the bulk of persons involved: *their* central cognitive and emotional investments are put into keeping their social acts together, into keeping going a show not apparently concerned with the strategy and change that are crucial to the controller. The awesome social pressure from which control is bled off at the margin comes and must come from the self-selected, self-interested, self-directed "natural" actions and emotions of the actors, constrained, to be sure, by corporate cultures and in more tangible ways (for an elegant case study, see Crozier and Thoenig 1976). It follows that in controlling, the controllers themselves necessarily also are exposed to the risk of being controlled, and this is another motive for relying more on agency relations in larger, rigid, impersonal structures.[3]

In all of the examples in this section, the quality of particular ties lies in between *shaliach* and arm's-length transactor. It is time to look at how such agency ties fit with others, to examine the differentials attributable to agency relations. What impacts do they have? Let us focus on the general problem of compensation, found in agency, bureaucracy, and market contexts alike.

Agency and Compensations

Agency as control is tied to compensation in at least three different manners. The first is a causal relation: compensation helps define the agency relation, much more than the reverse. Compensation's conventional motivational role (giving the agent incentives to act in the principal's interest) is less important, I think, than its role in informing agents of what their responsibility is and how it changes. In the Medici Bank account, as in Vancil's modern survey, there are many indications that agents' actual compensation is not nearly as variable with outcome as the scheme would suggest *ex ante;* yet great care was given to reshaping continually these terms of compensation. On the other hand, agents also used great care in interpreting them. Compensation schemes are ways of structuring the elusive and changing nature of the agency situation.

Performance-related compensation for managers may be primarily a vehicle for defining what it is they are to do. The extent of such flexible compensation can become an accurate gauge of the extent to which agency has been intruded into the formal organization. But if the bonus scheme or other form of incentive compensation is mechanical, conveying little about the *kind* of performance to be elicited, the scheme does not signal agency relations. When the full array of monetary and nonmonetary rewards projected to managers is considered, some companies that offer "straight salary" may reflect a more contingent, agency-designing atmosphere.

This first connection between compensation and agency has to do with bringing agency into the formal organization, as in the example of decentralized profit centers. The second connection brings agency into public markets or arenas, as in the procurement management example. It also reverses the normal expectation of the direction in which the cash component of compensation should flow.

Liturgy is the original Greek term for an ingenious form of taxation. If a city-state wanted to mount a cycle of drama, it would do so by awarding a liturgy to some wealthy citizen, who would pay for and activate the traditional and expensive production arrangements, his recompense being the public honor of the liturgy. Athletic games were organized in the same way, and still other examples can be found in Finley's *Ancient Economy*. This is an early example of achieving control for a definite purpose by assigning agency relations to actors prominent in the public arena. In effect, liturgy was a form of procurement management. In the modern business world similar *pro bono* agency relations are used for getting many tasks performed, not least trade association coordination and investigations. And, of course, modern governments are adept at reaching into markets to pull out prominent business leaders for liturgies. Liturgy is a reverse or dual form of agency. It would be interesting to explore thoroughly whether the reversal yields efficiency.[4] In the last section of the paper, I return to agency reversals in more general form.

As a third illustration of the relation between agency and compensation, consider the question of appointments to corporate boards of directors. The firm's officers, as one authority put it, "are agents not of the shareholders but of the board, while the board itself is conceived of not as an agent of the shareholders but as an independent institution. . . . Any study of corporate structure must therefore consider two very different interfaces: that between the shareholders and the managerial organs taken together, and that between the managerial organs themselves" (Eisenberg 1976, 2–3). It is the latter interface that is considered here.[5]

Such director appointments are excellent examples of creating ties of agency in my sense. Appointment often is seen as an important form of compensation in itself, and one that is contingent upon performance in many ways fitting into control plans of the appointing authorities. These appointments can be inside officers, financial world figures, or confreres from the same industry. (The three types will be discussed in the next section.) In the United States some of these kinds of director appointments are in possible conflict with business laws. Analytic treatment is fuller and less cramped for other economies.

One extensive study of the Canadian director interlock situation gave attention to both financial and industry competitor effects (Berkowitz et al. 1978–79; Carrington 1981). A new study of precision and scope has recently appeared on the German and Austrian economies (Ziegler 1982; see Chandler and Daems 1980, 90–92, for the special role of banks). The main finding of the Berkowitz group is that director interlock patterns can be interpreted in reciprocal control terms only after the analyst has collapsed together into a single entity and board each cluster of firms that are heavily connected through ownership— within the cluster, directors are used in all kinds of erratic and cosmetic ways. Ziegler (1982) finds that high intraindustry concentration is consistently associated with *lower* profit margins, and hence concludes that director interlocks are not used to concert behavior of big producers within a market (pp. 47, 55); but joint directorships and other cooptive devices become more likely with increasing severity of constraints from monopoly and high concentration in *supplying* or in *consuming* industry markets (pp. 114, 139–40). The direction of cause and effect is another matter: there was *no* indication of increased profits following the higher density of cooptive ties. Both these foreign studies suggest that U.S. results will be similar despite differences in antitrust statutes.

The Berkowitz and Ziegler studies imply that both operational control and strategic control purposes are served by these agency-type interventions, which simultaneously operate inside the boundaries of big formal organizations and across the inner workings of the markets that complete the economic structure. Detailed insider studies have also examined the meaning of these directorships to particular individuals and the business culture they contribute to and reflect; such explorations are necessary to validate the inferences drawn from large-scale statistical studies. In particular, Paul Hirsch (1982) has found, on the basis of intensive interviewing across a spectrum of *Fortune* 500 boards, that directors have little sense of representing any organization in their role as board members. Rather the membership is part of one's *own* job description, one's process of advancing in reputation and contacts. "Absence of variance reveals a widely shared normative structure of appropriate behavior and forms of control. As

CEOs themselves, outside directors are part of a self-regulating collectivity which knows and plays by widely understood rules of the game" (p. 12). Directorships are compensation in, and mechanisms of, flexible control by agency within a circumscribed arena, which, however, crosscuts both organizations and markets.

In contingent compensation, I argue, it is the contingency that reflects control through agency, while the regularized aspect of compensation mirrors the formal organization. Both aspects are oriented to the "bottom line" as a control goal, but the interpretation of that magic phrase differs. It is time to look more closely at just how agency can be imbedded in market or organization and the multiple kinds of audience for and ties among those in agency relations.

Agency Embedded in Constituencies: Multiplex Networks

The matter of whom one is compared to—which other managers and with what similarities in constraint and mission—can by itself do much to structure one's efforts, as shown in the previous section. (Bower 1970, 261, makes a similar point.) More generally, assigned targets of comparison shape your sense of the identity and nature of the agency relationship, which always encompasses more than one tie and more than one short stretch of time. These comparisons, built into contingent compensation, do much to mesh the flexible agency relation into the formal organization. Comparisons outside the firm are also important.

Let me continue to focus on executive compensation schemes in order to keep discussion tangible. A 1982 *Fortune* article noted that, "In a totally rational world, top executives would get paid handsomely for first-class performance, and would lose out when they flopped. But to an extraordinary extent, those who flop still get paid handsomely" (Loomis 1982, 42). In other words, the external world, especially the financial world, presumably expects hard-nosed payment by results, and is puzzled that this outcome is not achieved. The article later remarks that recent "squishiness" introduced by several major companies "tips the truth about bonuses: they are much less a reward for performance these days than an institutionalized variety of salary" (p. 46). Compensation schemes for profit center managers must recognize another constituency as well. Large companies incorporate dozens of sequential layers of ranks, each to be paid more than the next below. When agency relations are embedded within this giant managerial society, the recognition of profit performance must be tempered by articulation into the hierarchical scheme.

For just these first two constituencies, Wall Street and employees of the firm, the best analytic treatment still is a monograph by Oliver E. Williamson (1970), who contrasts hierarchical principles for pay scales with performance-related pay. He assesses the extent to which outside capital markets can influence contingent compensation schemes. The most extensive empirical treatment I know of this same contrast is the cogent monograph by Llewellyn (1968) derived from 10-K reports on total compensation of top executives, which the Securities and Exchange Commission requires of all publicly held corporations. His main finding is that although bonus and other performance-contingent payments represent a substantial part of total compensation, their variation is determined far more by the general state of the economy than by variations in corporate performance.

A third, and very significant, constituency for the contingent compensation accorded executives resides in what I construe as agency relations between firms. As the *Fortune* piece observed, companies look outside their own boundaries: "No major oil company would today pay that much because no other major oil company does. Compensation committees spend enormous amounts of time checking what peer companies pay, so that the committees can satisfy themselves they are not getting grossly out of line" (Loomis 1982, 45). In addition to satisfying the organization's own ranks and outside financial analysts, that is, compensation structures must be devised in light of standards set by other corporations perceived as comparable, in the same industry.

Consider a striking recent case of compensation change, detailed in a Harvard Business School case study of Connecticut General Corporation (1982). An incoming chief executive officer was paid $200,000 in 1976; by 1981 the same man was being paid a total of $950,000, over half in contingent compensation features. The company's size, in sales volume and employees, did not increase more than 400 percent during these five years, so one could not argue that the increased compensation was warranted by sheer growth in responsibility. One pressure for higher compensation came from the internal organization constituency: the CEO, at rank 32, was conceded a certain earnings multiple over his immediate subordinates in rank 30 (31 was not assigned), and so on down the line, so that all had a keen interest in increases for the CEO! The constituency of financial analysts, looking at the doubling of earnings and dividends over this era, may have felt an urge to cheer large bonus awards. But whatever subtle long-term evolutionary effects financial market judgments may have, none of the many studies has shown much sign of a direct short-run causal connection.

Indeed, the case study makes it clear that performance-based compensation increased so strikingly because of the third constituency, the perceived industry. And here the significant point is that the nature of this environing industry changed sharply. In 1981 Connecticut General defined itself as a participant in the new "financial services" industry, which encompassed many banks but also included such firms as Household Finance and American Express (p. 18). Only three insurance companies were among the fourteen leading companies with which Connecticut General compared itself in seeking to determine appropriate CEO compensation. The reality of the agency nature of the redefined executive ties is underlined by a striking change in mobility patterns. Before 1973 Connecticut General had never hired an officer from outside, but in the changes of the late seventies they turned outside repeatedly for new expertise—and could expect to begin losing some executives elsewhere in a real managerial market for the first time.

Just this multiplicity of constituencies increases the need for and importance of introducing agency relations partially into these firms and markets. The flexibility and fluidity of agency helps loosen a structure that can become ever more rigid as further constituencies are able to impose some of their views. Control toward new and definite purposes is better effectuated with the use of agency.

The divergences in atmosphere among constituencies are truly striking. Read the market analysts' section of *Forbes* or the *Wall Street Journal* for a bracing atmosphere of impersonal, critical assessment. How different is the ambience within a market or industry, where "the close, multifaceted, and continuing relations that exist between industrial buyers and sellers must often be based on a strong spirit of trust and fairness" (Corey 1983, xii). These are the same firms whose sales executives in other conferences will be talking sternly about brisk change and strong measures to achieve such and such a target growth in the bottom line. Clearly there are several analytically distinct networks of ties among managers in related firms and to financial markets. In sociologese, we are dealing with *multiplex networks*, each one of which may have its own kind of formal and informal order imposed to the extent possible given the presence of the others.[6]

Similar issues surround agency relationships introduced into more formal government settings. The observations of the English historian J. H. Plumb in *The Growth of Political Stability in England 1675–1725* can be recast in my present terms. In that period the Whigs raised patronage to new heights, binding much larger numbers of gentry and aristocrats to a no-nonsense political machine reminiscent of Mayor Daley's Chicago, unhampered by civil service notions. It was a social invention of some note. Persisting employment at positions of some definiteness was awarded on the basis of tangible ties of obeisance to high Whigs; in this way the machine of government was permeated, made malleable, and controlled through flexible clusters of ties only informally connected in a party-ambience network. These patronage ties had to function effectively in diverse social, county, court, and economic constituencies at the same time.[7]

My impression from many serious case studies is that similar processes are indispensable to getting things done and achieving real control in modern businesses, for example, as an incoming CEO takes charge. As in politics, the flexible agency ties are defined as well as rewarded by contingent and personalized payments in various coin, and these skeins of agency relations are intruded both into bureaucracy and into arenas of market transaction.

Clientela in Political Life and Business Contexts

Before attempting to connect the question of asymmetric information with significant issues of structure and control for agency, I need to lay some further groundwork. Agency as described so far seems a short-term matter, despite the strategic aspect of control it is purported to deal with. Each agency tie casts shadows ahead and behind in time, but I have not yet shown how the shadows reflect and articulate to a larger ambience of agentry. The Roman Republic is a classic setting for beginning this task. I shall start with ties among individuals but show how these grew into sinews for an enormous state, and then conclude with specific analogues in modern business and industry.

"The relation of patron and client is one of the most characteristic features of Roman life lasting, in some form, from the origins to the downfall of the city and beyond." Thus Badian (1958) begins his classic treatise on the generalization of *clientela* to the foreign relations of Rome. "The client may be described as an inferior entrusted, by custom or by himself, to the protection of a stranger more powerful than he, and rendering certain services and observances in return for this protection. . . . There are many ways of forming this relation of trust, some resting on status and some on contract (in the widest sense of these terms)." That is, both voluntary and dependent contexts were included. Badian goes on to say that this institution is "in that penumbra of religion and inescapable custom that is not quite law—or is more than law."

In the case of Rome, this apparently personal and local type of tie was cumulated into the larger skeleton of social life in a creation that gradually far outgrew its face-to-face village origin. "The mystery of the cohesion of the Empire through successive civil wars, and despite manifest misgovernment, now becomes intelligible. The Empire was based on the personal loyalty of leading men throughout the provinces to leading families at Rome, and this attachment proved to be independent of political vicissitudes and, as we have seen, on the whole unaffected even by the fortunes of those families" (Badian 1958, 262). "The all-pervasive nature of this phenomenon and its extreme importance in fashioning and preserving the fabric of Roman rule through generations of trial and (often all but fatal) error in policy and administration. It was *clientela* in its private aspects that enabled Rome to assert and maintain that dominance over ostensibly independent states" (p. 165). Thus the *clientela* relation was also generalized to become the basis for relations of other states to the Roman state.

The Roman *clientela* relationships are directly analogous to the agency prototypes in American business I described earlier. Consider the conundrums of decentralization, especially to profit centers, and the ambiguity that Vancil (1979) emphasizes is at the core of the delegation of authority there. After the blitzkrieg of the First Illyrian War, Rome turned to the principle of association-without-treaty with a chain of states dependent upon Rome, and a "friend" of Rome, Demetrius of Pharus, was made de facto ruler of the Illyrian "kingdom." Demetrius became convinced of the reality of his freedom and adopted an entirely independent policy. So long as Rome's limited interest in flank security was maintained, the Senate did not interfere. But then within ten years, "on a thin pretext and without much ceremony, a Roman army invaded Illyria and after a short struggle drove Demetrius into exile. . . . Rome's purpose had been very limited. . . . The example of Demetrius, the ungrateful client, showed them the importance of remembering Rome's *beneficia*. The nature of political *clientela* was becoming clear: the client must not forget his station and the benefits he had received from Rome" (Badian 1958, 46–47). "For the interpretation of the client's obligations rests largely—as in private *clientela*—with the patron" (p. 54).

Corey's account of how procurement relations reach through supposedly arm's-length market interfaces also has a large-scale analogue in Badian's Roman context. The core city-state of Rome relied increasingly on massive wheat imports. In one sense this wheat was obtained on the market from the enormous Sicilian wheat farms. But the actual mechanism depended heavily on intricate ties of dependency from foreign *clientelae*. Some, like Demetrius, failed their test and were suppressed, with pure market or other kinds of relations taking over. Others, like Hiero of Syracuse, took care as faithful friends; he was able to retain a wealthy little kingdom supplying wheat on a secure basis and yet also had much more scope than a puppet.

The Roman context is unique in some respects. In particular, it was the universal conscious recognition and approbation of the *clientela* institution that made possible the chaining together of such ties of agency into a long-enduring and huge structure for a sizable Western part of the Mediterranean world, and the subtle intertwining of these ties with the formal organization frames that began to be constructed with the Empire. Moreover, the clarity of form of Roman institutions makes it easier to see some of the mechanics of agency. A key aspect of agency is interrelations among principals. The Senate as an institution, as well as the official nature of subordinate classes, such as the Equites, throw these relationships open to public view, as it were.[8] The strategic aspect of control, which especially concerns principals, involves them heavily with one another's moves; since they are on comparable footings, their choices and acts must have the sophisticated and robust character that can enable them to survive in strategic interaction with competent peers (Leifer 1983).

Though more transparent in the Roman context, some such features of agency can be recognized in modern business contexts. Isaacs pointed out sixty years ago that agency ties cast a long shadow that permits the manufacturer to control resale prices. In the next section I go back two centuries to the beginning of the industrial system, to the awkward period of transition from the sophisticated mercantile network economy (already foreshadowed in the Medici Bank's situation) to what we take for granted as an economy, a transition signaled by emerging new class relations among principals.

The main concern is not with large systems, which seem to consist primarily in stackings-up of agency relations, but let me just cite other modern business contexts in which one can see some approximations to the Roman example. The Japanese economy (Yoshino 1971), as is now widely known, makes much use of networks of traditional small firms clustered in client-like patterns around the large showcase firms. A generation ago David Granick (1960) reminded us how extensively the realities of Soviet Russian industrial management depended upon "expediters" and other kinds of hustlers and hustling roles among line management in Soviet firms. Supposedly the embodiment of central planning, the Soviet system seemed, on the ground, very much like an ad hoc agency system writ large. The new matrix formulation of American management systems, observed first in federal government contractors (Davis and Lawrence 1977), sometimes seems to me to come close to being a rationalization of how agency expediting must be overlaid on orderly organization structures and markets that are not sufficiently fine-grained (Stigler 1951; Eccles 1981; Chaiken and Larson 1972). The example of Rome retains pride of place, however, as the one case in which agency relations are fully approved, recognized, and institutionalized, and thus can bear the weight of coordinating huge systems.

Small-Time Control: Weak Ties for Agency

It is not just big shots—Roman Senators or U.S. CEOs—who use devices of agency. Most of us use slithery techniques of network contacts in finding jobs and forging careers. Mark Granovetter (1973; 1982) has described how we shape much of our social lives through "weak ties"—that is, acquaintances much less close than kin or friends but much more tied to us as distinctive individuals than are officeholders with whom we have only official communication. Surely this amounts to a mass-production middle-class version of agency, a sort of horizontal form in which many parties can engage simultaneously. The tie in this sort of agency also is middling in type, between *shaliach* and arm's length. Its nature is to be symmetric, in information and motivation and the like, on the average over time, but to exploit at each particular instant the exact asymmetry holding at that moment. Mutual back-scratching proceeds one back at a time. Boorman (1975) has published a powerful mathematical and simulation analysis that exploits just this symmetry-asymmetry.

Weak ties can be the actual structural base of major systems. Let me sketch a weak-tie system in the European economy in the period since the Roman Empire. It is a parallel to *clientela* in scope but without the intense commitment within ties on which the Roman system rested. I take my general guidance from Braudel's (1982) massive account; let him pose the problem: "Above all . . . there certainly was no natural and logical transition from the manufactory to factory" (p. 302).

Rome already had manufactories and sophisticated trade (see Badian 1972), and the economy that came into being early in medieval times resembled its Roman predecessor in its reliance upon trust, upon strong ties to keep the merchant networks running. Within the past century, at least, a different system including huge formal organizations has taken hold. Our concern is with the transition regimes, which relied on weak ties. (For economists' views see Landes 1969 and North 1981).

From the Middle Ages on, the tasks of cutler, blacksmith, nailmaker, miller, and the like involved a minimal division of labor and little interaction between workshops. Increasingly dominant, however, was a further set of workshops that, though just as scattered, were connected by the intermediary of the merchant entrepreneur, advancing raw materials and organizing production in a serial form. Thus, for example, in the textile process, product moved from spinner to weaver through to the fuller, dyer, and finisher. Such serial processes were also found in some ironmaking trades. Let us restrict the term "putting out" to just this early and rather separable form, and the system which it dominated. It involved a sequence of manufacturing operations, and it involved forms of wage labor, but it is a howling anachronism to import back to that era the modern terms of "industry," "labor," and the like.

For some time and across much of Europe, this "putting-out" system was an invertebrate form of socioeconomic organization in which the most alert participants, entrepreneurs, subcontractors, and sublettors were constantly weaving and reweaving a substantial flow of production for a market economy but without a continuing frame. (One wonders if our big social frames would have emerged as soon and decisively had it not been for the development of technical means of producing power in great concentrations and, later, of machines in the modern sense to exploit the new possibilities for power.) For a time, a stable and large-scale system existed that was not based on either traditional kin ties or on formal organization, but instead on the concatenated and imaginative use of weak ties. Agency relationships were the basis of a surprisingly effective system of continuous production, through a web of entrepreneurs and subentrepreneurs as complex as a patronage scene in Rome. Reliance on preexisting family relations, between husband and father and other nuclear family members, was a major instance of agency's use of autochthonous fields of ties, parallel to patronage's use. Unlike the patronage web, this entrepreneurial network permitted frequent reversals of principal with agent as economic fortunes changed.

It is worth going a step further to follow how the putting-out system fared as factories, and eventually industry, grew into the new systems. The outwork system (Bythell 1978) preceded and then long coexisted with emerging factory systems (M. Anderson 1971). Agency, in this nineteenth-century version of an England at its apogee, intruded into both larger formal organizations and market interfaces, and its entrepreneurs had simultaneously acute problems of strategic and of operational control. The outwork entrepreneur was unlike either trading merchants or the new factory builders and owners. Outwork was a distinct further stage beyond "putting out," in which substantial production, comparable to that from factories, was built up as regular continuing flows from a diverse and scattered work force. No longer were reversals common in agency ties.

The work force sometimes was provided with the requisite tools and sometimes had its own; it was always supplied with coordinated flows of materials as needed. This was real standardized production, with no attempts at differentiated quality, and it was tuned to the emerging mass markets of a new form of economy. Yet at the same time outwork seemed a holdover form of organization. The entrepreneur was not dealing with a homogeneous and concentrated pool of labor, but rather had to intervene in a various array of familial and kinship clusters and networks to find and maintain production. The paradox is that to a considerable extent outwork yielded a closer approximation to an ideal labor market than the new industries did, so far as pressure toward low and uniform wages was concerned.

The form of the outwork system was very plastic; it varied according to the degree to which it became a mere detail-work appendage of the factory system.[9] Manufactories, such as tanneries, breweries, and glass works, did centralize the work force and had some advanced division of labor. But the manufactories regularly employed outworkers, and centralized production only insofar as its technical requirements placed it beyond the capabilities of the domestic outworker. The early factories used outworkers as "outside departments" of the factory, but departments better characterized as weak-tie congeries than as any sort of self-reproducing organizations.

Procurement management, as Corey describes it, resembles the out-work system adapted from the freestanding "putting-out system"—an outwork system on the grand scale. Certainly agency devices today often are survivals of earlier systems. My main point here, however, is that an enlarged scope of operation does not in itself require going beyond agency devices; in the putting-out example it seems techno-logical developments were necessary to the supersession of the sys-tem. Oddly enough this large system of putting out is one of the poorest examples of agency-as-control. The putting-out system spread far in a horizontal sense but seemed ill-adapted to the crisp and far-reaching manipulation that in our minds is associated with control. I now turn back to a crucial early case of centralization and strong control in a field of agency.

Specialization and Reversal

There are asymmetries in agencies, and they can lead to difficulties, but I think it is misleading to focus our attention on "information," as in the economist's customary formulation of the agency problem. Asymmetry in information is better thought of as a by-product and an implication of asymmetry in control, rather than the cause of prob-lems in control. Problems in social organization and process always are, mainly and in the first instance, problems of reproducibility, of how participants can be led to recreate by their normal actions the motivations and context that will continue just the normal structures and processes. These are problems of coordination of an eminently social kind. I think it a delusion to try to turn the problems into atomistic cognitive ones. Most of the models I see proposed, especially by mathematical economists, to represent and give guidance for prob-lems of agency seem to me to draw attention away from the structural context in which abstraction can be effective. So much by way of an aside to the formulators of this symposium.

There is, I think, a natural history of agency problems. Control needs engender the construction and use of agency relations, usually as "add-ons" to the existing pattern and process of organization. Over time, in its continued operation across a variety of occasions, agency tends to encourage specialization within its practitioners and pat-terns. I recognize two main and quite different sorts of specialization:

specialization in analytic skills, whether through practice or training, and specialization by localization, by accumulating familiarity with the details of local situations. I think of them as professional specialization, in modern imagery, and rooted specialization.

The problem, the generic problem in both these species, is a tendency toward reversal of control; as Llewellyn (1930) put it, the principal comes under the control of the agent after the latter becomes a specialized purveyor. I see this as a problem, because it would be expected to interfere with the achievement of the purposes for which the agency relationship was originally created. The operational control aspect is likely to be sharply decoupled from its rightful partner, strategic control, once the goals of action move away from principals and into the hands of agents (Abbott 1981). Both in professional and in rooted specialization, the identity of principals tends to become vague and shifting, while agents are in focus.

These are problems for which the clinician, the case expert, must be the main resource. And the problems will be complex and intricate. A profession is not a matter just of agency, nor of expertise in a simple cognitive sense; profession is all these and more, a historically evolved yet culturally crisp phenomenon (Sarfatti-Larson 1977). It would be artificial to isolate a problem with agency on its own.

It may be useful, however, to consider some very early and clear-cut instances of growth of specialization in agency. I choose as an example the evolution of the early Church, in the first few centuries of the Christian Era. I refer only to the pre-Nicene years before the deliberate cooptation by the Roman Empire complicated the meaning and interpretation of church government.

In the first century, during the era of the apostles, the Church shows an unusually clear-cut split between what I think of as operational control (the running of local congregations—in effect all Christians in a given small ancient city) and strategic control (formulating creeds and giving directions for proselytizing). Two totally segregated sets of agents become the sites for these two aspects of control. Each local church was defined by a presbytery, a council or committee of peers who lacked distinctive sacerdotal powers but had full operational responsibility and authority for the local community of this semisecret and oppressed society. The apostles, and the additions to their number assimilated to that status, were wholly other from the presbyteries. They had no local identity; they had complete and absolute sacerdotal authority.

206 AGENCY AS CONTROL

This division of control did not last. Instead, a then-extraordinary figure emerged: the bishop, a complex and contradictory creation reminiscent in some senses of the complex and contradictory modern business position of CEO. To understand why operational and strategic control came to be united in a single figure, I think, will suggest much about the complexities of agency in more developed contexts.

"The true ministry of the first generation," Turner (1911, 143) has written, "was the ordered hierarchy": first apostles, leading down to the local ministry with narrowly limited powers. This early church was a laity grouped in local communities and a ministry that moved from place to place. In the words of Dix (1946, 286), "the virtual breakdown of the old, jealously corporate notion of the local church and its local ministry . . . is the final result of the adjustment to one another of two originally distinct institutions, the *shaliach* with his personal commission from our Lord Himself of a quite undefined scope, and the *zeqenim* with a collegiate not a personal authority, for specific purposes within a local society. . . . In the second century they are roughly adjusted by the 'localization' of an apostolate within each presbytery." Elsewhere Dix remarks, "that curious duality and apparent mutual exclusiveness which we have noted in the material relating to the bishop and presbyterate in Hippolytus, therefore, goes right back into the roots of the Church in the apostolic age" (p. 237).

Turner (1911, 145) poses the central question thus: "When we have explained how the supreme powers of the general ministry were made to devolve on an individual who belonged to the local ministry, we have explained the origin of episcopacy." This suggests to me that segregation between the agents of operational control and those of strategic control cannot sustain itself. Considerable tension is built into positions that deny neat segregation to the two sides of control via agency. The new "bishop," for example, was an extraordinary creation. "The pre-Nicene bishop is, indeed, in a singular sense 'the man' of his own Church—its priest, offering its corporate sacrifice . . . and the minister, in person or by delegation, of all sacraments to all its members. . . . He is the creator of its lesser ministers; its representative to other Churches; the administrator of its charity; the officer of its discipline; the center of its unity; the hub of its whole many-sided life, spiritual and temporal, inward and outward" (Turner 1911, 198).

This unique position suggests an overshooting in the attempt to reconcile in a new way the local and the apostolic—that is, the rooted versus the professional aspects of control through agency. The attention given to the issue of "translation" of bishops is revealing: "There were then no retired bishops . . . no translations from see to see . . . [the latter] was denounced by a long series of councils . . . as a sin, often actually classed with adultery." And yet at the same time the bishops were long claimed to be additions to the apostles, not merely successors, and the apostles were not localized.

What happens to the previous localized agents? Against all declamations the clergy become in fact movable, and thus too they become priests with sacerdotal and liturgical powers akin to—though kept dependent upon—the bishops. But the presbytery loses its heretofore overwhelming corporate power in local matters. And over time, the bishop, who claims apostleship with almost purely unrooted, abstract, strategic, and creedal authority, becomes one of a decidedly rooted and concrete local corporate group, the synod of his peers.[10]

The transformation is completed in a way suggestive of modern solutions to the problems of asymmetry of control in agency. "The idea that the various 'orders' were a series of 'promotions,' each 'order' containing within itself, so to speak, the powers of all those 'below' it, begins to come only [later]. . . . This introduction of the principle of 'hierarchy' in place of that of an 'organism' (distinct functions vis-à-vis the body as a whole) is important in its effects . . . it completes the destruction of the idea of the ministry of each local Church as an organic whole. . . . It opens the possibility of a clerical career by a regular succession of 'promotions' " (Dix 1946, 284). In the words of another authority (Goguel 1964, 156): "Each community is an isolated cell with a life independent. . . . There were therefore two parallel tendencies, one toward an increase in the authority of the ecclesiastical ministries, the other toward a diversification of functions. The two tendencies were harmonized by a hierarchical organization of ministries, the three essential orders being bishop, presbyters and deacons."

Conclusion

Agency is flexible, so that it can penetrate most situations, however organized, and yet be changed or removed. This is a social flexibility that depends on underlying cultural context.[11] Agency depends on types of ties that cast shadows of commitment. Kinship was such a context in early societies, where son could be full plenipotentiary for father in one system, for mother's brother in another, and so on.

In this paper I have tried to build up, through comparative historical examples, a sense of the range of agency. This range can help one understand better some important practices of upper management in the tapestry of big firms and segregated markets that characterizes the United States today. Colleagues and I are engaged in a series of papers with this aim. We show agency embedded variously in markets and in hierarchies, and interconnecting exemplars of these; via agency we come to see how hierarchy and market cannot be fully separated because they interpenetrate.

Flexible and simple, yes, but agency is also enmeshed in complicated conundrums of human social organization. I shall conclude by designating two. These are the conundrums of *specialization* and *boundaries*, which together yield the ambiguities of autonomy. All three rest on the paradoxical connection of agency to authority; so let me first set out my meaning for that. Authority means transferability of efforts from some to other definite, timely purposes at one's discretion. Control is the process enactment of authority.

All agency can be seen as specialization in some sense. This specialization is perhaps the source of early formal organization via delegation and spreading of agency in multiple copies and chains. The conundrum is that specialization tends to yield reversal of control between principal and agent, a reversal that upsets the root source of agency, the desire of authority to enlarge the reach of its full control. The evolutions of such business intermediary roles as factor and banker provide examples. One might imagine that such reversal on a large scale has as end product what we see as the professional-client relation, today imbedded in curious guildlike organizations on large scales. In sum, agency generates multiple copies of itself by other principals as well as to further agents, and the funneling of access that may result can lead to reversal of control just because of the enhancement of particular capacity to which specialization leads. The early Church was an example.

Boundaries must be defined simultaneously in cultural terms and in group membership.[12] A theme throughout this paper has been the decrease in control associated with clear boundaries. Agency is a way to sidestep some of this decrease, by introducing fluidity in membership. Yet in many respects agency requires even sharper cultural boundaries, to yield strongly defined ties. The boundary conundrum follows from the interaction. The criterion for agency in business, for example, usually has to do with profit, which is one of the least operational terms in the whole range of business, in part because the boundaries, in time and membership, for the reckoning remain fluid, despite or perhaps because of the preeminent and sharp nature of profit in business culture.

Contingency, as from the "environment," is not the problem to which organization adapts using agency mechanisms, as the conventional view has it; rather, contingency is the solution, the justification for continuing adjustments in boundaries, social and cultural, which are needed by authority to loosen the grip of specialization upon authority, without passing the reins to autonomy. Specialization yields some measure of autonomy, which measure is curtailed by the use that authority makes of continuing realignment in boundaries.

Autonomy is ambiguous because of these usages. Reasons given for introduction of agency into organizational schemes invariably cite increases in autonomy of subordinate actors, and corresponding increases in profit, efficiency, and the like. The examples in this paper, and our continuing work, turn this standard reasoning upside down: agency, at the same time as it enhances autonomy in certain restricted cultural spheres, sharply increases control, and thence authority, and it is reasonable to conclude that these latter effects are the chief reasons for agency, in the Roman polity as in modern multidivisional firms. "Autonomy" sums up and incorporates the two conundrums of agency.

References

Abbott, Andrew. 1981. "Status and Status Strain in the Professions." *American Journal of Sociology* 86:819–35.

Allen, Patrick M. 1981. "Power and Privilege in the Large Corporation: Corporate Control and Managerial Compensation." *American Journal of Sociology* 86:1112.

Anderson, M. 1971. *Family Structure in Nineteenth Century Lancashire.* Cambridge: Cambridge University Press.

Anderson, Perry. 1974. *Passages from Antiquity to Feudalism.* London: New Left Books.

Badian, E. 1958. *Foreign Clientelae.* Oxford University Press.

———. 1972. *Publicans and Sinners: Private Enterprise in the Service of the Roman Republic.* Ithaca, N.Y.: Cornell University Press.

Behavioral Research Service of General Electric. 1965. *A Study of the Salary Exempt Program.* Crotonville, NY EBR-24 (2,000).

Berkowitz, S. D., Peter J. Carrington, Yehuda Kotowitz, and L. Waverman. 1978–79. "The Determination of Enterprise Groupings through Combined Ownership and Directorship Ties." *Social Networks* 1:391–413.

Boorman, Scott A. 1975. "A Combinatorial Optimization Model for Transmission of Job Information Through Contact Networks." *Bell Journal of Economics* 6:216–49.

Bower, Joseph L. 1970. *Managing the Resource Allocation Process*. Boston: Division of Research, Harvard Graduate School of Business Administration.

Braudel, Fernand. 1982. *The Wheels of Commerce*. Translated by S. Reynolds. New York: Harper and Row.

Breiger, R. L. 1979. "Toward an Operational Theory of Community Elite Structures." *Quality and Quantity* 13:21–57.

Breiger, R. L., Scott A. Boorman, and Phipps Arabie. 1975. "An Algorithm for Clustering Relational Data with Applications to Social Network Analysis and Comparison with Multidimensional Scaling." *Journal of Mathematical Psychology* 12:328–82.

Bythell, D. 1978. *The Sweated Trades, Outwork in Nineteenth Century Britain*. London: St. Martin's Press.

Carrington, Peter. 1981. "Anticompetitive Effects of Directorship Interlocks." Working Paper Series, Structural Analysis Program, Department of Sociology, University of Toronto, No. 27.

Chaiken, J. M., and Richard C. Larson. 1972. "Methods for Allocating Urban Emergency Units: A Survey." *Management Science* 19:110–30.

Chandler, Alfred D., Jr., and Herman Daems, eds. 1980. *Managerial Hierarchies: Comparative Perspectives on the Rise of the Modern Industrial Enterprise*. Cambridge: Harvard University Press.

Cohen, Michael D., James G. March, and Johan P. Olsen. 1972. "A Garbage Can Model of Organizational Choice." *Administrative Science Quarterly* 17:1–25.

"Connecticut General Corporation." 1982. Boston: Harvard Business School Case Services 0-183-116.

Corey, E. Raymond. 1978. *Procurement Management: Strategy, Organization, and Decision Making*. Boston: CBI Publishing.

———. 1983. *Industrial Marketing*. 3d ed. Englewood Cliffs, N.J.: Prentice-Hall.

Crozier, Michel, and J. C. Thoenig. 1976. "The Regulation of Complex Organized Systems." *Administrative Science Quarterly* 21:547–70.

Davis, James A. 1970. "Clustering and Hierarchy in Interpersonal Relations: Testing Two Graph Theoretical Models on 742 Sociograms." *American Sociological Review* 35:843–52.

Davis, Stanley M., and Paul R. Lawrence. 1977. *Matrix*. Reading, Mass.: Addison-Wesley.

Dix, G. 1946. "The Ministry in the Early Church" in *The Apostolic Ministry*, ed. K. E. Kirk. New York: Morehouse.

Eccles, Robert G. 1981. "The Quasifirm in the Construction Industry." *Journal of Economic Behavior and Organization* 2:335–57.

Eisenberg, Melvin A. 1976. *The Structure of the Corporation*. Boston: Little, Brown.

Fama, Eugene F., and Michael C. Jensen. 1983. "Separation of Ownership and Control." *Journal of Law and Economics* 26 (June).

Faulkner, Robert R. 1983. *Music on Demand: Composers and Careers in the Hollywood Film Industry*. New Brunswick, N.J.: Transaction Press.

Finley, M. I. 1973. *The Ancient Economy*. Berkeley and Los Angeles: University of California.

Goguel, Maurice. 1964. *The Primitive Church*. Translated by H. C. Snapl. London: Allen & Unwin.

Goldsmith, Raymond W. 1969. *Financial Structure and Development*. New Haven, Conn.: Yale University Press.

Granick, D. 1960. *The Red Executive.* New York: Doubleday.

Granovetter, Mark S. 1973. "The Strength of Weak Ties." *American Journal of Sociology* 78:1360–80.

———. 1982. "The Strength of Weak Ties: A Network Theory Revisited." In *Social Structure and Network Analysis,* eds. P. V. Marsden and N. Lin. Beverly Hills: Sage Publications.

Hinson, E. Glenn. 1981. *The Evangelization of the Roman Empire: Identity and Adaptability.* Macon, Ga.: Mercer University Press.

Hirsch, P. 1982. "Network Data versus Personal Accounts: The Normative Culture of Interlocking Directorates." Graduate School of Business, University of Chicago, unpublished manuscript.

Hirschman, Albert O., and Charles E. Lindblom. 1962. "Economic Development, Research and Development and Development, Policy Making: Some Converging Views." *Behavioral Science* 7:211–22.

Holland, Paul W., and Samuel Leinhardt. 1981. "An Exponential Family of Probability Distributions for Directed Graphs." *Journal of the American Statistical Association* 76:33–49.

Isaacs, Nathan. 1924–25. "On Agents and 'Agencies.' " *Harvard Business Review* 3:265–74.

Jensen, Michael C., and William H. Meckling. 1976. "Theory of the Firm: Managerial Behavior, Agency Costs and Ownership Structure." *Journal of Financial Economics* 3:305–60.

Kent, Sherman. 1966. *Strategic Intelligence for American World Policy.* Princeton, N.J.: Princeton University Press.

Landes, David S. 1969. *The Unbound Prometheus: Technological Change and Industrial Development in Western Europe from 1950 to the Present.* Cambridge: Cambridge University Press.

Leifer, Eric M. 1983. "Robust Action." Ph.D. diss., Department of Sociology, Harvard University.

Llewellyn, Karl N. 1930. "Agency." *Encyclopedia of the Social Sciences* 1:483.

Llewellyn, W. G. 1968. *Executive Compensation.* New York: Columbia University Press.

Loomis, Carol J. 1982. "The Madness of Executive Compensation." *Fortune* (July 12), 42–52.

Nadel, S. F. 1957. *The Theory of Social Structure.* London: Cohen and West.

North, Douglass C. 1981. *Structure and Change in Economic History.* New York: W. W. Norton.

Padgett, John F. 1980. "Managing Garbage-Can Hierarchies." *Administrative Science Quarterly* 14:583–603.

Plumb, J. H. 1967. *The Growth of Political Stability in England 1675–1725.* London: Penguin.

Pocock, J. G. A. 1975. *The Machiavellian Moment: Florentine Political Thought and the Atlantic Republican Tradition.* Princeton, N.J.: Princeton University Press.

Roberts, David R. 1959. *Executive Compensation.* Glencoe, Ill.: Free Press.

de Roover, Raymond. 1966. *The Rise and Decline of the Medici Bank 1397–1494.* New York: W. W. Norton.

Sarfatti-Larson, M. 1977. *The Rise of Professionalism.* Berkeley and Los Angeles: University of California Press.

Schweizer, Edward. 1961. *Church Order in the New Testament.* Translated by Frank Clarke. Napierville, Ill.: A. R. Allenson.

Simon, Herbert A., D. Smithburg, and N. Thompson. 1950. *Public Administration*. New York: Knopf.

Stigler, George J. 1951. "The Division of Labor Is Limited by the Extent of the Market." *Journal of Political Economy* 3:185–93.

Thrupp, Sylvia. "The Gilds." Chap. 5 in *Cambridge Economic History*, vol. 3.

Turner, C. H. 1911. "Organization of the Church." Chap. 6 in *Cambridge Medieval History*, vol. 1.

Vancil, Richard F. 1979. *Decentralization: Managerial Ambiguity by Design*. Homewood, Ill.: Dow Jones-Irwin.

———. 1983. "Management Systems: Structure and Process." Harvard Business School Working Paper 0-183-182.

Williamson, Oliver E. 1970. *Corporate Control and Business Behavior*. Englewood Cliffs, N.J.: Prentice-Hall.

Yoshino M. Y. 1971. *The Japanese Management System*. Cambridge: M.I.T. Press.

Ziegler, Rolf. 1982. *Market Structure and Cooptation*. Institut für Soziologie Ludwig-Maxmilians-Universitat, Munich.

CONTRIBUTORS

JOHN W. PRATT is professor of business administration at Harvard Business School. He was educated at Princeton and Stanford, specializing in mathematics and statistics. Except for two years at the University of Chicago, and a sabbatical in Kyoto on a Guggenheim fellowship, Pratt has been at Harvard for his entire professional career. Editor of the *Journal of the American Statistical Association* from 1965 to 1970, he is a fellow of four professional societies and has chaired National Academy of Sciences committees on environmental monitoring and census methodology. His recent research has been on utility theory, incentives, proxy variables, and the nature and discovery of stochastic laws, statistical relationships that describe the effects of decisions.

RICHARD J. ZECKHAUSER is professor of political economy at the John F. Kennedy School of Government, Harvard University. His academic career, from freshman to his present position, has all been at Harvard. His research focuses on microeconomic theory, with an emphasis on incentives and uncertainty, and on policy issues related to health, the environment, human resources, and financial markets. His continuing work on principals and agents is sponsored by Harvard's Business and Government Research Center. Zeckhauser is the coauthor of *A Primer for Policy Analysis* and *Demographic Dimensions of the New Republic.*

KENNETH J. ARROW is Joan Kenney Professor of Economics and Professor of Operations Research at Stanford University. Educated at City College, New York and Columbia University, he has also taught at the University of Chicago and Harvard University. He has received the Nobel Memorial Prize in Economic Science and is currently president of the International Economic Association.

ROBERT C. CLARK is professor of law at Harvard Law School, where he teaches and writes in the fields of corporate law, corporate finance, and the regulation of financial institutions. After earning his Ph.D. in philosophy of science at Columbia and a J.D. at Harvard Law School, he spent several years in private practice before beginning his academic career at Yale Law School. He is currently completing a treatise on corporate law.

FRANK H. EASTERBROOK is the Lee and Brena Freeman Professor of Law at the University of Chicago and formerly a deputy solicitor general of the United States. He was educated at Swarthmore College and the University of Chicago.

An editor of the *Journal of Law and Economics*, he is also affiliated with the consulting firm Lexecon, Inc.

ROBERT G. ECCLES is assistant professor of business administration at the Harvard Business School. He was educated at the Massachusetts Institute of Technology and Harvard University. His most recent work has extended his research on transfer pricing to examine more generally the relationship between profit centers in a firm and the relationship between a firm and its suppliers and customers. The results of his research on transfer pricing are discussed more extensively in a book, *The Transfer Pricing Problem: A Theory for Practice*, which will be published in 1985.

RICHARD A. EPSTEIN is James Parker Hall Professor of Law at the University of Chicago, where he has been teaching since 1972. Educated at Columbia, Oxford, and Yale Law School, he was on the faculty of the University of Southern California from 1968 to 1973. From 1977 to 1978 he was a fellow at the Center for Advanced Study in the Behavioral Sciences, and since 1981 he has been the editor of the *Journal of Legal Studies*.

HARRISON C. WHITE, professor of sociology at Harvard University, was educated at the Massachusetts Institute of Technology and Princeton University. He was formerly on the faculties of the University of Chicago and Carnegie-Mellon University. His previous books include *Chains of Opportunity*. Recently his work has focused on mathematical models of control in firms and markets.

MARK A. WOLFSON, associate professor of accounting at Stanford University, was educated at the University of Texas and the University of Illinois. With the exception of the academic year 1981–82, which he spent at the University of Chicago, he has been on the faculty at Stanford since 1977. His recent work has focused on taxes and contracting behavior.

Notes

Chapter 1

1. In fact golden parachutes may actually be in the interest of shareholders, if they are a cheap way of "bribing" the corporate management to leave. For similar reasons, efforts to recruit high-level officers often include the assurance of generous severance pay. Even new ventures sometimes create arrangements that in effect provide golden parachutes for their executives.

2. In a number of societies, descendants play an important role as apparently unmonitored agents of their ancestors. But some of these societies may believe that nonhuman monitors or the ancestors themselves are actually looking down.

3. A popular brain-teaser illustrates this kind of sorting-out process and its difficulty. Each of three people has a sticker placed on his forehead. Each sticker is either white or green. Each person can see the color of the others' stickers, but not his own. The rules of the game are that everyone who sees a green sticker raises his hand. When a player figures out the color of his sticker, he announces it by putting his hand down. When play begins, everyone puts up his hand. After several minutes, one person brings his hand down. What color is his sticker? (HINT: What would an information untangler do almost immediately if he saw a white and a green sticker and both other players with their hands up?)

4. Some commentators on the economic scene suggest that we may be moving into an age of information, in which most of us will be employed in eliciting, processing, and providing information. This prediction may well be a bit overstated, for although information helps improve the allocation of resources, it provides little consumption benefit of its own (leaving aside the pleasures of learning). In any case, the widespread discussion of an information society suggests that the inability to monitor perfectly and costlessly is a significant phenomenon.

5. An aside to our technical friends: Having contributed to the theory of risk aversion, we take the liberty of ignoring it here to facilitate exposition. We also ignore nonpecuniary costs to the snatchee.

6. Similarly, the person who rents an auto at someone else's expense will almost certainly purchase collision damage insurance even at rates that are actuarially quite unfavorable. Foregoing this coverage would save the individual nothing and would expose him or her to considerable risk.

7. Some simple fee schedules that emerge from conceptual models are also hard to find in real-world contexts. Thus a risk-neutral agent could simply be given all profits or returns in exchange for a fixed price. The manager of a firm owned by an absentee principal might be in such a situation. In essence, he or she would rent or buy the firm.

In the more realistic case of a risk-averse agent, possible solutions include two simple schedules we call the *slam* and the *sliver*. When monitoring costs are high, random inspections or other low-probability forms of discerning "bad behavior" by agents can be employed. When deviation from the prescribed action is strongly suspected (or detected), the slam is imposed; that is, the agent is penalized mightily. Even if the agent is strongly risk averse, the slam scheme will be prescribed whenever there is a way to impose a penalty that is arbitrarily great in utility terms and that makes the ratio of the probability of a penalty given prescribed behavior to the probability of a penalty given a deviation arbitrarily small. If, for example, the agent's deviation from prescribed behavior can be estimated with an error representable as normal with known, bounded, or estimable variance, then by imposing the penalty only when the estimated deviation is extreme enough, we can get below whatever ratio is required.

The sliver is employed when the agent must make choices on behalf of the principal, but need not devote any effort. This might be nearly the case with a portfolio manager serving an investor who has no idiosyncratic needs distinguishing him from the manager's many other clients. The manager will select stocks correctly if, in addition to a fixed fee, he receives or pays a sliver, a small percentage of whatever gains or losses are reaped by the portfolio.

These elegantly simple solutions, alas, tend not to work when complications enter. For example, if the agent must make any effort at all, the sliver is too slender a reward.

8. If the taxi industry is competitive, as in the freight-cost case above, then each company is small enough that it has no control over the market supply and demand curves, which determine the new equilibrium, hence the division of surplus. If the taxi company has a monopoly, it can set the rental price and taxi rates (if not regulated) wherever it wishes. But we should expect it to set the rent and rates that maximize its profits allowing for the response in the numbers of riders and drivers. In so doing, it will determine how the efficiency gain from the improved arrangement is shared. If there are just a few firms in the industry, strategic considerations enter, and the new equilibrium would be difficult to predict.

9. Of course individuals who are not players in the game, such as producers of substitute products, may lose, as would players in the game if the new contract or equilibrium not only gave them no part of the efficiency gain but took something from them.

10. Microeconomics also offers a solution to an agency problem that often arises between landlord and tenant. Consider the hard-pressed owner of a Victorian extravaganza who lives on the first two floors and rents out a third-floor apartment. The apartment's electrical circuits cannot be separately metered. Even if the tenant shares the electric bill, he has an incentive to make use of electricity when the value to him is less than its real cost, because the cost to him is less. His incentive can be corrected by having him pay the entire electric bill, presumably in return for a fixed reduction in rent. But he will rightly complain that the owner can now use electricity at no cost and will be no more restrained from excessive use than the tenant would if the owner paid the bill. The only solution is for the owner also to pay the entire bill, or the entire bill less a fixed amount. Who should collect the extra payment? If the owner or the tenant collects it, incentives are again distorted. A third party is needed. Presumably many should be willing to bid the expected value of the bill, less transactions costs, for the right to receive the extra payment. Both owner and tenant can be made better off by an appropriate split of the proceeds than if either uses too much electricity because it costs him too little.

Chapter 3

1. See especially Armen A. Alchian and Harold Demsetz, "Production, Information Costs, and Economic Organization," 62 *American Economic Review* 62 (1972): 777; Eugene F. Fama, "Agency Problems and the Theory of the Firm," *Journal of Political Economy* 88 (1980): 288; Michael C. Jensen and William J. Meckling, "Theory of the Firm: Managerial Behavior, Agency Costs and Ownership Structure," 3 *Journal of Financial Economics* 3 (1976): 305; Oliver E. Williamson, *The Economics of Discretionary Behavior: Managerial Objectives in a Theory of the Firm* (Englewood Cliffs, N.J.: Prentice-Hall, 1964).

2. See Victor Brudney and Robert C. Clark, "A New Look at Corporate Opportunities," *Harvard Law Review* 94 (1981): 998, 1001-6.

3. See William A. Klein, "The Modern Business Organization: Bargaining Under Constraints," *Yale Law Journal* 91 (1982): 1521.

4. Throughout this paper, the term *managers* includes both directors and officers.

5. This point is embodied in a leading definition: " 'Agency': the fiduciary relation which results from the manifestation of consent by one person to another that the other shall act on his behalf and subject to his control, and consent by the other so to act" (American Law Institute, *Restatement [Second] of Agency*, sec. 1 [1]).

The point is explicated and driven home by cases and commentary. "The agent differs from most other fiduciaries such as executors, trustees, etc., in that he remains under the continuous control of the principal as to matters relating to the object of his agency, throughout the entire period of his agency. The agent has a duty, at all times, to obey the directions of his principal, even though the principal may have initially indicated he would not give such additional instructions" (W. Edward Sell, *Agency* 2 (Mineola, N.Y.: Foundation Press, 1975). "Further, the agency relation differs from other fiduciary relations in that it is the duty of the agent to respond to the desires of the principal. . . even if the principal is guilty of a breach of contract by interfering, the agent will still commit a breach of duty by acting in a manner opposed to his principal's wishes" (Harold G. Reuschlein and William A. Gregory, *Agency and Partnership* (St. Paul, Minn.: West Publishing, 1979), 11–12.

6. See, for example, Harry G. Henn and John R. Alexander, *Laws of Corporations*, 3d ed. (St. Paul, Minn.: West Publishing, 1983), chap. 9. The points made in this and the next two paragraphs of the text are not only elementary but fairly stable over time. They are true today and were true long before Henn wrote his treatise.

7. See, for example, *Long Park, Inc. v. Trenton-New Brunswick Theatres Co.*, 297 N.Y. 174, 77 N.E.2d 633 (1948); *Kennerson v. Burbank Amusement Co.*, 120 Cal. App. 2d 157, 260 P.2d 823 (1953). Today a state's statute or case law may allow extended delegation of the directors' authority. Virtually all such legal rules were adopted for the purpose of facilitating business planning in closely held corporations. See, for example, *Galler v. Galler*, 32 Ill.2d 16, 203 N.E.2d 577 (1964).

8. Del. Gen. Corp. Law sec. 351. See also Minn. Bus. Corp. Act sec. 302A.457, which authorizes shareholder control agreements, but only if *all* shareholders sign—a requirement that by itself makes the authorization meaningless in the public corporation context. The Minnesota provision was part of a major 1981 revision of that state's corporation law, and followed extended study and debate by the bar; the revision was geared almost entirely to liberalizing the

law to fit the preferences of participants in closely held corporations. See *Report to the [Minnesota] Senate by the Advisory Task Force on Corporation Law* (1981); Note, "Minnesota Business Corporations Act: Greater Freedom for Corporations," *Minnesota Law Review* 66 (1982): 1033.

9. Useful selections of cases on agency law are presented in Alfred F. Conard, Robert L. Knauss, and Stanley Siegel, *Agency, Associations, Employment, Licensing and Partnerships: Cases, Statutes and Analysis*, 3d ed. (Mineola, N.Y.: Foundation Press, 1982), 232–407. See also Philip Mechem, *Selected Cases on the Law of Agency* (Chicago: Callaghan, 1954).

10. Ronald H. Coase, "The Nature of the Firm," *Economica* 4 (n.s.) (1937): 386.

11. Alchian and Demsetz, 777–78.

12. Jensen and Meckling.

13. The work of Frank Easterbrook and Daniel Fischel (both lawyers) is basically centered on the problem of agency costs, yet is aware of the legal concept of the fiduciary and tries to develop rigorous arguments for particular rules they think should govern managers. See their "The Proper Role of a Target's Management in Responding to a Tender Offer," *Harvard Law Review* 94 (1981): 1161, and "Corporate Control Transactions," *Yale Law Journal* 91 (1982): 698. Perhaps the same could be said for most recent writing by other legal commentators on hostile takeover bids. See also Brudney and Clark.

A legal writer on fiduciary duties who is only partially persuaded by the economic literature is Alison G. Anderson, "Conflicts of Interest: Efficiency, Fairness and Corporate Structure," 25 *UCLA L. Rev.* 738 (1978). See also Tamar Frankel, "Fiduciary Law," 71 *Cal. L. Rev.* 795 (1983).

14. Note that the persons who lobby about changes in corporate law are not restricted to representatives of the investing and managerial classes.

15. Richard Posner, *Economic Analysis of Law*, 2d ed. (Boston: Little, Brown, 1977), 404.

16. Posner, 292–96.

17. Ralph K. Winter, Jr., "State Law, Shareholder Protection, and the Theory of the Corporation," *Journal of Legal Studies* 6 (1977): 251.

18. Peter Dodd and Richard Leftwich, "The Market for Corporate Charters: 'Unhealthy Competition' vs. Federal Regulation," *Journal of Business* 53 (1980): 259 provides empirical data consistent with one of Winter's beliefs—that stockholders suffer no measurable loss when corporations reincorporate in Delaware—but these data do not go to the issue of whether the "market" for charters reaches efficient outcomes.

19. Jensen and Meckling.

20. For example, *Auerbach v. Bennett*, 47 N.Y.2d 619, 393 N.E.2d 994 (1979); *Lewis v. Anderson*, 615 F.2d 778 (9th Cir. 1980) (applying California law). Less deferential to litigation committees are the decisions in *Zapata Corp. v. Maldonado*, 430 A.2d 779 (Del. 1981) and *Joy v. North*, 692 F.2d 880 (2d Cir. 1983) (Winter, J.).

21. *Panter v. Marshall Field & Co.*, 646 F.2d 271 (7th Cir. 1981); *Crouse-Hinds Co. v. InterNorth, Inc.*, 634 F.2d 690 (2d Cir. 1980); *Treadway Cos. v. Care Corp.*, 638 F.2d 357 (2d Cir. 1980); *Johnson v. Trueblood*, 629 F.2d 287 (3d Cir. 1980).

22. See Donald C. Langevoort, "State Tender-Offer Legislation: Interests, Effects and Political Competency," *Cornell Law Review* 62 (1977): 213.

23. See *Edgar v. MITE Corp.*, 102 S. Ct. 2629 (1982).

24. Easterbrook and Fischel, "Corporate Control Transactions," 702–15, 737.

25. I think my statement in the text reflects their argument fairly accurately. In subsequent correspondence Easterbrook tells me that the unanimity

theorem, not diversification, was the *main* point of their gain-sharing argument. That is, shareholders unanimously prefer maximum value for their shares, even if each shareholder holds only a single company, and unequal distribution is sometimes necessary to maximize value. Nevertheless, he goes on to admit that the diversification possibility was introduced because a unanimity theorem can be defeated if investors have a substantial degree of risk aversion. My suggestion is that investors are often significantly risk averse but diversification possibilities do not fully destroy the relevance of this risk aversion for legal policy making.

26. See, for example, *Levin v. The Great Western Sugar Co.*, 406 F.2d 1112 (3d Cir. 1969); *David J. Greene & Co. v. Dunhill International, Inc.*, 249 A.2d 427 (Del. Ch. 1968).

27. Easterbrook and Fischel, "Corporate Control Transactions," 734.

28. For a recent attempt, see Frankel. Older efforts include Austin Scott, "The Fiduciary Principle," 37 *California Law Review* 37 (1949): 539; Ernest Weinrib, "The Fiduciary Obligation," *University of Toronto Law Journal* 25 (1975): 1.

29. 224 N.Y. 483, 121 N.E. 378 (1918).

30. 224 N.Y. at 489.

31. In addition to being specified in meaning for certain recurring transactions, the fiduciary principle is often stated by courts in highly general formulations that can be, and sometimes are, applied to new or unusual fact patterns.

32. See *Kerrigan v. Unity Savings Assn.*, 58 Ill. 2d 20, 317 N.E.2d 39 (1974).

33. 308 U.S. 295 (1939).

34. See, for example, *Jones v. H. F. Ahmanson & Co.*, 1 Cal. 3d 93, 460 P.2d 464 (1969) (Traynor, C.J.); *Lebold v. Inland Steel Co.*, 125 F.2d 369 (7th Cir. 1941), cert. denied, 316 U.S. 675 (1942).

35. 308 U.S. at 311.

36. Two classic, moralistic, oft-quoted descriptions of fiduciary duty are those in *Guth v. Loft, Inc.*, 5 A.2d 503, 510 (Del. 1939) (Layton, C.J.) and *Meinhard v. Salmon*, 249 N.Y. 458, 164 N.E. 545 (1928) (Cardozo, C.J.). The language of the two opinions cited in note 34 is also striking (even apart from the Douglas quotation).

37. Compare Posner, 121–22 (why theft is inefficient).

Chapter 4

I thank Walter J. Blum, Dennis W. Carlton, Daniel R. Fischel, Ronald J. Gilson, Richard Leftwich, Henry G. Manne, Kenneth E. Scott, and the participants in the Law & Policy Workshop of the Boston University School of Law for helpful comments on earlier drafts.

1. *Dirks v. SEC*, 103 S. Ct. 3255 (1983), and *Chiarella v. United States*, 445 U.S. 222 (1980), discuss the pertinent legal history and current rules. See also Dooley (1980) and Easterbrook (1981).

2. Despite the increasing interest, even among judges, in the economics of insider trading, this attitude persists in some quarters. Consider this statement by Justice Blackmun, dissenting in *Dirks* (see note 1) from the Supreme Court's holding that Dirks's tips to investors about the Equity Funding scandal did not violate the law. "The [Court's conclusion] not only has no basis in law, but it rests implicitly on a policy that I cannot accept. The Court justifies Secrist's and Dirks's action because the general benefit derived from the viola-

tion of Secrist's duty to shareholders outweighed the harm caused to those shareholders [citing economic articles]—in other words, because the end justifies the means. Under this view, the benefit conferred on society by Secrist's and Dirks's activities may be paid for with the losses caused to shareholders trading with Dirks's clients" (103 S. Ct. at 3272-73). (Citations, including one to Manne (1966), have been omitted.) Justice Blackmun obviously subscribes to a moral, irrefutable view of the vices of insider trading. He also does not grasp the economic arguments. When investors know that insiders may trade, prices of stock reflect this in advance, and shareholders do not suffer losses. Justice Blackmun's portrait of investors being sacrificed to "society's" gains misses the point that if management by inside traders yields gains for the firm, these gains are received by the firm's investors. The insiders' profits are no more "at the expense of" investors than are the insiders' salaries and bonuses. See Carlton and Fischel (1983). The combination of moral outrage and misstatement of the economic position is distressingly common.

3. Manne (1970) offers the further argument that trading by insiders improves the efficiency of the capital markets. This is a less powerful claim, for reasons developed in Easterbrook (1981, 335–37) and Gilson and Kraakman (1984, 629–34), and is outside the scope of this essay. Manne appears to have retreated from this position by observing that the market may infer information from the lack of trading as well as from trading (1974).

4. If, however, all managers are compensated under the same schedule, and investors select the schedule before they know the probability distribution of projects and outcomes, Dye's model does not operate. In such a case, a no-trading approach may get information out faster (Trueman 1983). Moreover, if managers' *ex ante* selection of a payoff schedule is not costlessly enforceable *ex post*, the model again does not give an optimal outcome. Managers might pick a no-trading schedule and trade anyway, confusing the signals. As I discuss later on, enforcement of a no-trading pledge is quite costly.

5. Compensation schemes that establish payoffs only after the event also require costly renegotiation and create still another moral hazard. What if the firm welches on the (implicit) deal and does not adequately compensate a manager for superior performance? A firm near the end of its expected life may conclude that the savings exceed the reputational costs.

6. A cynic might remark that I have smuggled into this discussion the assumption that the opportunity costs of judges and lawyers are positive.

7. Volume 11 of the *Journal of Financial Economics* (1983) contains a symposium on this subject. Of particular interest are Dodd and Warner (1983) (proxy contests), and Jensen and Ruback (1983) (survey article). See also DeAngelo, DeAngelo, and Rice (1984) (going private).

8. This does not, however, explain why the public rule is mandatory. Most other public enforcement, such as the use of criminal law to penalize theft by a firm's employees, simply states a rule that prevails in the absence of contract. If a firm agrees to give a sum of money to an employee, the transfer of wealth becomes salary or bonus rather than theft. It is not possible to contract around the insider trading rules in this manner.

9. Jaffe (1974) and others have examined the records of insiders' activities for evidence that changes in the law affected the frequency or profitability of trading. These studies find few or no effects. But the studies look only at data the insiders voluntarily disclose; it is unlikely that they file reports condemning themselves. The records Jaffe and others use contain trades on public or nonmaterial private information that are not objectionable under existing rules. Thus such studies are biased toward finding no effect.

Chapter 5

I have benefited from discussions with David Baron (Harvard MBA), Peyton Galloway (Harvard MBA), Charles Horngren (Harvard MBA), Robert Wilson (Harvard DBA), David Kreps (Harvard Economics), and Joel Demski and James Patell (unblemished). The editorial assistance of Nancy Jackson is also gratefully acknowledged.

1. *Investor's Tax Shelter Report,* January-February 1983.

2. Haft (1973, 5-53).

3. These costs include "delay rentals, location and surface damage, labor utilized in drilling wells, drilling mud and chemicals, drilling tests and core analysis, footage and day-work drilling costs, engineering and well site geological expenses, deductible completion or rework expense on productive wells, and expenditures for leases and equipment following the drilling of a noncommercial or unproductive well ('abandonment loss costs')" (Haft 1973, 5-5).

4. Capitalized costs, not all of which are eligible for the investment tax credit, include "expenditures for purchasing depreciable and salvageable equipment on productive wells, such as casing, tubing, rods, pumping units, and related equipment, and lease bonuses, screening, seismic and other costs incurred as a part of lease acquisition and title approval, except for those lease acquisition and equipment expenditures which are written off as abandonment loss costs" (Haft 1973, 5-6).

5. An alternative here is a Subchapter S Corporation, which permits flow-through of tax losses to individual shareholders, but there are more restrictions on the use of this organizational form than there are for partnerships.

6. The prospectus for Dyco Petroleum Corporation's 1983 Oil and Gas Program states:

> In the opinion of counsel for Dyco . . . the Functional Allocation of costs and revenues contained in the Drilling Agreement will be recognized for federal income tax purposes as having "substantial economic effect" as required by Section 704(b) of the Internal Revenue Code as amended by the Tax Reform Act of 1976. . . . This opinion is based upon the fact that such deductions will be charged to the capital accounts of the respective parties which capital accounts are taken into account on distribution of assets in liquidation of the Program. . . . Further, the costs so allocated will actually be paid from capital contributions by such parties or from their share of revenues so that the amount of each class of costs will actually affect the contributions by or distributions to the parties so charged (p. 66).

7. In addition to drilling programs, there also exist public oil and gas income programs (where outside investors enter the picture after the well has been completed) and oil and gas completion programs (where outside investors enter the picture after the well has been drilled but before it has been completed). Neither of these two types of ventures could be characterized as tax shelters in the same sense that drilling programs are, but their popularity has increased explosively over the past year or two. This is due largely to demand by such entities as Individual Retirement Accounts, Keogh plans, and pension funds.

8. *Investor's Tax Shelter Report,* January-February 1983, 14.

9. Some items, like sales commissions, are not immediately deductible. Furthermore, deductions are not permitted until the funds are actually spent or irrevocably committed to operators for the drilling of specified prospects.

10. Dyco (1983, 47).

11. *Stanger Register,* April 1983, 24.

12. Stanger (1982a, 63).

13. Ibid.

14. *Stanger Register*, April 1983, 74.

15. Haft (1973, 5-37).

16. Damson (1982, 43).

17. Dyco (1983, 47).

18. Apache (1983, 24).

19. Mission Resources (1982, 27).

20. Hilliard Fund (1982, 22).

21. Once the prospect has been drilled, R_i is assumed no longer to be a random variable to the general partner; however, there is no loss of generality.

22. Dyco (1983, 45–46).

23. Hilliard Fund (1982, 44–45).

24. Templeton (1982, 15).

25. The costs include not only the obvious direct costs (e.g., salaries), but also indirect costs (e.g., loss of control over private information that the partnership would otherwise expect to exploit).

26. Harris and Holmström (1982) and Holmström (1982) provide a formal analysis of this phenomenon in a multiperiod wage model setting. In these models, there is a dynamic moral hazard problem induced by wage-earner effort aversion along with effort unobservability. In my simple model, the undercompletion problem is driven by adverse selection (the general partner becomes privately informed). I could easily show that an undercompletion problem persists in my setting if there is no adverse selection problem, but the completion expenditure by the general partner is unobservable and gives rise to a random payoff. Because the functional allocation arrangement requires that completion costs be borne entirely by the general partner, a classic externality problem arises, and the general partner will spend fewer completion dollars than he would if he were keeping 100 percent of the resulting revenues. Completion expenditures play exactly the same formal role in this tax model without effort aversion, as worker effort aversion plays in the Holmström (1982) taxless model.

Another scenario in which reputation effects would lead to increased completion is where general partner tastes are uncertain. Suppose that general partners are of two types: either they derive considerable disutility from breaking commitments or they do not. Recall that prospectuses often include (largely unenforceable) "promises" not to take actions that enrich the general partner at the expense of limited partners. Hence, other things equal, limited partners will be willing to pay a premium for the right to buy into a partnership managed by an inherently honorable general partner. Limited partners will rationally use track records to draw inferences about general partner types. General partners who are not inherently honorable may nevertheless have incentives to act as though they possess such a characteristic by completing more wells than would privately be optimal in a single-period setting. See Kreps and Wilson (1982) and Milgrom and Roberts (1982) for examples of reputation models of this variety.

27. Haft (1983, I-4).

28. Stanger (1982a, 59). Robert A. Stanger is probably the industry's leading expert.

29. *Stanger Register*, 74.

30. Stanger (1982b, 3).

31. Theory requires us to use as explanatory variables a vector that captures all the relevant information limited partners use to forecast general partner performance.

32. Woods (1983, 26, 47).

33. Haft (1973, 5-16).

34. Stanger (1982a, 60).

35. Also note that a risk-neutral general partner will *not* generally find it efficient to enter into a fixed fee rental contract with the limited partners, thereby eliminating incentive problems. Recall that the primary motivation for the limited partnership organizational form is to enable the general partner to sell tax benefits to limited partners.

36. Mission Resources (1982, 26). A farmout is an agreement whereby the owner of a leasehold or working interest agrees to assign its interest in certain specified acreage to the assignees, retaining some interest such as an overriding royalty interest, an oil and gas payment, or other type of interest, subject to the drilling of one or more specified wells or other performance as a condition of assignment.

37. Actually, the completion problem exists in a programwide reversionary interest structure as well, but to a much lesser extent, as will become obvious.

38. Increasing $\sigma(R_j)$ means that both very high and very low R_j realizations become more likely. Since the marginal payoff to the general partner is s_2 for very high R_j realizations and s_1 for very low R_j realizations, and since s_2 exceeds s_1, the mean payoff to the general partner increases, holding the mean of R_j constant.

39. To see the effect of increasing $\sigma(R_j)$, consider the more general case in which $\tilde{R}_j = KC_i + \tilde{u}_j$, where $\sim$ denotes a random variable and $\tilde{u}_j$ takes on the value of $+ \$400,000$ half the time and $- \$400,000$ half the time. The special case of $\sigma(R_j) = 0$ corresponds to $\tilde{u}_j$ taking on the value of $\$0$ with certainty. The payoff to the general partner is now $s_1 C_i$ plus the maximum of $s_1(R_j - C_i)$ and $s_2(R_j - C_i)$. Half the time the general partner gets $\$10,000 - \$2,000 = \$8,000$; the other half the time he gets $\$10,000 + \$150,000 = \$160,000$. On average the general partner gets $\$84,000$, versus $\$60,000$ when $\sigma(R_j) = 0$, despite the fact that $E(R_j) = \$1.2$ million in both cases.

40. To offset the undercompletion incentive, it may actually help to allow the general partner (or an affiliate) to receive a noncompetitively high price for completing wells.

41. There is a relatively small noncompletion problem in carried interest programs because of the relatively small increase in the general partner's share of revenues after payout. See Table 1 for details.

42. Total net wells drilled is equal to the sum of the partnership's fractional interests in gross wells drilled.

43. Not all reversionary programs revert on a prospect-by-prospect basis, and I do not have sufficiently detailed data to identify the basis for reversion in all programs.

44. This prediction ignores the potentially favorable implications of the option-like features of the arrangement and the consequent inducement of risk-taking behavior on the part of the general partner. While this consideration might be important if limited partners were much more risk tolerant than the general partner, the typical general partner is a reasonably large corporation.

45. Although analysis of nondrilling oil and gas programs is beyond the scope of the present study, oil and gas completion programs also suffer from an incentive problem along the completion dimension, but the incentive is to complete *more* wells than the limited partners would prefer. The reasons are quite similar to those that explain undercompletion in functional allocation programs. In completion programs, the operator pays all costs to drill a hole,

just as limited partners do in functional allocation drilling programs. However, whereas the party paying the completion cost renders the completion decision in functional allocation drilling programs, it is the party who has paid the drilling cost who makes the decision in completion programs.

46. *Forbes*, October 11, 1982, 148.

Chapter 6

I thank Janet Hedrick for her helpful research assistance in the preparation of this paper.

1. The term originates in a classic article, Michael C. Jensen and William H. Meckling, "The Theory of the Firm: Managerial Behavior, Agency Costs, and Ownership Structure," *Journal of Financial Economics* 3 (1976): 305.

2. See, for example, *Limpus v. London General Omnibus Co.*, 1 H. & C. 526, 158 Eng. Rep. 993 (1862), for an early statement of the general rule. A convenient summary of the rules mentioned hereafter is found in William L. Prosser and W. Page Keeton, *The Law of Torts*, 5th ed. (St. Paul, Minn.: West Publishing, 1984), secs. 69–72.

3. See, for example, Y. B. Smith, "Frolic and Detour," *Columbia Law Review* 23 (1923): 444, listing nine possible rationalizations: control, profit, revenge, carefulness and choice, identification, evidence, indulgence, danger, and satisfaction.

4. For an elaboration of this theme in the context of corporate control, see Frank H. Easterbrook and Daniel R. Fischel, "The Proper Role of a Target's Management in Responding to a Tender Offer," *Harvard Law Review* 94 (1981): 1161.

5. For an overview of the problems with derivative actions, which always assume aspects of class actions, see Harry G. Henn and John R. Alexander, *Laws of Corporations*, 3d ed. (St. Paul, Minn.: West Publishing, 1983), 1035–1146. These suits are brought by individual shareholders in the name of the corporation against the directors and officers who it is claimed have abused their position of trust. The procedural complications raised by these suits are fearsome, and the number of cases in which they are successful turns out to be very small, given that the directors and officers typically have a "business judgment" defense that protects them in their exercise of judgment, at least where there is no self-dealing involved.

6. On the merits of which, see Easterbrook and Fischel, "The Proper Role of a Target's Management," 1172–74. See also Lucian A. Bebchuk, "The Case for Facilitating Competing Tender Offers," *Harvard Law Review* 95 (1982): 1028; Frank H. Easterbrook and Daniel R. Fischel, "Auctions and Sunk Costs in Tender Offers," *Stanford Law Review* 35 (1982): 1; Ronald J. Gilson, "Seeking Competitive Bids Versus Pure Passivity in Tender Offer Defense," *Stanford Law Review* 35 (1982): 51.

7. See Nelson, "Information and Consumer Behavior," *Journal of Political Economy* 78 (1970): 311. Note here the contrast to the ordinary cash sale, in which the seller does not have to worry about the ability of the buyer to perform. Sales contracts become more difficult to control when the obligations are deferred on both sides (i.e., when there are warranties of merchantability, or credit terms). Employment contracts of necessity face the question of in futuro risks, and always on both sides.

8. "The basic principle for the measurement of those [contract] damages is

that of compensation based on the injured party's expectation. He is entitled to recover an amount that will put him in as good a position as he would have been in had the contract been performed." E. Allan Farnsworth, *Contracts* (Boston: Little, Brown, 1982), 839. The origin of the modern terminology is found in L. Fuller and W. Perdue, Jr., "The Reliance Interest in Contract Damages," *Yale Law Journal* 46 (1936): 52 (pt. 1), 373 (pt. 2).

9. "It may be said with safety that mere notice to a seller of si me interest or probable action of the buyer is not enough necessarily and as matter [sic] of law to charge the seller with special damage on that account if he fails to deliver the goods." *Globe Refining Co. v. Landa Cotton Oil Co.*, 190 U.S. 540, 545 (1903) (Holmes, J.).

10. *Gainsford v. Carroll*, 2 B. & C. 624, 107 Eng. Rep. 516 (K.B. 1824).

11. *Flureau v. Thornhill*, 2 W. Bl. 1078, 96 Eng. Rep. 635 (C.P. 1776).

12. *Hadley v. Baxendale*, 9 Ex. 341, 156 Eng. Rep. 145 (1854). This case contains the reference to losses "in the contemplation of both parties," a phrase that was very narrowly interpreted on its facts.

13. See, for example, *Kerr Steamship Co. v. Radio Corporation of America*, 245 N.Y. 284, 293–294, 157 N.E. 140, 143 (1927). The standard clause there used reads:

> It is agreed between the sender of the message on the face hereof and this company, that said company shall not be liable for mistakes or delays in transmission or delivery, nor for nondelivery to the next connecting telegraph company or to the addressee, of any unrepeated message, beyond the amount of that portion of the tolls which shall accrue to this company; and that this company shall not be liable for mistakes or delays in the transmission or delivery, nor for delay or nondelivery to the next connecting telegraph company, or to the addressee, of any repeated message beyond the usual tolls and extra sum received by this company from the sender for transmitting and repeating such message; and that this company shall not be liable in any case for delays arising from interruption in the working of its system, nor for errors in cipher or obscure messages.

14. See *Ebasco Services, Inc. v. Pennsylvania Power & Light Co.*, 460 F. Supp. 163 (E.D. Pa., 1978); *Soo Line Railroad Co. v. Fruehauf Corp.*, 547 F.2d 1365 (8th Cir. 1977).

15. See *Posttape Associates v. Eastman Kodak Co.*, 537 F.2d 751, 753 (3d Cir. 1976):

> This film will be replaced if defective in manufacture, labeling, or packaging, or if damaged or lost by us or any subsidiary company even though by negligence or other fault. Except for such replacement, the sale, processing, or other handling of this film for any purpose is without warranty or liability.

16. See, for example, *Griffiths v. Earl of Dudley*, 9 Q.B.D. 357 (1882); *Clements v. London & North Western Ry. Co.*, [1894] 2 Q.B. 482. These contracts are discussed in Richard A. Epstein, "The Historical Origins and Economic Structure of Workers' Compensation Law," *Georgia Law Review* 16 (1982): 775.

17. "Compared with the extensive power that contracting parties have to bargain over their substantive contract rights and duties, their power to bargain over their remedial rights is surprisingly limited." E. Allan Farnsworth, *Contracts* (1982), 895.

18. U.C.C., §2-719(3). The comments to the section reflect the indecision over the contracting out of standard remedies.

19. See, for example, "Note, Protecting At Will Employees Against Wrongful

Discharge: The Duty of Terminate Only In Good Faith," *Harvard Law Review* 93 (1980): 1816.

20. Ibid., note 2.

21. Thus tenure in universities is an exception to the general rule, which in part is explained by the want of a clearly defined ownership structure in universities. That structure may in part be required in order to induce charitable gifts, by guaranteeing the donors that the contributions made will not be diverted to private purposes. See Eugene Fama and Michael C. Jensen, "Agency Problems and Residual Claims," *Journal of Law and Economics* 26 (1983): 327, 347–48. The price paid for tenure is high, given the cost of supervising academic output, but there is no alternative institutional arrangement that is superior. Complete discretion in deans raises the question of abuse. Term contracts for individual faculty members raise the spectre of eight or ten renewals in the course of a given year (five-year terms with fifty-person departments); the opportunities for coalition and faction, within and across years, are simply manifest.

22. The parallel situation is one in which there are variations in the timing of deliveries instead of shifts in the price term. See Dennis Carlton, "Reexamination of Delivered Pricing Systems," *Journal of Law and Economics* 26 (1983): 51.

23. Indeed where employment (or other) relationships are drafted so as to give the greater power to the employer (or the landlord), the decision may well be perfectly sound from the point of view of both parties. The reputational constraints exercise a greater discipline over the firm than over the individual; the imbalance in the legal rights is designed to compensate for that imbalance, with appropriate adjustments being made in the wage rates.

24. For arguments of this sort, see "Note, Protecting At Will Employees," 1830:

> The at will doctrine should be altered not because of "unequal bargaining power," but rather because it is inefficient. Courts must intervene, according to this view, in order to bring about the substantive outcome that the parties would have reached had transaction and information costs not precluded informed negotiation. When high costs of bargaining prevent negotiation between individual employees and employers, and inadequate access to information prevents parties from properly valuing the benefits of job security, judicial intervention is justified to ensure a more efficient result.

25. See, for example, *Monge v. Beebe Rubber Co.*, 114 N.H. 130, 316 A.2d 549 (1974). The bulk of the common law jurisdictions still permit at-will contracts. See, for example, *Hinrichs v. Tanquilaire Hospital*, 352 So. 2d 1130 (Ala. 1977). The bulk of the legal academic commentary has been strongly against the doctrine. See Lawrence E. Blades, "Employment At Will Vs Individual Freedom: On Limiting the Abusive Exercise of Employer Power," *Columbia Law Review* 67 (1967): 1404; Clyde W. Summers, "Individual Protection against Unjust Dismissal: Time for a Statute," *Virginia Law Review* 62 (1976): 481.

26. For an extended discussion on the yellow-dog contract, see Epstein, "A Common Law for Labor Relations: A Critique of the New Deal Labor Legislation," *Yale Law Journal* 92:1357 (1983). The traditional legal literature was highly critical literature and supportive of the ban. See, for example, A. Cox, *Law and the National Labor Policy* (Institute of Industrial Relations, University of California, Los Angeles, 1960), 1–12.

27. See Summers, 526–27.

28. See, for example, *Vaca v. Sipes*, 386 U.S. 171 (1967), still the leading Supreme Court case on the so-called duty of fair representation.

29. Summers, 506.

30. See, for example, Richard B. Freeman and James L. Medoff, "The Two Faces of Unionism," *Public Interest* 69 (Fall 1979).

31. See, for example, *Hitchman Coal & Coke Co. v. Mitchell*, 245 U.S. 229 (1917).

32. Section 8(3) forbade the employer "By discrimination in regard to hire or tenure of employment or any term or condition of employment to encourage or discourage membership in any labor organization." For one recent criticism of the collective bargaining provisions of the National Labor Relations Act, see Dan C. Heldman, James T. Bennett, and Manual H. Johnson, *Deregulating Labor Relations* (Dallas: Fisher Institute, 1981), chap. 5.

33. For the most recent Supreme Court effort to allocate the burden of proof in cases in which workers allege that their dismissal has been motivated by antiunion animus, see *N.L.R.B. v. Transportation Management Corp.*, 103 Supreme Court (1983), 1176.

34. The point was repeatedly made in *Hitchman*, 254–55: "Every Hitchman miner who joined Hughes' [the UMW's organizer] 'secret order' and permitted his name to be entered upon Hughes' list was guilty of a breach of his contract of employment and acted a lie whenever thereafter he entered plaintiff's mine to work." See note 31.

35. Section 8(5) made it an unfair labor practice "To refuse to bargain collectively with the representatives of his employees, subject to the provisions of Section 9(a)," which provides: "Representatives designated or selected for the purposes of collective bargaining by the majority of employees in a unit appropriate for such purposes, shall be the exclusive representatives of all the employees in such unit for the purposes of collective bargaining in respect to rates of pay, wages, hours of employment, or other conditions of employment: *Provided,* That any individual employee or a group of employees shall have the right at any time to present grievances to their employer."

36. The origins of the doctrine are found in *Steele v. Louisville & Nashville R.R. Co.*, 323 U.S. 192 (1944).

37. For an exhaustive account of the matter, see generally Mayer G. Freed, Daniel D. Polsby, and Matthew L. Spitzer, "Unions, Fairness and the Conundrums of Collective Choice," *Southern California Law Review* 56 (1982): 461.

38. See Benjamin Klein, Robert G. Crawford, and Armen Alchian, "Vertical Integration, Appropriable Rents, and the Competitive Contracting Process," *Journal of Law and Economics* 21 (1978): 297.

Chapter 7

I would like to thank Charles Christenson, Michael Jensen, Robert Kaplan, Eric Leifer, Dutch Leonard, John Pratt, Harrison White, and Richard Zeckhauser for extremely helpful comments and criticisms on previous drafts of this paper. I also benefited from the discussion of the paper at the colloquium at which it was first presented.

1. A division performs most of the functions of an independent firm (e.g., R&D, manufacturing, sales, finance) under the authority of a division general manager who has profit responsibility. Firms can also establish other types of

profit centers, as in matrix organizations, where profit center managers share authority with other managers over the resources they need. In some cases profit center managers are responsible for the costs of resources over which they have no authority. For simplicity the term division general manager (DGM) will be used throughout to refer to all types of profit center managers. Reece and Cool (1978) found that 95.8 percent of the *Fortune* 1000 firms used some profit center form of organization. From surveys by Vancil (1978), Mautz (1968), and Tang (1979), it can be estimated that about 85 percent of these firms make internal transfers between profit centers, which amount to 7 to 10 percent of the cost of goods sold.

2. Hirshleifer (1956), in the first formal analysis of the transfer pricing problem, showed that when the intermediate or transferred good is sold in a perfectly competitive market, the use of market price maximizes corporate profits whether or not divisions trade with each other. For imperfectly competitive markets he showed that marginal cost was the solution. These two solutions apply only when four assumptions hold: (1) the selling division has spare productive capacity, (2) there is only one buying division, (3) technological independence exists (the unit costs of each division are independent of the volume of the other), and (4) demand independence exists (the sales of one division do not affect the sales of the other). When any one of these assumptions does not hold, mathematical programming techniques must be used. The iterative nature of these techniques makes them too complex and unwieldy in practice, they are not incentive compatible and are subject to gaming by DGMs, and it is extremely difficult to reach consensus on the mathematical representation of the real-world situation. For critiques of the use of economic theory and mathematical programming, see Abdel-khalik and Lusk (1974), Kaplan (1982), and Verlage (1975).

3. Jensen and Meckling (1976) emphasize the importance of viewing the firm as a "legal fiction which serves as a nexus for contracting relationships" between principals and agents, and not as an individual profit maximizer, as is done in classical microeconomic theory.

4. The president may be the chief executive officer (CEO) or only the chief operating officer (COO) when the chairman of the board is the CEO. The president can be the CEO even when there is a separate chairman of the board, and sometimes one person is both president and chairman of the board.

5. Complexities are introduced by the potential for coalition formation, the existence of many hierarchical levels, and the possibility of randomized behavior by the agent as an optimizing strategy (Baiman 1982, 177).

6. However, Zimmerman (1979, 520) recognized that "the major obstacle to developing this positive analysis is in gaining access to data in order to test theories, which will generate new insights and produce richer theories, thereby better assessing the empirical magnitudes of the various costs and benefits." These data could include the informal theories by which managers explain their own practices.

7. The term *sourcing decision* usually applies to the selection of a supplier by a buyer. Here it will also be used to refer to the symmetric problem of customer selection by the seller.

8. The product sold by the selling division is often called the *intermediate good.* It is purchased by the buying division and incorporated in the product it produces, often called the *final good.*

9. Formal economic theory has techniques for translating all other variables

into the present value of future income streams, and economists often assume that managers can and do make these translations, usually with some adjustments for uncertainty. I do not make this assumption. Nor do I take a position on how the vertical integration decision and the distinct business versus manufacturing unit decision affect firm profitability.

10. Porter (1980) identified a number of advantages of vertical integration including economies of integration (from combined operations, internal control and coordination, information, avoiding the market, and stable relationships), tapping into technology, assuring supply and/or demand, offsetting bargaining power and input cost distortions, enhancing ability to differentiate, elevating entry and mobility barriers, entering a higher-return business, and defending against foreclosure.

11. Standard costs are engineering estimates of what the unit costs should be for a given technology in an efficiently run plant at a given volume. Actual costs are those actually incurred. A division selling all of its output internally can be turned into a profit center in a technical sense simply by including a profit on internal transfers. Such divisions are often referred to as "quasi" profit centers or "pseudo" profit centers. Kaplan (1982, 477) defined a profit center as "a unit for which the manager has the authority to make decisions on sources of supply and choice of markets. In general, a profit center will be selling a majority of its output to outside customers and is free to choose sources of supply for a majority of its materials, goods, and services." Just as there are variations in the ratio of external to internal sales, so are there variations in the authority of DGMs to choose their suppliers and markets.

12. Often this autonomy is primarily given to the buying division. Unless the selling division is operating at full capacity, a small volume of internal sales at a price less than could be obtained externally will not create major problems even if the selling division is required to accept internal business.

13. In cases of monopoly sellers or monopsony buyers, exchanges may take place that are not totally acceptable to one party but to which there are no alternatives.

14. For discussions of industrial marketing see Corey (1976), Oxenfeldt (1975), and Webster (1979). For a discussion of industrial purchasing see Corey (1978).

15. Although he meant that internal buying divisions were given the lowest priority, and used a common colloquial expression of this condition, I have been told that the "hind tit" actually produces the richest milk and is the choice of the strongest of the offspring. I did not explore this issue in any depth on this research project because of anticipated difficulties in getting it funded by the Division of Research at the Harvard Business School.

16. I am indebted to John Pratt for making this point clear to me.

17. These "market prices" on external transactions may be established by any one of the three pricing conventions identified by Corey: cost plus markup, market bidding, and competitive bidding.

18. I am indebted to Michael Jensen for suggesting this change in the decision rights of the buying division general manager.

19. See Kaplan (1982) for a good discussion of this point.

20. Corey (1976, 178) in his discussion of the product pricing problem noted:

As must be apparent, the art of pricing is attended by a good deal of uncertainty. Sellers cannot in practice chart supply and demand curves, setting price where the two intersect. Instead, the pricing process must be viewed as a dynamic one in which moves are made, responses are analyzed, and further action is taken.

21. I am indebted to Michael Jensen for suggesting this possibility.

22. This is a different use of the term *dual pricing* from that in linear programming.

Chapter 8

Financial support under Grant SES 8008658 from the National Science Foundation and from the Division of Research of the Harvard Graduate School of Business Administration is gratefully acknowledged. I am indebted to Andrew Laing and Peter S. Bearman for assistance with this research and for stimulating commentary to Richard F. Vancil, Robert G. Eccles, Eric M. Leifer, Ronald L. Breiger, Robert H. Scott, John W. Pratt, and Richard Zeckhauser.

1. For an apt illustration, see the brilliant account by Robert Faulkner (1983) of how composers of the music for movie sound tracks build their careers. Hollywood today is an arena in which producers and financiers float around putting together one-shot combinations of story, script, director, camera, composer, and so on. As these combinations are formed, all the parties are eyeing and relying on each other's track records, as judged *Variety*-style by market gross, in previous one-shot combinations.

2. I have simplified in several ways. Agency "ties" always imply third parties and so are triads even in their simplest form. The *locus classicus* for theoretical exposition of triadization in social structure is Nadel (1957). See Davis (1970) for extended discussion and Holland and Leinhardt (1981) for technical specification of triad models of network data. Another issue is whether facts of agency relation are completely open and known by all (as in the Roman *clientela* example developed below) or concealed, as when a naive contestant is used as a cat's-paw or stalking horse in a contest for control. Both these aspects tend to be disregarded because of our obsession with contracts as a definitive polar type—see my earlier discussion of Isaacs.

3. A beautiful working-out of consequences from these themes can be found in recent theoretical work in American political science. I refer to John Padgett's (1980) application of the "garbage can" theory of James G. March and collaborators. "The thrust of this theory's approach was to focus less on the details of individual decision making, and more on the aggregate flows of people, problems, and solutions through organizational networks. These flows determine the perceived issue or meaning context of choice, and in turn are constrained by access structures, energy loads, and attention-focusing rules.... Explaining this changing 'meaning context' of choice as a function of organizational processes operating under conditions of ambiguity is the core analytic task" (pp. 583, 586).

Padgett's mathematical model of these stochastic processes shows that a chief executive officer's " 'intervention begets intervention' for both heterogeneity and contagion reasons. This result is parallel to the Cohen, March and Olsen conclusion that 'one would expect decision makers who have a feeling that they are always working on the same problems in somewhat different contexts, mostly without results' (1972: 10). In the present model, however, these decision flows can be substantially modulated by structural centralization policy" (p. 596). In fact Padgett proves, for his model, that optimal presidential control—which is second-best in terms of stability properties as well—comes from a Dwight Eisenhower approach of strict hands-off. The punch line, for my purposes, is that intermediate officers must be chosen and manipulated by the president, in just the ways I ascribe to agency relations, in order to achieve optimum control by hands-off regular bureaucratic proceedings. The "independent" manager of a profit center in a decentralized firm is just such a mixture of intermediate official and agent of those in ultimate control of the firm.

4. I cannot resist suggesting that in our society lawyers sometimes act as principals inducing laymen to perform liturgies for them as a corporate body. Thousands of persons are induced by lawyerdom to bring asbestos-related suits (*New York Times*, July 28, 1983, p. A19) from which, even when "victorious," they obtain but a third of payments, the rest going to lawyers in various guises and roles.

5. Despite the obvious involvements of agency, I do not attempt to deal with ownership and control issues here; for a recent attempt to dissolve the controversy, see Fama and Jensen (1983).

6. Systematic techniques for analyzing such multiplex networks, mathematical models implemented in user-oriented computer programs, have been available for some time, so far applied mostly to political and government organization—cf. Breiger (1979); Breiger, Boorman, and Arabie (1975).

7. Reading Plumb (1967) will also bring to your attention my neglect in this paper of yet another contextual dimension for agency, namely ideology. A fascinating aspect of Plumb's argument is how very essential it was to the operation of this crass machine to have a hostile party and ideology, the Tories. In fact, the Tories were so weak it seemed possible they might disappear without occasional judicious support from the Whig powers-that-be. I find a rather similar theme present implicitly in the excellent analysis of intelligence systems, written during the un-self-conscious Cold War period, by Sherman Kent (1966). And see Pocock's (1975) distinguished treatise, 523–28, 423–27, and especially 349.

8. At the risk of appearing overimaginative, I suggest a similarity between the institutional form of the Roman Senate and the upper reaches of a firm as described by Jensen and Meckling (1976): "a legal fiction . . . a nexus for contracting relationships . . . also characterized by the existence of divisible residual claims on the assets and cash flows of the organization which can generally be sold without permission of the other contracting individuals." And conversely, Badian (1972, 72) sees an analogy with our boards of directors: "The *socii* of large companies met from time to time for formal purposes, rather like modern shareholders, and (it seems) with no more real power."

9. Perhaps the Japanese system of satellite firms should be discussed here, rather than in the section on *clientela*. This system might be seen as a variant of the outwork mode as it develops toward the larger scale in which the outworker becomes a "sublettor" of labor on a larger scale than that of the domestic outworking in the European nineteenth century. The main issues are the intensity of the tie—it appears to me much more persistent and imbued with *fides* than in European outwork—and the degree of control—does the satellite bargain with several of the larger firms or is it usually completely under the thumb of one?

10. I see an analogy between the synod as a context for the bishop, and the board of directors as a context for CEOs as Hirsch (1982) describes it. Papal legates' roles in synods are like investment bankers' participation in corporate boards of directors. Both systems remind one how hard it is to distinguish

analytically between specialization as profession and specialization by localization.

11. Agency ties by no means suppose a permissive cultural ambience. In the words of Hinson (1981, 287): "Early Christianity grew for the same basic reasons that conservative American churches are now growing. . . . It is doubtful whether many modern Christians would look with favor on the disciplinary procedures or on the authoritarian ministry of the early centuries."

12. Interpenetration of the cultural and social in agency is hard to unravel. Schweizer (1961, 14), for example, observes, "We are concerned with the much more difficult question of recognizing in the actual ordering of the New Testament Church, and in what is said about it, the theological concerns that caused it to take that form and no other." Schweizer goes on to urge that the New Testament is to be read as a gospel, not as laws.

Index

Abbot, Andrew, 205
Accounting, 10, 25, 95–96, 152, 154–155
Add-ons, 204, 207
Adverse selection, 38, 40
  and insider trading, 87–89, 94
  in oil and gas tax shelters, 222 n. 26
Advertising, 6, 11, 13
Agency costs
  and agency structures, 17, 154
  and bargaining, 11
  and bargaining around legal rules, 64
  and contracts, 16, 49, 138
  and corporations, 55–59
  defined, 3
  distributing, 65–67
  and fiduciary duties, 62
  and fiduciary relationship, 55–79
  and employee misbehavior, 129–130
  and firm, 60
  and information, 11, 32, 86, 87
  and insider trading, 83–85, 91–93
  and legal rules, 63, 66, 67
  and managers as agents, 55–59
  and monitoring, 2–3, 16, 65, 67
  in oil and gas tax shelters, 103, 110, 221 n. 3,
    n. 4; 222 n. 25
  and optimal contracts, 65–66
  and transfer pricing, 167, 178
  and unions, 127, 144
Agency loss
  defined, 3
  and information asymmetries, 11
  and interests, 25
  and monitoring, 5, 6, 10
  and reputation, 30
Agency problems, institutional responses to, 3,
    26–32, 53–148
  employment contracts and, 30–32, 127–148
  and fiduciary duties, 26–27, 28
  and insider trading, 28–29, 81–100
  and tax incentives, 29, 101–125
  and transfer pricing, 151–186
  unions and, 141–148
Agency relationship, 1–51, 188
  changes in, 17–22, 28, 46, 216 n. 8
  and *clientela*, 198–201, 202
  defined, 2, 151, 217 n. 5
  and interests, 14–15, 25
  and law, 58, 128–129
  long-term, 6, 7, 14, 16

  and market, 190–191
  optimality of, 65–66
  in organizations, 33, 35, 151
  and procurement, 190–191
  reciprocal, 2
  as social plumbing, 34, 188–189
  and transfer pricing, 159–167
Agency reversals, 193, 203, 205–207, 208
Agency structures, 3–4, 15–22
  changes in, 17–22, 45
Agency ties, 188–204, 231 n. 9, 232 n. 11, n. 12
  and evolution of organizations, 201–204
  and executive compensation, 192–198
  and information asymmetries, 230 n. 2
  long-term, 198–201
  short-term, 198
  and society, 232 n. 12
  as triads, 154, 230 n. 2
  weak, 201–203
Agency
  definitions of, 187–189
  purpose of, 187
  specialization in, 188, 208
"Agency," 188
Agents
  and agency relationship, 37–38
  corporate officers as, 56
  and decision making 153, 159, 164–165, 167
  defined, 2, 128
  as distributors, 198
  employees as, 144
  heterogeneous, 20
  and hidden action model, 38
  and hidden information model, 39
  managers as, 56
  measuring performance of, 152
  multiple, 3, 46–47, 153–154, 159
  shaliach as, 189, 192, 201, 206
  and transfer pricing, 164–165, 185
  union officials as, 144
Alchian, Armen A., 59, 91, 167
Ancient Economy, 193
Anderson, M., 203
Antitakeovers, 66–67
Apache Oil & Gas, 121, 122
Apache Petroleum, 107–108, 113
Aquinas Chemical, 170, 172
Arm's length transaction, 32, 192, 200, 201
Arrow, Kenneth J., 16, 17, 25, 26, 37–51, 81, 87,
  213

This volume is set in ITC Zapf Book, one of the first typefaces commissioned and designed especially for computer-driven, high-speed, photographic, digitally reproduced letterforms.

Herman Zapf, a designer of metal printing types, turned his talent to designing traditional letterforms in current technology with the introduction of this face in 1976.

The book was printed by offset lithography on acid-free paper.